Early
Schools and School-Books
OF
New England

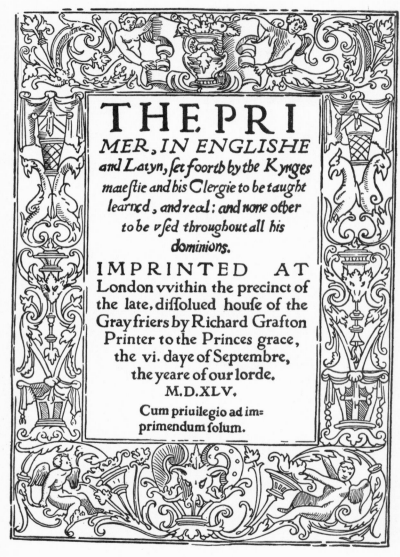

THE PRI
MER, IN ENGLISHE
and Latyn, set foorth by the Kynges
maieftie and his Clergie to be taught
learned, and real: and none other
to be vfed throughout all his
dominions.

IMPRINTED AT
London vvithin the precinct of
the late, diffolued houfe of the
Gray friers by Richard Grafton
Printer to the Princes grace,
the vi. daye of Septembre,
the yeare of our lorde.
M.D.XLV.

Cum priuilegio ad im=
primendum folum.

Early
Schools and School-Books
OF
New England

By

George Emery Littlefield

NEW YORK

RUSSELL & RUSSELL · INC

1965

FIRST PUBLISHED IN 1904
REISSUED, 1965, BY RUSSELL & RUSSELL, INC.
L. C. CATALOG CARD NO: 65—13932

PRINTED IN THE UNITED STATES OF AMERICA

Contents

Illustrations

Early Schools of Europe

EARLY SCHOOLS
OF EUROPE

The Beginnings of Education

EDUCATION is the art of drawing out, or developing the faculties, of training human beings for the functions for which they are destined. To educate is from the Latin *educere*, to lead out, to bring up, as to bring up a child mentally or physically. The definition of "educate" as given by Webster is: "To bring up, as a child; to lead out and train the mental powers of; to inform and enlighten the understanding of; to form and regulate the principles and character of; to prepare and fit for any calling or business, or for activity and usefulness in life."

Education is properly to draw forth, and implies not so much the communication of knowledge as the discipline of the intellect, the establishment of the principles, and the regulation of the heart. Instruction is that part of education which furnishes the mind with knowledge, and the one whose business it is to instruct others is known as a teacher.

All questions of education rest upon two main points; namely, what is the end or aim that the education ought to pursue, and what are the best means to attain that end. Before we can hope to mould a human being in a desired way, the nature of that being must be well known. The knowledge of man's nature is usually comprehended under three divisions: physiology, the constitution of his body; psychology, the constitution of his mind; ethics and religion, his moral and religious nature. As these sciences are in an imperfect and unsettled state, we cannot look for any complete science of education. Education has existed as an art from the very infancy of society, but it is as yet mostly an experimental art, the rules and methods of which have been arrived at by the blind groping of experience, by the process of trial and error.

In the widest sense of the word a man is educated, either for good or evil, by everything that he experiences from his cradle to his grave; but in the more limited and usual sense, the term " education " is confined to the efforts made, of set purpose, to train men in a particular way; to the efforts of the grown-up part of a community to inform the intellect and mould the character of the young; and more especially to the labors of professional educators or schoolmasters.

The means employed in education fall naturally under two heads: discipline, or moral training; and instruction, or the imparting of information. Although the two often run into each other, home and neighborhood are the chief educators of moral training, while the imparting of information has become more particularly the business of the schoolmaster.

As a preliminary step, and as a medium through which all other knowledge is conveyed, there is required a knowledge of the mother tongue and the faculty of reading and writing it; to which should be added a knowledge of counting and measuring. These three branches are the first and indispensable steps in instruction. With this knowledge information may be acquired at any period of life; without it the grand access to knowledge remains forever closed.

The following anecdote is related of Edmund Stone, a distinguished mathematician: " Stone was born about the year 1700; his father was gardener to the Duke of Argyle, who, walking one day in his garden, observed a Latin copy of Newton's *Principia* lying on the grass, and thinking it had been brought from his own library, called some one to carry it back to its place. Upon this, Stone, who was then in his eighteenth year, claimed the book as his own. 'Yours!' replied the Duke; 'do you understand geometry, Latin, and Newton?' 'I know a little of them,' replied the young man. The Duke was surprised, and having a taste for the sciences conversed with the young mathematician and was astonished at the force, the accuracy, and the candor of his answers. 'But how,' said the Duke, 'came you by the knowledge of all these things?' Stone replied: 'A servant taught me ten years since to read. Does one need to know anything more than the twenty-four letters in order to learn everything else that one wishes?' The Duke's curiosity redoubled; he sat down on a bank and requested a detail of the whole process by which he had become so learned.

"'I first learned to read,' said Stone: 'the masons were then at work upon your house. I approached them one day, and observed that the architect used a rule and compasses, and that he made calculations. I inquired what might be the meaning and the use of these things, and I was informed that there was a science called arithmetic. I purchased a book of arithmetic and I learned it. I was told there was another science called geometry: I bought the necessary books and I learned geometry. By reading I found that there were good books of these two sciences in Latin; I bought a dictionary, and I learned Latin. I understood also that there were good books of the same kind in French; I bought a dictionary, and I learned French. And this, my Lord, is what I have done; it seems to me that we may learn everything when we know the twenty-four letters of the alphabet.'

"Under the patronage of the Duke of Argyle, Stone, some years after, published in London a *Treatise on Mathematical*

Instruments, A Mathematical Dictionary, and was chosen a Fellow of the Royal Society."

As geology, by offering us an insight into the mighty revolutions through which the earth has passed since the days of its creation and before it became the fit abode for man, enables us to understand the history of the earth, so comparative philology, a science of the nineteenth century, by analyzing and comparing the language of the various nations of the world, enables us to trace the history of man. Without this science of language, ages about which all traditions and all histories are silent would be sealed books to us. It is now established as a fact beyond all doubt that the nations on the banks of the Ganges and the Indus, and the ancient Persians, spoke a language radically identical with the language spoken by the nations of Europe from the earliest times, including the Greek and Latin. Therefore there must have existed at one time a close connection between these nations, and all must have sprung from one stock. Further investigations will probably show that all the languages spoken by man are traceable to one common parent, and that all mankind is descended from one common father and one common mother.

As there are no records, the extent of the knowledge of our first parents and the language spoken by them are wholly matters of speculation. Whether this language was of human invention or divine origin is a question which has employed the ingenuity of many eminent men, and probably never will be settled.

Diodorus Siculus, the Greek historian, says : " Necessity was man's first instructor, which made him skilful in everything, being an ingenious creature, assisted (as with so many servants) by hands, speech, and a rational soul, ready to put everything in execution."

Whether of human invention or divine origin, it is very evident that our first parents possessed only the first principles

of knowledge, which were to be improved from actual obser-
vation and experience as necessity might give occasion. The
primeval man lived upon the fruits of the earth and the
products of the chase, and found shelter from the inclemency
of the weather in natural caverns and recesses of the earth. As
the numbers of the people increased, the uncertainties of the
chase rendered it necessary to tame some of the wild animals
and raise flocks and herds which would furnish the necessary
food and clothing. By roaming over the plains suitable pastur-
age was secured, and the owners dwelt in tents. The defending
of these flocks and herds, not only from wild beasts, but also
from more powerful neighbors and robbers, taught the necessity
of several individuals or tribes uniting together for mutual protection if they wished to live in peaceful possession of their
property. Naturally, in the beginning the father was the head
of the family, and his authority was supreme. When family
joined family and tribe joined tribe for mutual protection, some
one of the leaders made himself conspicuous among his fellows
by his success and good fortune and by his interest in the
general welfare of his tribe, and a fortunate leader stood a good
chance to be chosen as ruler of all the tribes. Thus of the
first monarch mentioned in the Sacred Scriptures it is written :
Nimrod " began to be a mighty one in the earth. . . . He
was a mighty hunter before the Lord. And the beginning of
his kingdom was Babel, and Erech, and Accad, and Calneh,
in the land of Shinar."

Another epoch in the progress of the human race was the
introduction of agriculture, or the art of cultivating the soil in
order to render it most productive. Agriculture in its most
extensive sense means not only the preparation of the soil, the
planting of the seeds, and the harvesting of the crops, but also
the rearing, feeding, and management of livestock, the building of warehouses and barns, and the construction of canals,

embankments, and roads. Agriculture necessitated the permanent occupation of a particular section of the country by a family or tribe, and the substitution of houses for tents. Villages, towns, and cities were formed, and a great nation, which, if we accept the statements of the Bible, attempting to build a tower which was offensive to the Deity, was confounded as to its language and dispersed into different nations.

Whether the science of agriculture was of divine origin or of human invention is still a matter of speculation. Diodorus Siculus says that it was owing to the care and industry of the Egyptian goddess Isis, supposed to be the same person with the Grecian Ceres, " who collected the wheat and barley she found growing here and there wild in the fields, among other herbs and weeds ; of this she taught her people how to make bread, which they found so sweet and delicious, and so much good did this discovery produce, that it made many leave off their barbarous course of life." Her brother Osiris, supposed to be identical with Bacchus, taught the people " how to till the land, to cultivate, gather, and preserve the corn. He also instructed them in the gathering and preservation of the fruits of the earth, to plant vines, make wine, and where vines would not grow he discovered the way to make a liquor, little inferior to wine in flavor, from barley, called in the language of Egypt, Zythen," which we understand by the familiar terms of beer and ale. The historian adds : " In the time of Osiris and Isis, projectors and ingenious artists were in great honor and esteem, and therefore in Thebes there were then goldsmiths and braziers, who made weapons for the killing of wild beasts, and other instruments for the husbanding of the ground and the improvement of tillage."

As the practice of agriculture furnishes the highest degree of certainty for supplying the daily wants of man, we find that man in all ages and in every nation has paid great attention to the cultivation of the soil, and there is no art or science that has risen to a higher degree of perfection.

Agriculture goes hand in hand with architecture, a science most beneficial to mankind. It erects for us domestic habitations, temples for sacred worship, and monuments for the dead; it unites different districts of the country by bridges and highways; it supplies us with water by raising aqueducts; it affords protection to cities by building walls and forts; provides homes for the unfortunate, hospitals for the diseased, and prisons for the vicious. Naval architecture affords the means of communication between countries separated by water, furnishes the conveyance by which nations are enabled to make an exchange of products, and by armed vessels preserves the comity of nations.

The first attempts at architecture were extremely rude, but as society advanced in knowledge, architecture advanced with equal steps, and it gives the best record of the mental progress of every people which can be collected. An English writer says: " It has been found to flourish best in Free states, and where the governors have possessed genius, virtue, and good taste. The most eminent era of Grecian architecture was when the Athenian republic was under the direction of Pericles; at this period also existed the first of statuaries, Praxiteles. When that eminent artist and their admirable architects were employed, in the words of Pausanias, ' they rendered the whole of the Acropolis as an entire ornament.' "

Vitruvius enumerates twelve requisite qualifications for an architect: that he be docile and ingenious, well educated, skilled in designing, in geometry, arithmetic, history, philosophy, music, medicine, law, and astronomy; he should also possess exquisite judgment and taste.

The uniting together for mutual protection and security necessitated the obedience to authority by the members of the community and submission to a code of laws. The object of

these laws was to prevent wrong, preserve right, protect inno-
cence, and punish guilt.   In this manner government was established, a governor was chosen, and obedience on the part of the
people to the governors was assured.   We have seen that the
first ruler was the father of the family; he was followed by
the ruler of a tribe, who was in turn succeeded by the ruler of
many tribes; and finally we find a ruler of nations, or an emperor.   In very early ages the object of government was the
happiness of the people, and the office of ruler was given to
that person who had been most useful to the people.   As the
office was not hereditary, but elective, the ruler naturally would
be induced to be kind and beneficent to the people.   This ideal
government, however, must have been short-lived, for, so far as
we can trace history, the strong has always subdued the weak,
the rich oppressed the poor, and the cunning has cheated the
simple.   He who had the power claimed the right to rule over
the weaker as his subjects or slaves, and the kingly power
descended from son to son, and from generation to generation.
Despotism, therefore, was the established form of government
among the earliest nations known to history, such as the Assy-
rians, Egyptians, and the nations of India.

A more or less complete system of caste prevailed among
these nations, whereby the descendants were bound to follow
the same pursuits as their parents.   The classes distinguished
for their knowledge, for their military prowess, or for wealth,
subdued the others, assumed higher powers, and tried to preserve them for their descendants.   Knowledge and valor naturally gained the ascendancy, and hence priests and warriors
appear as the first and most powerful.   As wisdom and knowledge were regarded as gifts by the Deity to his ministers, the
priests were the teachers and advisers not only of the people,
but also of the rulers, and their power was often greater than
that of a king, whose authority was that of the sword.   The

military caste from which the ruler was usually taken formed a kind of nobility which kept the rest of the population in subjection by the constant practice and exercise of arms, and secured to their descendants the same rights and privileges by early training and habit.

In India the caste system was the most fully developed. There the four chief castes were the priests, or Brahmins, the warriors, the tradesmen, and the servants. Although the priests and warriors were separated from the other castes by a great interval, yet the first three were treated as belonging to one another and as far superior to the servants, or fourth caste, who were forbidden to read the sacred books. The Brahmins, or priestly caste, were always the first and most influential caste, and concentrated in their own body the intellectual life of the nation. At the creation they are said to have issued from the mouth of Brahma. They were commanded to live a pure and holy life, to devote themselves to the service of the gods, to study the sacred books, to expound their contents to the members of the second and third castes, and to perform sacrifices for themselves and others. They were to draw up and interpret laws, but the administering of them was vested in the warrior caste. They were supposed by their imprecations to destroy kings with all their troops. Hence the Brahmin was to be treated with the most profound respect even by kings.

In Egypt the priests and warriors were the two highest and most honored castes, the priests ranking above the soldiers. The kings were hereditary, and when a dynasty became extinct a new king was chosen from the priestly or military caste. Although the king's authority was very great and he was profoundly reverenced by his people, yet he was bound by certain rules and regulations framed by the priests, who were not only the king's counsellors and advisers, but also saw that their regulations were observed. The caste of the priests was divided into several ranks, and they were distinguished according to the divinities they served and the temples to which they were attached. They were the sole depositaries of all knowledge, human and divine, and they might also be distinguished according to their profession as politicians, lawyers, scholars, physicians, architects, etc.

The nations which have had the greatest influence on the education of the world were the Egyptians, Phœnicians, Greeks, and Romans.

Among the Egyptians the greater portion of the people was instructed only in the useful arts, or the arts which are the offspring of necessity, such as the art of procuring clothing for the body, building homes, manufacturing weapons for the hunt or for offence and defence in war, constructing boats, the art of agriculture, and a knowledge of the medicinal properties of plants. As it was always the custom for the children to follow the profession of the father, the common people imparted instruction to children at home and generally taught them only those things which belonged to the successful carrying on of the particular occupation into which they were born. A very few only were taught anything of literature, and those principally of the better class of mechanics. The sons of the soldiers were sent to the barracks to be trained for their future business as defenders of the country; the children of the priests alone received what we should call a liberal education both in the arts and sciences. The higher education, or the study of the sciences, was in the hands of the priests, who were the educators or teachers of their day.

Aristotle informs us that the priests consumed the greater part of their time in abstract studies; and when Herodotus or Diodorus Siculus relate any fact with regard to the sciences in Egypt they always inform us that they received it from the mouths of the priests. The Egyptians were very superstitious, and the priests veiled their actions with much mystery, using a written character called hieratic, or priestly, which contained the secrets of their religion, was unintelligible to the rest of the Egyptians, and was taught only to their children or to those who intended to become priests. To other children they taught the hieroglyphic and demotic. The hieroglyphic was originally the only written character, from which was derived the hieratic, for the sole use of the priests, and the demotic, for all ordinary purposes. It was therefore only those children who were taught one or the other of these written characters who could read and write; all others had practically no education. The priests, however, were not confined to their religious and educational duties, but filled the highest offices of state. They had the custody of the public records; it was their province to impose and levy taxes, to regulate weights and measures; and out of their order were chosen all the magistrates and judges.

Although the Egyptians were great inventors and reached a high degree of civilization, yet they seem never to have been able to advance beyond a fixed point nor to develop their inventions. The arts in which they were the greatest and which will secure to them the admiration of all ages were architecture and sculpture, and yet it remained for Greece to carry them to far greater heights. The Egyptians appear to have been a home-loving people, content with their own institutions, laws, and customs, and shunned coming in contact with other nations. They reached the height of their power, and their art reached its highest point, during the reign of Rameses the Great, about 1300 B. C., who extended the dominions of Egypt south and west, and is said to have traversed Syria and Asia Minor, but the conquests in Asia do not appear to have been lasting. During the reign of Psammeticus, which lasted from 670 B. C. to 617 B. C., the ancient policy of seclusion was changed. The ports of Egypt on the Mediterranean and the Red Sea were opened to foreign merchants, particular encouragement was given to the Greeks to settle in Egypt, and efforts were made to overcome the illiberal prejudice which had kept the people sequestered from all other nations.

The Egyptians are credited with having invented a written character, but it was the Phœnicians who evolved from this character a system of alphabetical writing which they are believed to have introduced into Greece. It was also through the more liberal institutions of the Phœnicians that the despotism of Asia was changed into the freedom of Europe. Although occupying only a narrow strip of land north of Palestine, bordering on the Mediterranean and extending inland only a few miles, yet the importance of the Phœnicians as a commercial people was not surpassed by any other nation of antiquity. Commerce and navigation were the only means by which they could secure their existence, and their dominion was extended only by planting colonies in nearly all parts of the Mediterranean. As the Egyptians were not a sea-going nation, it was left to the enterprise of the Phœnicians to extend their commerce to Europe and Africa, and all the islands of the Mediterranean. In connection with the Jews they are said to have sailed down the Red Sea to a country called Ophir, whence they returned laden with valuable products. During the reign of the Egyptian King Necho (617–601 B. c.) they are said to have circumnavigated Africa. Herodotus says: " King Necho was the first to prove that Lybia (Africa) is surrounded by the sea, except the part where it is connected with Asia. For he sent out Phœnician sailors and ships, ordering them to return by the pillars of Hercules to the Mediterranean and Egypt. These Phœnicians accordingly sailed down the Red Sea into the southern ocean. Each autumn they landed on the coast of Lybia, which happened to be near; they then sowed corn and waited for the harvest ; after reaping the corn they again embarked and continued the voyage. In this manner they returned in the third year to Egypt by way of the Pillars of Hercules." They thus anticipated the discovery of the Portuguese by more than two thousand years. They also sailed as far north as the Scilly Islands, on the southwest coast of England, whence they brought back tin, and probably visited the Prussian coast of the Baltic, where they obtained amber. Cadiz was founded by them 1100 B. c., and Carthage about 814 B. c. As Phœnicia ultimately became subject to Persia, and as its cities and towns were destroyed, we possess scarcely any means of forming a correct opinion of its civilization. It was patterned, however, largely upon Egypt, but its religion and political institutions were greatly modified by its intercourse with other nations. It was through the Phœnicians that the knowledge, language, and religion of Egypt were introduced into the countries bordering upon the Mediterranean, and especially Greece.

Education in Greece and Rome

THE whole system of education among the Greeks was peculiarly calculated for the development and improvement of the powers of the mind and of the body in common. Gymnastics constituted an essential part of it, and was taught and practised in the gymnasia, or schools for bodily exercise. All that part which related more especially to the cultivation of the mind went under the term "music." In later times music was used in the restrictive sense, and grammar comprehended those branches not included under the term "music." Thus the education of a Greek was divided into three parts : grammar, music, and gymnastics. The republics of Lacedæmon and Athens differed very much as to the grand aim in education which gave rise to two systems of education, the Spartan and Athenian.

Lycurgus, the celebrated Spartan lawgiver, travelled extensively in Asia Minor, Egypt, and India, examining and comparing the political institutions of these various countries, and thus acquired a knowledge fitting him to become one of the greatest legislators in the world. He is reputed to have been selected by the Spartans to draw up a code of laws for the better government of the state. He consented, and the constitution which he framed was adopted by the Republic of Lacedæmon. One of the principal objects of the institutions of Lycurgus was the education of the youth of the republic, on which the legislator bestowed the most particular attention.

The Spartan citizen lived habitually in public; being prohibited from commerce and his farms operated by his slaves, his days were passed in military and gymnastic drill; his meals were taken at the public mess, to which he contributed and of which he was compelled to be a member; and his nights were spent in the public barracks. He had but little time to spend with his family and seldom saw his younger children, who were in charge of the mother and who were taught at home the lessons of obedience and frugality.

According to the laws of Lycurgus, when the boys had attained the age of seven, they were no longer the charge of their parents, but of the state. They were enrolled in classes, and under public masters their education was such as to train them up to that species of heroism and the practice of the severer virtues which so strongly marked the Spartan character. They were taught to despise equally danger and pain. Their sports and amusements were such as are fitted to promote a strength of constitution and vigor and agility of the body. To run, to swim, to wrestle, to hunt, were the constant exercises of youth. The discipline was more strict after the age of twelve. At the age of sixteen they were called σιδευναί; at eighteen they were considered to have arrived at the age of manhood and entered the classes termed ἔφηβοι; at twenty they received the appellation εἴρενες, or those permitted to speak in the assemblies, and were admitted to the public banquets; at thirty they were ranked as men, ἔξηβοι, and were allowed to undertake public offices. With regard to the culture of the mind, Spartan discipline admitted none of those studies which tend to refine or embellish the understanding. But the duties of religion, the inviolable bond of a promise, the sacred obligation of an oath, the respect due to parents, the reverence for old age, the strictest obedience to the laws, and the love of their country were early and assiduously inculcated. From their compulsory attendance at the public tables from their earliest youth and listening to the conversation of their elders, they became acquainted with all the important business of the republic. They knew thoroughly the constitution, the powers of the several public officers, and the rights and duties which belonged to the kings, magistrates, and citizens. They were thus educated to become obedient citizens and excellent soldiers.

Sparta was a great military establishment. Among the Spartans war was considered the only honorable and manly occupation. The arts and sciences were despised, and those who cultivated them. They had no occupations for a season of peace. The distinction of professions which gives rise to separation of interests and which inspires life and vigor into the whole community was totally unknown. The Spartan was active only when engaged in war. In peace his manner of life was idle and listless. When some one was vaunting to him the contempt which the Spartans had for death, Alcibiades, the Athenian wit, replied : " It is no wonder, since it relieves them from the heavy burden of an idle and stupid life."

At Athens peace was the natural state of the republic, and the institutions of that other great lawgiver, Solon, tended to form his fellow-citizens for the enjoyment of civil happiness. Every citizen was compelled to industry and to the utmost exertion of all his talents. The luxury of the rich constantly employed the industry of the poor. Commerce was encouraged, and the arts and sciences were cultivated with the greatest ardor. Common schools were established in which elementary instruction was given in music and grammar ; the gymnasia were furnished with a corps of instructors, some to maintain order among the youth, some to attend to their health and diet, some to teach the art of wrestling, and others to teach gymnastic exercises.

Philosophy was always a favorite study with the Athenians. This name was applied to all inquiries about the nature of the Deity, the origin and destiny of man, and the phenomena and powers of the physical world. Public schools of philosophy were established, among the most famous of which were the Academy, of which Plato was the first teacher; the Lyceum, the school of Aristotle; Cynosarges, where Antisthenes taught; the Stoa, where Zeno of Cyprus opened his school; and the garden which Epicurus bought in which to instruct his pupils, who are thence called "philosophers of the garden."

The three branches of instruction recognized among the Athenians as the essential elements of a liberal education at the time of Socrates were grammar, gymnastic training, and music. Up to the age of sixteen the education of youth was left entirely to parents or guardians. The boy first attended the grammar school, where he was taught his alphabet and how to speak and write correctly; later he studied grammar, under which was included not only a knowledge of the language, but also something of poetry, eloquence, history, and the elements of philosophy. He also attended the palestra, where he learned the exercises, and received instruction from the professional harper or flute-player, who taught him the rudiments of music. At the age of sixteen he entered the gymnasium, where he was trained in gymnastic exercises under public teachers who kept him under severe discipline. At the age of eighteen he entered upon his apprenticeship in arms, during which he had to perform several duties for the protection of his country. At the end of two years he was admitted to the rights of a citizen, and until the age of sixty was liable to be called upon to perform military service.

If, however, it was intended the boy should occupy a place in the upper ranks on a level intellectually with those who gave the tone to society and were regarded as finished gentlemen, there must be acquired a knowledge of literature, and especially of poetry, above all, an intimate acquaintance with the classic writings of Homer; to which should be added a familiarity with philosophical systems and skill in composition and oratory. These accomplishments, which correspond to the higher education of to-day, were acquired in the celebrated schools of philosophy.

Among the means for promoting knowledge were the public libraries, some of which are celebrated in history. Pisistratus, who reigned from 560 B. C. to 527 B. C., is said to have been the first Greek who formed a library for the good of those who wished to avail themselves of it. It was also during his reign that the works of Homer were collected into one body and constituted the first production that circulated among the Greeks in a written form. Sylla gained possession of the library when he took the city of Athens 85 B. C., and removed it to Rome. Another library of great value, said to have been collected by Aristotle, was also carried to Rome by Sylla.

The most flourishing period in the history of Greece was during the time intervening between Solon and Alexander. The arts and sciences were cultivated with great success, eloquence and poetry were raised to the greatest eminence, and Greek literature rose to its greatest splendor. After the death of Alexander 323 B. C., Greek literature gradually declined. Among the causes were the increasing luxury and consequent effeminacy of the people, the various internal political commotions, the loss of their independence, the establishment of schools at Rhodes, Alexandria, and Constantinople, and finally the suppression of the philosophical and rhetorical schools of Athens by the Emperor Justinian, because the teachers opposed his efforts to exterminate paganism.

The most brilliant age of Roman literature began with the capture of Corinth and Carthage 146 B. C., and continued to the death of Augustus, A. D. 14. The progress of the Romans in the arts and sciences was so great that it has excited the admiration of posterity, and secured them a rank among the nations of antiquity second only to the Greeks. Familiarity with Greek civilization caused them to imitate the best Grecian models. They began to admire poetry and study the principles of language They applied themselves to historical researches, studied jurisprudence, took a great interest in Grecian philosophy, and cultivated the art of oratory. Great improvements were made in the system of education. The methods of the Greeks were adopted, the instructors were Greeks, and Grecian letters and arts constituted the principal study. Public schools were established in which were taught not only the elements of the Greek and Latin language, but also the principles of poetry and oratory, the principal works of which were analyzed and explained.

From Kennett's *Antiquities* we learn that " at the age of six or seven, children were sent to masters called literatores, who taught them to read and write. They were then sent to the grammar schools to learn the art of speaking well and the understanding of authors; frequently to the houses of great men, where some eminent grammarian was employed not only to instruct the children, but also to assist the master of the house in his oratorical exercises. At the age of seventeen, when the youths put on the manly toga, they were brought in a solemn manner to the forum and entered in the study of pleading ; not only if they designed to make this their chief profession, but although their inclinations lay rather to the camp. For we scarce meet with a good captain who was not a good speaker, or any eminent orator who had not served some time in the army. Thus it was requisite for all persons who had any thoughts of rising in the world to make a good appearance both at the bar and in the field ; because if the success of their valor and conduct should advance them to any considerable post it would have proved almost impossible without the advantage of eloquence to maintain their authority with the senate and people; or if the force of their oratory should in time procure them the honorable office of prætor, or consul, they would not have been in a capacity to undertake the government of the provinces without some experience in military command."

Collections of books were quite numerous at Rome. Besides the public libraries there were several distinguished private libraries, many citizens having them in their palaces or at their country villas. The library occupied one of the principal apartments in the house, usually on the eastern side of the building. They were ornamented with paintings and with statues and busts of distinguished writers. The books were arranged along the walls in cases which were numbered and had subdivisions. Grammarians, and Greek slaves or freedmen, were appointed for the librarians.

The decline of Roman literature may be dated from the end of the reign of Augustus, A. D. 14, and its history is considered as terminated with the overthrow of the Western Empire, A. D. 476. The establishment of Christianity necessarily tended to encourage a new system of education and a new form and spirit of literature.

Historical Review

THE limitations of our subject allow only a brief mention of the subjugation of Media, Phœnicia, Asia Minor, and Egypt by Persia under Cyrus, Cambyses, Darius, and Xerxes; of the struggle for supremacy between Persia and Greece which resulted in the defeat of Persia after the battles of Marathon, Thermopylæ, Salamis, Platæa, and Mycale; of the rise of Greece and the extension of its civilization over the whole of the ancient world, — a civilization which in many respects has never been surpassed by either ancient or modern nations; of the establishment of the republics of Lacedæmon and Athens, where the government was in the hands of the people, and where resided those great lawgivers Lycurgus and Solon; of the supremacy of Athens, which saw the most brilliant epoch in its history under the leadership of Pericles, at which time lived Herodotus, Lysias, Æschylus, Sophocles, Euripides, Aristophanes, Phidias, and Apelles; of the extension of the dominions of Greece and of the building of Alexandria about 330 B. C. by Alexander the Great, which under the Ptolemies became the centre of commerce and Greek culture for the eastern and western worlds; of the rise and progress of Rome until it became mistress of the world under Constantine the Great, who transferred the seat of empire from Rome to Byzantium, which from him received the name of Constantinople. He openly embraced Christianity, raising it to the rank of a state religion, discountenanced all the old rites and superstitions, pulled down many of the heathen temples, and had others purified and consecrated as Christian churches. At the death of Constantine, A. D. 337, the Empire was divided into the Eastern and Western Empires. The Eastern Empire continued until about the middle of the seventh century, when Mahometanism swept over Asia and Africa and still remains the religion of a large portion of these countries. The Western Empire struggled along until A. D. 494, when Odoacer, a prince of the Heracli, defeated Orestes and became King of Italy. Britain, Gaul, Spain, and the south of Germany were invaded and subdued by other barbarians, and new and independent kingdoms established in these countries. It is a law of history that wherever a barbarous nation conquers a civilized people and rules over it, the barbarians generally adopt the civilization of the conquered and become absorbed by them. These barbarian nations in Britain, Gaul, Spain, and Italy soon became Romanized, adopting the language, customs, laws, and religion of the conquered people; hence at the present day these countries form the links which connect our modern civilization with that of the Roman Empire, and their languages are living monuments of the dominion of Rome.

Only a slight reference can be made to the great historical events of the ten centuries following the overthrow of the Western Roman Empire, — a period in history known as the Middle or Dark Ages. As the Greek and Latin classics were at variance with the teachings of Christianity, they were prohibited by the Fathers of the Church, men's minds were deprived of the means of enlightenment, and ignorance, superstition, and barbarism overspread the countries of Europe, until the revival of the study of classical literature, the spirit of which is called the Renaissance; and freedom from the spiritual tyranny exercised by the papacy over all Christendom, which kept the human mind in bondage, led to an advance in civilization which at the present day has reached a point which in many respects is much superior to that of any country in the ancient world.

Among the more important events were: first, the rise of the feudal system, or the system by which the proprietors of the lands held them on condition of performing military service when required by their sovereign. Second, the rise of the monarchy of the Franks, which under the dominion of Charles the Great had revived the Western Empire of the Romans and rivalled in extent of territory and power the proudest times of Ancient Rome. Although the state of the arts and sciences was very low, Charles the Great employed every means in his power to improve them. He endeavored to promote education, agriculture, arts, manufactures, and commerce. He projected great national works and built sumptuous palaces at Aix-la-Chapelle and Ingelheim, and many churches. He possessed a knowledge unusual for his age, could speak Latin and read Greek. He gave great encouragement to literature, and invited learned men from all quarters to reside in his dominions. He invited Alcuin of England, the most distinguished divine and philosopher of his time, to become his instructor and counsellor, and employed him to promote the cause of education and learning in the schools and colleges which he founded. Third, the progress of Christianity until at the time of Charles the Great it was the religion of nearly the whole of Europe, Asia, and Africa. As the Church grew stronger costly cathedrals were built, numerous rites and ceremonies were added to the public worship, fasts and festivals were observed, and pictures and images of Christ and the Apostles adorned the walls of the churches. The festivals of the Church were celebrated with such pomp and ceremony that the difference between the religion of the pagans and the Christians would appear to be in name only. Not satisfied with spiritual power, the Church aspired to temporal power, which was granted by the Emperor Pepin and confirmed by Charles the Great. Fourth, the era of the crusades and the rise of chivalry and romance. Fifth, the invention of printing, the discovery of America, and the circumnavigation of Africa. Sixth, the Renaissance, or a revival of the taste for classical literature, which was greatly assisted by the dispersion of the Greeks, by the taking of Constantinople by the Mahometans in 1453, which sent forth over Western Europe the pent-up stream of all the learning of the old world which had so long stood stagnant in that seat of ancient splendor. Seventh, the Reformation, or that great spiritual and ecclesiastical movement begun by Luther at the beginning of the sixteenth century and as a result of which the Protestant Church separated from the Roman See. A Reformed Church entirely independent of Rome was established in Denmark, Sweden, Norway, Holland, and many parts of Germany, France, and Switzerland, which separated from the Church of Rome, threw aside its superstitions, renounced the supremacy of the Pope, and embraced a more scriptural form of faith.

In England, however, the readjustment of ecclesiastical affairs which was brought about by Henry VIII. was rather a change of rulers than a reformation. The throne had taken the Pope's place as the head of the Church, the monasteries had been suppressed, and the spoils divided with otherwise as little change as possible. The Protestants and Presbyterians were not satisfied, but wished a reconstruction of the whole ecclesiastical fabric. During the reign of Mary many of them were obliged to seek safety in exile on the continent, and while there learned Calvin's ideas of theology and church government. On their return to England after the accession of Elizabeth they wished to carry into practice the new ideas. They assumed that the liturgy, ceremonies, and discipline of the Church of England required further reformation ; that the Church as then constituted did not separate itself markedly enough from Roman Catholicism ; and that it was desirable in the interest of religion to abandon everything that could boast of no other authority than tradition or the will of man, and to follow as far as possible the " pure " word of God. Hence they were called Puritans. The queen, however, would not tolerate their notions, and during her reign and also during the reigns of James I. and Charles I. all who refused to obey the Episcopal ordinances were severely punished. The hardships to which they were exposed became so great that many of them emigrated to New England and there cultivated unmolested that form of Christianity to which they were attached.

Institution of the Public School

I T must be kept in mind that certainly as late as the beginning of the seventeenth century education in the modern sense of that term was confined to the children of the upper classes, such as the nobles, gentry, small freeholders and merchants. The children of the farm laborers, mechanics, and servants received practically no education. At Athens in the time of Pericles the free citizens numbered fourteen thousand; of the slaves there were four hundred thousand. Among the Romans, Horace considers ten slaves the minimum, even for one of restricted means, and talks of the ridicule thrown upon Tullius the prætor, because he had no more than five slaves to accompany him from the Tiburtine villa to Rome. In 1500 the population of England is estimated to have been three millions, a very small portion of which received any education. London was the great city, containing about sixty or seventy thousand inhabitants, and there were perhaps a dozen considerable towns besides; but the large majority of the population lived in the country on the large estates of the nobles and knights, — "an indiscriminate mass of workmen and farm-laborers of both sexes who slept on the premises and ate at the table of their employer." In the language of an act of Parliament of 1530 there were "huge routes and companyes of vagaboundes and beggers strolling about in great and excessive nombres whereby hath insurged and sprung continual theftes, murders, and other sundry and heynous offences and great enormities, to the high displeasure of God, the inquietation and damage of the King's people, and to the marvelous disturbance of the common weal of this realm." Henry VIII. hanged seventy thousand robbers, thieves, and vagabonds.

For many centuries knowledge was confined to the clergy, although under this term were comprehended many who were not clergymen. Hence the word *clericus*, or *clerk*, became synonymous with *penman*, in which sense it is still most usually employed. If a man could write or read, it was considered a proof presumptive that he was in holy orders. Among the Anglo-Saxons children learned the psalms and other books by heart. They were brought up religiously at home under their parents or masters, then at monasteries or under bishops, who either made of them monks or clerks, or sent them when young men, armed, to the king.

The laity, or the people who were not clerks, had but little use for letters. Commerce was carried on principally by truck or barter, or by payments in money. Amounts were cast up by means of an abacus, an instrument for performing arithmetical calculations by balls sliding on wires, familiar to us in our childhood days and which are to be seen in every Chinese laundry office. Many important transactions which now require writing were effected by word of mouth, and whenever it was necessary to convey intelligence from place to place an oral message was sent through a courier despatched for the purpose, or some person going in that direction.

The credit of instituting the public school for the elementary education of the poor belongs to the Christian Church. In order to promulgate the doctrine of Christianity it was necessary to have a succession of teachers. The injunction of Saint Paul to Timothy was, " And the things that thou hast heard of me among many witnesses, the same commit thou to faithful men who shall be able to teach others also," and the command was carried out most effectually. Schools for the education of young Christians were established at Ephesus, Alexandria, and Rome by Saint John, Saint Mark, and Saint Peter. As the numbers of the Christians increased, it became necessary to build or set apart houses for the express purpose of holding assemblies for public worship, and whenever a Christian church was planted, a school for the nurture of children and youth for the service of religion and the duties of society was also established.

As the disciples themselves came from the more humble walks of life, so the pupils of these theological schools were drawn from the poorer classes. In A. D. 529 the Council of Vaison strongly recommended the establishment of village schools. In A. D. 800 a synod at Mayence ordered that the parochial priests should have schools in the towns and villages, that the children of all the faithful might learn letters from them : " Let them receive and teach these with the utmost charity that they may themselves shine as the stars forever. Let them receive no remuneration from their scholars unless what the parents through charity may voluntarily offer." A council at Rome in A. D. 836 ordained that there should be three kinds of schools established throughout Christendom : episcopal, parochial in towns and villages, and others wherever there could be found place and opportunity. A decree was promulgated to establish eight public schools in some of the principal cities of Italy, " in order that opportunity may be given to all, and that there may be no excuse drawn from poverty and the difficulty of repairing to remote places." In A. D. 1215 the Council of Lyons decreed " that in all cathedral churches, and others provided with adequate revenues, there should be established a school and a teacher by the bishop and chapter, who should teach the clerks and other poor scholars gratis in grammar, and for this purpose a stipend should be assigned him."

On this point we quote Henry Barnard, LL.D., superintendent of common schools in Connecticut : " Such was the origin of the popular school, as now generally understood, everywhere the offspring and companion of the Church ; sharing with her, in large measure, the imperfections which attach to all new institutions and all human instrumentalities ; encountering peculiar difficulties from the barbarism of the age and people through which it passed, and which it was its mission to enlighten ; and everywhere crippled by insufficient endowments, unqualified teachers, and the absence of all text-books, and necessary aids to instruction and illustration. The discovery of the art of printing in 1440, and the consequent multiplication of books at prices which brought them within reach of the great mass of the people ; the study and use of the vernacular language by the scholars and divines, and particularly its employment in the printing of the Bible, hymns, popular songs, school-books, and in religious instruction generally; the recognition by the municipal authorities of cities, and at a later period by the higher civil power, of the right, duty, and interest of the state, in connection with, or independent of, the Church, to provide liberally and efficiently for the education of all children and youth ; and, above all, the intense activity given to the human mind by the religious movement of Luther, in the early part of the sixteenth century ; the assertion of the right of private judgment in the interpretation of the Scriptures ; the breaking up of existing ecclesiastical foundations, and the diversion of funds from religious to educational purposes, — all these causes, combined with the general progress of society, co-operated to introduce an advantageous change in the organization, administration, instruction, and discipline of the popular school. But the progress actually made from year to year, and century even to century, was slow; and after three hundred years of effort, there is much yet to be done even in those states and communities which have accomplished the most toward improving the outward organization and instrumentalities of the schools, and, above all, its internal life, in the improved qualification and position of the teachers, for as is the teacher, so is the school."

The Early Schools in England

I N England the earliest mention of a school dates back to the permanent introduction of Christianity. One of the oldest schools of which anything is known is the school of Canterbury, which is stated to have been established probably by Saint Augustine, who in A. D. 596 was sent with forty other monks by Pope Gregory I. to convert the Anglo-Saxons to Christianity and to establish the authority of the Roman See in Britain. Instruction was given not only in divinity, but also in astronomy, medicine, arithmetic, and the Greek and Latin languages. The Archbishop of Canterbury is primate of all England, metropolitan, and first peer of the realm. He ranks next to royalty and crowns the sovereign. Among his privileges he can confer degrees in divinity, law, and medicine.

For many centuries schools were found only in connection with monasteries and cathedrals. Among the most famous of these monastic schools was that founded by Bishop Benedict about 670 A. D., in his abbey at Wearmouth, where he also established a famous library made from books and pictures collected by him in Rome and Vienna, to which places he made several journeys for the purpose of securing books for the education of his monks. Among his pupils was the Venerable Bede, author of the ecclesiastical history of Britain. Another famous school was the cathedral school of York, founded by Archbishop Egbert, who had been a friend and fellow-pupil with Bede at Yarrow. At this school was educated Alcuin, the most distinguished scholar of the eighth century, the confidant and adviser of Charles the Great, and to whom that emperor committed the superintendence of education in his dominions.

The ravages of the Danes, which began in A. D. 787, totally destroyed the institutions of learning by dispersing the monks and burning their monasteries and libraries. About A. D. 880, after completely defeating the Danes, King Alfred wished to raise his people from a condition of ignorance and vice by promoting education among all classes. He addressed a circular letter to the bishops earnestly recommending the translations of "useful books into the language which we all understand, so that all the youth of England, but more especially those who are of gentle kind, and at ease in their circumstances, may be grounded in letters, for they cannot profit in any pursuit until they are well able to read English." "When I took the kingdom," says Alfred, "very few on this side of the Humber, very few beyond, not one that I could recollect south of the Thames, could understand their prayers in English, or could translate from Latin into English."

He invited learned men from all quarters of Europe to reside in England. He himself acquired a sufficient knowledge of Latin in his thirty-eighth year to translate the only book of Saxon history then extant. He re-established many of the old monastic schools and insisted that the officers of government should qualify themselves for their office, and in case they refused rejected them. Aldermen, magistrates, and governors were compelled to go to school for this late instruction or else give up their emoluments and office. He enjoined every freeholder possessed of sixty acres of land to send his children there for instruction. These schools were intended for every person of rank and substance, who, either from age or want of capacity, was unable to learn or read himself, and who was compelled to send to school either his son or a kinsman, or if he had neither, a servant that he might at least be read to by some one. He established a seminary, which was attended not only by the sons of the nobility, but also by many of the inferior clans, and this seminary is claimed to have been the foundation of the University of Oxford.

In the following centuries schools were established by eminent prelates. Joffrid, Abbot of Croyland, established a school at Cottenham in A. D. 1110, which is thought to be the origin of the University of Cambridge. In A. D. 1190 Sampson, Abbot of St. Edmunds, founded a school for forty boys at Bury St. Edmunds. William of Wykeham, Bishop of Winchester, " to relieve poor scholars in their clerical education, and for the support and exaltation of the Christian faith, and the improvement of the liberal arts," founded a college at Oxford in A. D. 1382. In the course of time other colleges were endowed by benevolent persons for the maintenance of the poorer students. The object of the colleges was to educate young men who were to devote their lives to study and for the service of the Church. The recipients of the endowments were known as *fellows*. The assistance was intended to last no longer than the completion of the course of study, but as most of the fellows belonged to the ecclesiastical order, and had no other means of support, aid was usually continued until the fellow succeeded in obtaining a benefice. Later, wealthy students who wished to receive an education in law, medicine, or other science were received as boarders and received the name of commoners, or students not on the foundation. Evidently these were not public schools in the modern sense. They were public only because any one could apply for admission either as fellow or commoner, and the number of fellows was limited to the amount of the foundation.

Education in its early stages was rarely conducted at home, but at courts, or in the houses of nobles. The period of infancy and boyhood was intrusted to women, and at the age of eleven years tuition was begun in earnest. In royal houses, the parents selected some veteran and able soldier of noble family, under whose roof their son was placed; and in whose castle, beginning his services as a page, he received instructions in the exercises and accomplishments befitting his conditions.

Plain education dates from the fourteenth century; reading and writing were the chief branches, but children were also taught grammar. Parochial grammar schools occur in the fifteenth century, but so few were they and so low was the grammar learning taught in them that in A. D. 1447 there was presented to Parliament a petition by four clergymen setting forth the lack of grammar schools and good teachers in the City of London, and praying leave to establish schools and appoint competent masters in their respective parishes. This is generally considered to have been the origin of free grammar schools, so called. The only one of the schools established in consequence of the petition, which has survived to the present time, is the Mercer's School, which was originally founded for seventy scholars of any age or place, subject to the management of the Mercer's Company. Those children whose parents could afford the expense received the rudiments of an education in the petty schools. Of these a few who showed an aptitude for letters and learning would be sent to the grammar schools, and later would be received at the colleges as fellows or commoners.

The greater portion of the people received but very little education. Few of the laity, even of the highest rank, could read or write, and their children spent their youth in idleness. Aubrey says, " from the time of Erasmus down to 1660, learning was downright pedantry. The conversation and habits of these times were as starched as their bands and square beards, and gravity was taken for wisdom. The doctors were old boys. Quibbles passed for wit even in sermons. The gentry and citizens had little learning of any kind."

John Timbs says, " In the year 1400 the average instruction of an English gentleman of the first class would comprehend common reading and writing, a tolerable familiarity with French, and a slight tincture of Latin, the latter attained, or not, according to his circumstances."

A passage in Camden's *Remains* reads, " A nobleman in the time of Henry VIII., in contempt of learning, said that it was for Noble men's sons enough to wind their horn and carry their hawk fair, and to leave study and learning to the children of mean men."

The ability to read gave to clergymen in early times exemption from criminal punishment in certain cases. They appeared in clerical habits and claimed the " benefit of clergy." This privilege was afterwards extended to all offenders who could read, but only for the first offence. In the time of Edward VI. it was enacted that any Lord of the Parliament might claim the benefit of clergy even if he could not read. The ignorance of the nobility is shown in a sermon preached by Bishop Latimer in 1548. He says : " Why are not the noblemen and young gentlemen of England so brought up in knowledge of God, and in learning, that they may be able to execute offices in the common weal ? If the nobility be well trained in godly learning, the people would follow the same train, for truly such as the noblemen be, such will the people be. Therefore, for the love of God appoint teachers and schoolmasters, you that have the charge of youth, and give the teachers stipends worthy their pains. The hundreds of young gentlemen should be so well brought up in learning and the knowledge of God that they would not, when they became of age, so much give themselves to other vanities."

The suppression of the monasteries by Henry VIII. and the diversion of the funds left by charitable persons for the education and support of the poor was followed by the destruction of a large portion of the schools. A portion of these funds, however, was used for the endowment of a class of schools now known as grammar schools. Twenty-one grammar schools were thus founded by Edward VI. (1547–1553), which are still flourishing. Mr. Barnard says : " The example continued to be followed during a century and a half; and many free grammar schools were established for the instruction of poor children in the learned language. From these often humble and unpretending edifices has issued a series of names illustrious in the annals of their country : a succession of men, often of obscure parentage and stinted means, who have justified the wisdom of the founders of grammar schools in providing education for those who would otherwise have been without it, and thus securing to the State the services of the best of her children."

These schools were not public schools in the modern sense. By Free School and Free Grammar School was meant a school for the teaching of Greek and Latin, and in some cases Latin only, and for no other gratuitous teaching. A few of the poor who were unable to pay for their education were to be selected, some according to the parish in which they were born, some on account of the name they bore, to receive instruction in the learned languages and under certain conditions to be supported through the university.

At the age of six or eight the boy enters the grammar school, which takes its name from the Greek *gramma*, a letter, and in which the pupil was to be taught the principles of language. As grammar schools were in existence before the English language was written, and as all knowledge of the principles of language could be obtained only through a study of the grammar of the Greek and Latin languages, and as even at the present time in many universities the ancient languages are recognized as the basis of a liberal education, the study of the ancient languages was the principal subject of instruction in the public or grammar schools.

From the sketch of a grammar school founded in Sandwich in 1580, by Sir Robert Manwood, it appears that *ciphering* was not considered a necessary acquisition by the young pupils. Latin and parsing words were the chief exercises. Mr. Ayscough, indeed, writing in 1797, says : " Whatever may be the present usage in grammar schools, it is within recollection that, fifty years ago, there were sent from capital schools, to the universities, youths of good abilities, and not by any means wanting in grammar and classical learning, yet so little versed in common figures, as to be obliged to have recourse to a master of a day school in the town for instruction in the four fundamental rules of arithmetic."

By " public schools " are meant the ancient foundations of Winchester, Eton, Harrow, Westminster, St. Paul's, Merchant Taylors, and the modern seminaries of Marlborough, Cheltenham, and Wellington College. The late Lord Pauncefote, after receiving his early education at Geneva and Paris, returned to England, and was one of the first boys to enter the gates of Marlborough College, which was incorporated in 1845.

Endowed grammar schools of the old foundation exist in all the principal towns of England, and are frequented both by day pupils and boarders from the country. The nucleus of these schools of course are the foundationers, to furnish whose board and education these schools were originally founded, but around them has grown up a large community composed of paying pupils from all parts of the country, tutors, and keepers of boarding-houses. As the course of instruction was intended to prepare for the universities, Latin and Greek formed the basis of the whole instruction ; geography, history, arithmetic, and mathematics occupying a subordinate place in the curriculum.

These schools were frequented by the sons of the professional classes and the wealthier tradesmen. It was not until about the time of the Revolution that free schools were established where poor boys could be clothed and taught the studies which were fitted to those destined to a life of traffic. These schools were founded by uneducated men who had pushed their way to fortune and honor and were generously resolved to do something for their own class. Then while the grammar schools were making divines, lawyers, and physicians out of the sons of the upper classes, the free schools were making clever handicraftsmen and thriving citizens out of the sons of the mechanics and laborers. When he arrived at the age of fifteen the free-school boy was ready to be apprenticed to a trade; at eighteen, and sometimes earlier, the grammar-school boy passed to the university.

Previous to the invention of printing, all books were in manuscript and were scarce and costly. One of the statutes of St. Mary's College, Oxford, in the time of Henry VI., shows the inconvenience to study arising from the scarcity of books. It reads: "Let no scholar occupy a book in the library over one hour, or two at most, so that others shall be hindered from the use of the same." Books were first kept in chests, and next chained to the desks, lest their rarity and value might tempt those who used them, and it was a very common thing to write on the first leaf of a book, "Cursed be he who steals or tears out the leaves, or in any way injures this book," — an anathema, but slightly changed, which may be found in books of the present day. After the invention of printing, the prices of books were greatly reduced. In 1396 the price of *Seven Books of Grammar in one Volume* was 4*s.*; seventy-five years later a printed copy could be purchased for 1*s.* or less.

English School=Books of the Seventeenth Century

I N March, 1902, Professor Foster Watson read a paper before the Bibliographical Society of London on *English Schools of the First Half of the Seventeenth Century*, from which is taken the following extract : —

"Elementary teaching in the first half of the seventeenth century in England is much more difficult to trace than is the (Latin) Grammar teaching. The best source of our knowledge of 'Petty' School teaching is to be found in Charles Hoole's *New Discovery of the Old Art of Teaching School* (1660). Brinsley, in his *Ludus Literarius* (1612), gives indications. Amongst text-books for elementary teaching, probably none was more popular than E. Coote's *English Schoolmaster*, first published in 1590, at the price of one shilling, the twenty-sixth edition of which was issued in 1656. From the latter it appears that elementary education was undertaken by tailors, weavers, shopkeepers, seamstresses, and others, along with their ordinary occupation. Hoole suggests that elementary teaching would keep some poor man or woman who knew not how to live otherwise.

"Reading, according to Brinsley, was taught, first, by Horn-book Alphabets; second, by The A B C, or, as we should say, Spelling; third, by The Primer (that is, prayers and religious exercises put forth by royal authority); fourth, by The Psalms in metre; fifth, by The Testament; sixth, by *The School of Virtue* and *The School of Good Manners*.

" The Catechism occupied an important position in elementary teaching. Andrew Maunsell, in 1595, enumerates sixty-eight different catechisms sold in London. William Loudon's Catalogue in 1658 includes a larger number. Hugh Peters, in 1660, says there ' are near an hundred several Catechisms in the Nation.' The Books of Manners, Civility, and Courtesy were numerous. Hoole recommends as reading-books Herbert's *Poems* and Quarles' *Emblems*, probably the first suggestion of English Literature in school-teaching.

" Brinsley gives directions for teaching writing and for the scholar to make and mend his own (quill) pens. But writing was chiefly taught by writing-masters, who seem to have formed a special class of private schools. Cocker was a writing-master rather than an arithmetic-master, though he taught both subjects. The writing-master in the country schools was peregrinatory, staying from a fortnight to a month in a place. The problem was often how to keep up the writing in a school between his yearly visits. Writing became a specialized fine art till it reached its climax in George Bickham's *Universal Penman* in 1741. Brinsley sends his pupils to the Cyphering School in 1612, and Hoole in 1660 sends his boys to Mr. Hodder for Arithmetic. As other subjects got added to the curriculum of the writing-master, writing schools developed into the modern private schools. Mr. Noah Bridges, in 1653, besides Writing and Arithmetic, includes Greek, Latin, Arts and Sciences, Mathematics, Merchants' Accounts, etc. Mulcaster, in 1581, said ' our country doth allow music ' in the schools, but this subject was lost during the Civil War. Sir Thomas Elyot and Mulcaster had advocated drawing, but it did not get a hold on the schools.

" The intensification of religious feeling especially traceable to the Marian persecution brought before the schools the function of interrogating children as to the sermons heard in church, and this gave rise to a whole series of shorthand text-books.

"But it is difficult to say how many of these subjects were taught in the elementary schools ; that is, petty schools, — probably only reading and a little writing.   Apparently Charles Hoole is the first to suggest the collocation, in the curriculum of the Petty School, of reading, writing, and arithmetic."

The foregoing sketch of the progress of education from early days to the beginning of the seventeenth century affords a slight glimpse of the school privileges in England in the latter part of the sixteenth and the earlier part of the seventeenth century, and it was during this period that the fathers of New England received their education.

Early Schools of New England

EARLY SCHOOLS
of NEW ENGLAND

𝕰𝖉𝖚𝖈𝖆𝖙𝖎𝖔𝖓 𝖎𝖓 𝕸𝖆𝖘𝖘𝖆𝖈𝖍𝖚𝖘𝖊𝖙𝖙𝖘

IN the early part of the seventeenth century there was in England a large body of men belonging to the more progressive middle class, — the class represented by Milton, Newton, and the illustrious men who later brought on the revolution of 1688, who were discontented with their condition, and were seeking a way out. Dissenting from the Established Church, they had suffered such persecution that residence in England had become almost unbearable. Indeed, the Pilgrims had already left England and were temporarily sojourning in Holland. The Puritans, although as strongly desirous of freedom, were more conservative, and had not entirely broken with the civil and ecclesiastical authorities. It finally became evident that the only way in which they could enjoy their religious, civil, and social faith was by planting themselves in a new country, far away from their oppressors; and between 1620 and 1640 about twenty thousand people sailed across the ocean and founded the colonies of Plymouth, Massachusetts Bay, New Haven, and Connecticut. They were endowed with an intelligent, industrious spirit, willing to toil for the cause of civil and religious liberty, and peculiarly fitted to lay the foundation of what is to-day the Great American Republic. Among them were many graduates of the English universities, who brought from home a good reputation for superior scholarship and honorable service in church and college.

In speaking of the Company of the Massachusetts Bay, Dr. Haven says : " Whether we consider the private history or the combined proceedings of this association, we are constrained to pronounce it a remarkable body of men. Purity of motive, greatness of purpose, boldness of action, and policy of conduct have seldom been so equally united. There were among them men of culture, in some cases to the extent of profound learning ; men of business talent, manifested by successful enterprise ; men of philanthropic zeal, and men of far-reaching political designs. To call them pious men, seeking to provide a refuge from religious persecution, expresses but a portion of the motives by which they were actuated. The idea of civil liberty was inseparably connected with that of religious freedom, in the conception and in the execution of their plans."

To people of such intelligence, about to plant themselves in a new country inhabited by savages, with an ocean between them and the fatherland, it was very important that the Company under whose auspices they proposed to venture, should guarantee that every facility should be furnished for the education and religious instruction of their children. Fortunately the leader in the organization of the Company of the Massachusetts Bay was the Rev. John White, Rector of Trinity Parish, in Dorchester, England, who has been called "the Father of the Massachusetts Colony." He was a moderate Puritan who conformed to the ceremonies of the Church of England. Actuated by religious and philanthropic motives, as well as by hope of gain, he had helped to found the Plymouth Colony. In 1624 he was a member of the Company which attempted to establish a colony at Cape Anne, for which moral and religious instruction was to be provided by ministers sent out by the Company. He is described as a person of great gravity and presence, and had always influence in the Puritanical party, near to and remote from him, who bore him more respect than they did to the diocesan. He is known to have been very much interested in education, and it is probable that it is owing to his influence that in the measures taken for the welfare of the Colony the religious and educational interests were so well protected.

From an examination of the Records of the various meetings of the Company held in England preparatory to removing to New England, we find that provision was to be made for sending ministers to New England, and in the contract of the ministers with the Company it was agreed in consideration of £20 a year and other inducements "to do their endeavor in their places of the ministry as well in preaching and catechizing, as also in teaching or causing to be taught the Company's servants and their children, as also the savages and their children, whereby to their uttermost to further the main end of this Plantation, being, by the assistance of Almighty God, the conversion of the savages."

The following extracts are taken from the Company's First Letter of Instructions to Governor Endicott and his Council:

"And for that the propagation of the Gospel is the thing we do profess above all to be our aim in settling this Plantation we have been careful to make plentiful provision of Godly ministers by whose faithful preaching, godly conversation, and exemplary life, we trust not only those of our own nation will be built up in the knowledge of God but also the Indians may in God's appointed time be reduced to the obedience of the Gospel of Christ. . . .

" . . . For the manner of the exercising their ministry and teaching both our own people and the Indians, we leave that to themselves, hoping they will make God's word the rule of their actions, and mutually agree in the discharge of their duties. . . .

" . . . We send you the particular names of such as are entertained for the Company's service, amongst which we hope you will find many religious, discreet, and well-ordered persons, which you must set over the rest, dividing them into families, placing some with the ministers, and others under such as being honest men and of their own calling as near as may be, may have care to see them well educated in their general callings as Christians, and particular according to their several trades or fitness in disposition to learn a trade. . . .

" . . . And to the end the Sabbath may be celebrated in a religious manner we appoint that all that inhabit the Plantation, both for the general and particular employments, may surcease their labors every Saturday throughout the year at three of the clock in the afternoon, and that they spend the rest of the day in catechising and preparation for the Sabbath, as the minister shall direct. . . .

" . . . We have entertained Lambert Wilson, chirurgeon, to remain with you in the service of the Plantation : and he is to educate and instruct in his art one or more youths, such as you and the said Council shall appoint, that may be helpful to him, and if occasion serve, to succeed him in the Plantation : which youth or youths, fit to learn that profession, let be placed with him."

In this last extract is the germ of the Medical School, undoubtedly the first contemplated in the English Colonies. These extracts make it very evident that the interests of the children were carefully protected by the Company, and that while the children of the masses were to receive an education in the fundamental principles of religion, and to be taught trades by master-workmen by which they could support themselves in later years and become dutiful citizens, the higher education of those who were to occupy official positions in after years was committed to the ministers.

Teaching was not a new thing to these ministers. It had been a general custom in England for ministers to receive scholars in their families who were to be prepared for the universities, and many of the Non-conformist and Dissenting ministers, when deprived of their benefices, supported themselves by teaching. The Puritan ministers were men of liberal education, and many of them, having studied medicine, were fitted for any emergency. They not only practised in their parishes, but took part in the medical controversies of the day. In the *Magnalia* Cotton Mather speaks of this union of the two professions as an " Angelic Conjunction " and says : " Ever since the days of Luke the Evangelist, skill in physic has been frequently professed and practised by persons whose more declared business was the study of divinity." They were also educated in the law, and frequently intricate cases were submitted to them for decision. Of the eight members of the Colonial Council chosen by the Company three were ministers ; and when the deputies of the freemen demanded a code of written laws, Mr. John Cotton and Mr. Nathaniel Ward framed models which were presented to the General Court for consideration.

At first the child received his primary education at home, but when able to stand alone, to read words of two syllables, and able to keep his place, he was sent to the minister, who was the superintendent of the secondary and higher education. The Company by its contract with the minister was obliged to furnish him with a house, and it is probable that the first schools, such as they were, were kept in these houses. Later, when meeting-houses had been built, they were transferred to them, as furnishing more suitable accommodations, and in these the children received the best education it was possible to obtain previous to the establishment of the College in 1636. But the rapid increase in the number of the colonists and the great demand for the assistance of the minister in civil as well as in religious affairs made it evident that the education of the children required the services of some one who could devote his whole attention to it.   The use of the meeting-house for various gatherings interrupted the sessions of the schools, and there was a necessity for buildings devoted only to school purposes.

Although the Company in its instructions to its agents had provided for a certain amount of education, yet it never contemplated the establishment of public schools ; and it was contrary to precedent for a government to undertake the public education of the children.   Therefore it would have been useless to appeal to the Court of Assistants, which had no authority to consider such an appeal and which had all it could attend to in managing the varied enterprises which had already been undertaken.   Accordingly, no action was taken until after the establishment of that grand institution which may well be called the cause of the American Republic, the New England Town Meeting.   Mr. Frothingham, in his *History of Charlestown*, speaks of it as follows : " These little assemblies, open to all, where debate was free as thought, were the primary school of freedom.   In selecting officers, in deciding about dividing the land, supporting schools and the university, making by-laws, and discussing parliamentary measures, there was evolved an independence of mind and a manliness of character that constituted a wide and admirable preparation for more important political action.   Their influence was decided.   Andros when he suppressed them, Hutchinson when he denounced them, and the British Parliament when it prohibited them, knew what they were about.   Such action on the part of their enemies is a solid testimonial of their value.   One of their friends (Judge Story) assigns to them the credit of having commenced the American Revolution."

At the beginning groups of colonists who wished to be neighbors were allowed to select their place of settlement and to govern themselves by their own rules provided these rules did not conflict with the Company's laws. In the first year eight such plantations had been settled. Others followed rapidly, and all adopted a similar form of government. They soon became known as towns, holding town meetings and electing town officers. The Court of Assistants, however, kept control of general affairs and enacted all the laws for the general welfare of the Colony. Although the charter provided for the admission of freemen into the Company, they were grudgingly admitted only after the Assistants had caused the passage of certain laws providing for their continuance in office and abridging the rights of the freemen. Soon after admission the freemen wished to exercise the rights provided for by the charter, among others that of having a part in the making of the laws. The Court of Assistants was reluctant to grant these rights, and made excuses for denying them. In 1634, just before the March meeting of the General Court, the deputies of the freemen demanded of the Governor a sight of the Charter. After examination they demanded a share in making the laws. Having met with a rebuff from the Governor, they carried the question into the General Court, and at the election deposed the Governor by electing in his place a man more to their liking. The influence of the towns was now felt in the management of Colonial affairs and led to great changes in the form of government. In March, 1636, the General Court passed a law regulating town governments, which has continued in force to the present day. It reads : " Whereas particular townes have many things which concern onely themselves and the ordering their own affairs, and disposeing of business in their owne towne, it is therefore ordered, that the freemen of every towne, or the major part of them, shall onely have power to dispose of their owne lands and woods, with all the previlidges and appurtenances of the said townes, to graunt lotts and make such orders as may concerne the well ordering of their owne townes, not repugnant to the lawes and orders here established by the Generall Court; as also to lay mulks and pinealties for the breach of their orders and to levy and distreine the same, not exceeding the some of XX^s; also to chuse their owne particular officers, as constables, surveyors for the highways, and the like; and because much business is like to ensue to the constables of severall townes, by reason they are to make distresses, and gather fynes, therefore that every towne shall have two constables, where there is neede, that soe their office may not be a burthen unto them, and that they may attend more carefully upon the discharge of their office, for which they shal be lyeable to their accompts to this Court when they shall be called thereunto."

This was the grand foundation of the town system of Massachusetts, which has proved to be the most perfect system of self-government ever devised or administered.

Dorchester claims the credit of having been the first plantation to establish the New England town meeting, when on the 8th of October, 1633, it passed an order establishing the form of government, which reads in part: " It is ordered that for the general good and well ordering of the affairs of the plantation there shall be every Monday before the Court by 8 o'clock A. M., and presently by the beating of the drum a general meeting of the inhabitants of the plantation at the meeting-house there to settle and set down such orders as may tend to the general good as aforesaid, and every man to be bound thereby, without gainsaying or resistance. It is also agreed that there shall be twelve men selected out of the company, that may, or the greatest part of them, meet as aforesaid, to determine as aforesaid." Attention is called to the use of the word " selected." When on the 6th of October, 1634, Boston chose a similar board, the members were designated as " the ten to manage the affairs of the town."

Edward Everett, in his Fourth of July oration in 1855, said of Dorchester: " It set the example in 1633 of that municipal organization which has prevailed throughout New England and has proved one of the chief sources of its progress."

During the first years the colonists had been so much engaged in the struggle for existence, in building homes in the wilderness, and in establishing the towns that they had not paid much attention to the education of the children. The author of *New England's First Fruits*, published in London in 1643, says: " After God had carried us safe to New England and we had builded our houses, provided necessaries for our livelihood, reared convenient places for God's worship, and settled the civil government, one of the next things we longed for and looked after was to advance learning and perpetuate it to posterity, dreading to leave an illiterate ministry to the churches when our present ministers shall lie in the dust. And as we were thinking and consulting how to effect this great work, it pleased God to stir up the heart of one Mr. Harvard, a godly gentleman and a lover of learning then living among us to give one half of his estate, towards the erecting of a college, and all his library. After him another gave £300, others after them cast in more, and the public hand of the State added the rest."

In 1636, when the entire population of the Massachusetts Bay Colony did not exceed five thousand persons, the General Court appropriated £400, a sum greater than the colonial taxes levied for all other purposes in a single year, to establish the school. It is said that this General Court, presided over by Sir Harry Vane, was the first body in which the people by their representatives ever gave their own money to found a place of education. The school or college, by order of the General Court, was erected in Newtowne, now Cambridge. In 1638 it took the name of Harvard, from its generous benefactor, who had bequeathed to it £770 and a library of two hundred and sixty volumes.

Boston, however, claims the credit of establishing the first public school for secondary education, or what is known to-day as the Boston Latin School. On the Boston Town Records under the date April 13, 1635, is recorded: " Likewise it was then generally agreed upon that our brother Philemon Pormont shall be entreated to become schoolmaster for the teaching and nurturing of children with us."

Philemon Pormont appears to have been a scrivener, or chirographer. In 1640 Thomas Lechford said of himself: " I am no pleader by nature; oratory I have little, . . . and as for the other part of pleading which consisteth in chirography, wherein I had some skill, I do not desire to use any of that." In the old law, a chirographer signified " him in the Common Pleas office that ingrosseth Fines in that Court acknowledged . . . and that writeth and delivereth the Indentures of them unto the parties." Webster defines " chirographer " as " one who practices the art or business of writing or engrossing." This would seem to indicate that the first Boston schoolmaster taught only the elementary branches and was little more than a writing-master. He married at Alford, England, Susanna, daughter of William Bellingham. With his wife and two children he came to Boston early in 1634, and on the 28th of August united with the First Church. April 13, 1635, he was chosen schoolmaster, and on the 6th of May was admitted a freeman. In the allotment of lands at Muddy River, now Brookline, made Jan. 8, 1638, he received thirty acres.

Coming from the same town in England as the noted Mrs. Anne Hutchinson, it is not strange that in the Antinomian controversy he should have favored her. When in October, 1637, Rev. John Wheelwright was banished from Boston and went to

Piscataqua, Pormont followed him early in 1638 and became one of the founders of the town of Exeter, receiving his dismission from the church in Boston to the church in Exeter, Jan. 6, 1639. In 1642, in order to get beyond the jurisdiction of Massachusetts, Wheelwright, accompanied by Pormont and others, went farther into the wilderness and settled the present town of Wells, Maine, where a church was formed of which Pormont became a member. In 1644, Wheelwright having made an apology, his sentence of banishment was revoked and he removed to Hampton. It is very probable that Pormont also left Wells and removed to Boston, as in 1645 he was in the employment of Valentine Hill, who was dealing very largely in real estate, and was in possession of a house and garden in the rear of the First Church, on which garden a part of Young's Hotel now stands. His name appears several times on legal papers, executed in Boston, which were probably drawn by him. In 1649, however, he had returned to Wells, as the original deed, dated Oct. 18, 1649, by which the early settlers of Wells obtained their title from the Indians, was drawn and witnessed by him, and Isaac Grose, who died in Boston in 1649, left in his will £10 to Philemon Pormont of Wells. On the 11th of January, 1653, he witnessed a legal document in Boston, and died before 1656, as in the record of the marriage of his daughter Elizabeth with Samuel Norden in 1656, she is described as " daughter of Philemon Pormott late of Boston."

The people of Boston, however, wanted something higher than an elementary school, and as soon as possible they chose a master who could teach Latin. The following entry appears on the first Book of Records of the Town of Boston : —

" 12th of the 6th, AUGUST, 1636.

" At a general meeting of the richer inhabitants there was given towards the maintenance of a free schoolmaster for the youth with us, Mr. Daniel Maud being now also chosen thereunto."

There is no record of the dismissal of Mr. Pormont, and it is probable that he remained as assistant to Mr. Maude. The superior attainments and the ministerial office of Mr. Maude would naturally give him the higher position.

Daniel Maude was born in England about 1585, and was educated at Emmanuel College, Cambridge, from which he received the degree of A.B. in 1606 and A.M. in 1610. He was ordained as a minister, but having been suspended for non-conformity, came to New England with the Rev. Richard Mather in the ship "James," of Bristol, arriving at Boston August 17, 1635. Concerning this voyage Mr. Mather says in his Journal : "It was not only safe, healthful, and delightful, but also comfortable by means of the fellowship of divers godly Christians in the ship and by means of our constant serving God morning and evening every day, the daily duties being performed one day by Mr. Maude, another by myself, and the Sabbath's exercises divided for the most part equally betwixt us two." Although Mr. Maude had been married, nothing is said about his wife, and probably she died in England before his departure. He was admitted to the Church Sept. 20, 1635, and made freeman May 25, 1636. On the 12th of August, 1636, we have seen he was chosen "a free schoolmaster." The phraseology is significant and shows that the subscribers intended to establish what was known in England as a "free school" where Latin should be taught and which Pormont was unable to teach. On the 17th of April, 1637, at a meeting of the selectmen, "it is agreed that Mr. Daniel Maude, schoolmaster, shall have a garden plott next unto Stephen Kinsleys houseplot upon like condition of building thereon if need be." This "garden-plott," consisting of half an acre, was situated on the east side of the present Tremont Street, and extended from the corner of Hamilton Place to a lot on the corner of Winter Street. Mr. Maude did not build upon this lot, but sold it

Oct. 13, 1643, to Edmund Jacklin. The reason for not building appears later.

Mr. Maude continued as schoolmaster until 1642, when he removed to Dover, N. H. The people of Dover, having been left destitute of a minister by the sudden departure of the Rev. Thomas Larkham, who had returned to England, wrote to Massachusetts for help. The Court, by recommendation of Richard Mather, sent them Daniel Maude, "an honest man of a quiet and peaceable disposition," qualities much wanting in his predecessors in the Dover church.

About this time Mr. Maude married as his second wife Marie Bonner, of Boston, a widow with four children, as on the Dover Records is the following entry: "1/6 1642. It is ordered that Mr. Daniel Maude and Mary his wife shall enjoy the house they now dwell in during their lives provided he continue among us as a teacher or pastor if please God to call him to it."

Mr. Maude died at Dover, July 3, 1655. In his will he bequeaths certain property to "Sister Cotton," "Brother Cotton," and their children Elizabeth, John, Sarah, and Seaborn, from which it is thought that the first wife of Daniel Maude and the second wife of John Cotton were sisters.

The opinion has been expressed that Philemon Pormont did not accept the position of schoolmaster which had been offered to him. The writer thinks he did accept and remained in the school until he went to Exeter in 1638. The subsequent appointment of Mr. Maude would not interfere with Mr. Pormont, as Mr. Maude would teach the classical branches, while Mr. Pormont would take reading, writing, and arithmetic, a plan which varied from the English system only in that both teachers were in the same building.

It is the opinion of the writer that Mr. Pormont received from his uncle by marriage, Richard Bellingham, either by purchase or gift, a small lot of land in the northeast corner

of his large allotment.   It is described as bounded with Mr.
Bellingham south and west, Mr. Cotton north, and the street
east.   Although taken wholly from Bellingham, it adjoined
Cotton's lot.   It was situated on the southern corner of the
present Tremont Street and the entrance to Pemberton Square,
measuring one hundred and thirty-seven feet on Tremont Street
by an average depth of eighty feet.   Upon this lot Mr. Pormont
built a house, probably in the latter part of 1634 or early in
1635, which he probably sold to Daniel Maude after Oct. 9,
1637, when he had decided to follow Wheelwright in his banishment.   We have shown that Maude was granted a lot farther
along Tremont Street in April, 1637, upon condition of building,
if necessary, before the first of March following.   If he bought
Pormont's house and garden, the condition would be no longer
binding.   It is a matter of record that Daniel Maude possessed
this house and garden, which he sold in 1642 to Hezekiah
Usher.   Although there is no record of any sale by Pormont
to Maude, yet if this supposition be true, the possession of this
property by Maude is consistently accounted for.

As Ezekiel Cheever, who opened a school in New Haven in
1638, taught in his own house, so it is very probable that the
first school in Boston was taught by Philemon Pormont in his
own house on the corner of what is now Tremont Street and
Pemberton Square.   The town built its first schoolhouse in
1645 on School Street, nearly in front of the present City Hall,
King's Chapel occupying part of the site.

Boston's claim of establishing the first public school for
secondary education is generally admitted to be a just one.
In later years this school is referred to in the Town Records
as the " Grammar School " and " Latin Grammar School."
This appellation was meant to signify a school of secondary
education, designed to prepare boys for college, where Latin,
Greek, and the mathematics were taught.   The term was

brought from England, where it long had been in use with the same meaning. It was in no sense an elementary school, and children under seven years of age were not admitted. Mr. Dillaway says: "This being the only public school in the town for about half a century, it is reasonable to infer that the elementary as well as the higher branches were taught. Its principal object, however, from its establishment to the present time, has been to prepare young men for college." There is no reason to suppose that the course of instruction followed by the first masters differed much from that pursued in the English grammar schools in their time, where the established period of school education in the classics preparatory to the college was seven or eight years.

The example of Boston was followed, and grammar schools were established in several of the plantations. It is claimed that a grammar school was established in Newtowne in the same year with the College, of which Elijah Corlett was master until his death in February, 1687, at the age of seventy-eight. In *New England's First Fruits* we read, "and by the side of the College a fair Grammar School, for the training up of young scholars and fitting of them for the academical learning, that still as they are judged ripe they may be received into the College. Of this school Master Corlet is the master who has very well approved himself for his abilities, dexterity, and painfulness in teaching and educating the youth under him."

In Charlestown, on the 3d of June, 1636, Mr. William Witherell agreed to keep a school for a twelvemonth at a salary of £40. In 1637 Mr. John Fiske opens a school in Salem. In 1639 the town of Newbury granted ten acres of land to Anthony Somerby "for his encouragement to keep school for one year."

On the 4th of March, 1635, the General Court granted to the inhabitants of Dorchester Thompson's Island on condi-

tion that they pay to the treasury 12*d.* yearly as rent.   From
the Dorchester Town Records we extract the following order :
" It is ordered the 20th of May, 1639, that there shall be a
rent of £20 a year forever imposed upon Thompson's Island
to be paid by every person that hath propriety in the said
Island according to the proportion that any such person shall
from time to time enjoy and possess there and this towards
the maintenance of a school in Dorchester.   This rent of £20
yearly to be paid to such a schoolmaster as shall undertake to
teach English, Latin, and other tongues, and also writing.
The said schoolmaster to be chosen from time to time by the
freemen, and it is left to the discretion of the elders and
the seven men for the time being whether maids shall be
taught with the boys or not."

It is claimed that this was the first public provision made
for a free school in the world, by a direct tax or assessment on
the inhabitants of a town.

Although called " free " schools and " public " schools, those
terms had a different meaning in those days from what prevails
now.   They meant a school " free " to all classes; that is, free
to all who paid their tuition and which was supported in part at
least by endowments and voluntary contributions.   In his address at the two hundred and fiftieth anniversary of the
establishment of the first public school in Dorchester, June 22,
1889, Dr. Mowry said, " But it is only a few years since this
great system of public schools became absolutely free.   Till the
Free Text Book law went into effect in 1885 there had always
been something to pay.   At first there was a ' rate bill,' then
the teacher ' boarded round,' the wood was sometimes contributed by the parents sending the children, and in proportion
to the number of children sent.   Even after these customs were
abolished, and all these things were paid for out of the public
money, it still remained that the books were furnished only at

the expense of the parent. Now, however, the schools of the Old Bay State are *absolutely free*, and she was the first of all the States to make them so."

The establishment of these grammar schools was undoubtedly largely due to the efforts of Rev. John Eliot, who arrived in Boston, Nov. 3, 1631, and Rev. John Cotton, who was a passenger in the "Griffin," which arrived at Boston, Sept. 4, 1633. Eliot was educated at Jesus College, Cambridge, where he took his degree of A. B. in 1622. After his arrival in New England he became interested in the Indians, and for fifty years labored for their conversion and civilization, preaching the Gospel to them, preparing school-books in their language, and translating the whole Bible into the language of the Massachusetts Indians. While in England he had been an assistant teacher in a school kept by the Rev. Thomas Hooker, and in New England he was the untiring friend of the early common school. After supplying the Boston pulpit for one year in 1632, he was established teacher of the church in Roxbury, where he continued until his death, May 20, 1690. Cotton Mather writes of him : —

"A grammar school he would always have upon the place, whatever it cost him, and he importuned all other places to have the like. I cannot forget the ardor with which I once heard him pray, in a synod of these churches which met in Boston to consider how the miscarriages which were among us might be prevented. I say with what fervor he uttered an exhortation to this people : 'Lord for schools everywhere among us ! O ! that our schools may flourish ! That every member of this assembly may go home and provide a good school to be arranged in the town where he lives ; that before we die we may see a good school arranged in every plantation in the country.' God so blessed his endeavors that Roxbury could not live quietly without a free school in the town and has afforded more scholars, first for the College, and then the public, than any town of its bigness, or, if I mistake not, of twice its bigness, in all New England." The grammar school was established in Roxbury in 1645 : " more than sixty families, well-nigh the whole town in those days, agree together to lay the foundation of a Grammar school, and for the maintenance thereof gave by a voluntary donation a small rent forever out of their several habitations and homesteads and settled a company of feoffees to gather and improve the said rents." By donations received in later years this school became richly endowed and its influence was second only to the Boston Latin School.

Rev. John Cotton was a graduate of Trinity College, Cambridge, and for twenty years a powerful and influential preacher at St. Botolph's in Boston, Lincolnshire. He was in every respect a man of mark and destined to exert a powerful influence in New England. Increase Mather says of him : " Both Bostons have reason to honor his memory and New England most of all, which oweth its name and being to him more than to any other person in the world." The Thursday Lecture and Market Day in Boston, New England, had their origin in him, having been transferred by him from Boston, England. There was also in Old Boston a Free Grammar School, established in 1554 by Queen Mary, in which Latin and Greek were taught, and with which he had been connected since 1613. The master of the English school had "a house rent free," and the master of the New England school had provided for him " a house to live in." The evidence would seem to prove that the Free Grammar School of Boston, England, was the model used in establishing the Free Grammar School in Boston, New England, and that it owed its origin largely to Rev. John Eliot and Rev. John Cotton.

Dorchester also claims to have been the first town in which was appointed a special school committee, whose members should have the entire oversight of the school. In the other towns the government and control of the schools was placed in the hands of the seven or more men who were to manage the affairs of the town, or, as they were called later, the selectmen. Boston did not have a special school committee until 1710. But " upon a general and lawfull warning of all the inhabitants of Dorchester the 14th of the first month 1645 rules and orders presented to the town concerning the school are confirmed by the major part of the inhabitants there present." The first order reads in part : " It is ordered that three able and sufficient men of the plantation shall be chosen to be wardens or overseers of the school abovementioned who shall have the charge, oversight, and ordering thereof and of all things concerning the same in such manner as is hereafter expressed and shall continue in their office and place for term of their lives respectively, unless by reason of any of them removing his habitation out of the town, or for any other weighty reason, the inhabitants shall see cause to elect and choose others in their room in which cases and upon the death of any of the said wardens the inhabitants shall make a new election and choice of others."

Dr. Mowry says : " The essential element of the public-school system is that these schools are supported by tax. The second feature is, that they are under control of officers appointed by the people for that purpose. Here was the beginning of the public management of schools by the municipality and here is the essential beginning of the American Public School System."

The advanced position of Dorchester was undoubtedly owing to the teaching of Rev. Richard Mather, who was pastor of the church there from 1636 to 1669. In his early youth, so great was his proficiency in his studies at Winwich School, in Lancashire, that in 1611, at the age of fifteen, he was invited to take charge of a public school at Toxteth Park, near Liverpool. Here he remained seven years, and fitted several scholars for the university, whither he himself removed, and entered a student

of Brazenose College, May 9, 1618, at the age of twenty-two.
He had been here only a few months when he was invited by
the people of Toxteth to return and become their minister.
The invitation was accepted, and after preaching fifteen years he
was suspended from his ministry for non-conformity.   He came
to Boston in 1635, and in 1636 was ordained pastor of the
church in Dorchester.   He is said to have been "a very powerful, awakening, and zealous preacher."   With Mr. Welde and
Mr. Eliot he made a new translation of the Psalms into English
metre, which was printed in 1640 by Stephen Day and was the
first book of consequence published in the English Colonies.   It
was adopted and used almost exclusively in the New England
churches until the Revolution.   At the Synod of Elders and
Messengers of the various churches held at Cambridge in
September, 1646, for the purpose of composing a System of Discipline, John Cotton, Richard Mather, and John Partridge
were appointed each a committee of one to draw up the plan of
a Scriptural model of Church Government, so that the three
might be compared at the adjourned meeting in June, 1647.   At
that meeting the Platform of Church Discipline agreed upon by
the synod was taken chiefly from the model submitted by Mr.
Mather.   The first edition of this famous Platform was published in Cambridge, Mass., in 1649, and was probably the first
work bearing the imprint of Samuel Green, the successor of the
Days.

Richard Mather was the father of Increase and grandfather
of Cotton Mather, and but very few families in New England
have had so great an influence as that of the Mathers.   The
object of these grammar schools was to fit the children for
public service, both in Church and Commonwealth, in succeed-
ing ages.   In the earlier years they were supported after the
English manner by voluntary contributions from the richer
townsmen who were interested in education, from bequests in

wills, and from lands rented on long leases, rather than by a direct support from the public treasury. It seems to have been the design of the community to endow their free schools, as they delighted to name them, with bequests in their wills.

But only a few of the boys comparatively could afford to spend the time necessary for the secondary and higher education. The great majority must get to work as soon as possible. At fourteen many of them were apprenticed to a master, and their education therefore was limited to what could be obtained previous to that age. The colonists were rapidly increasing, and families were taking up grants farther and farther away from the centres. If the family lived at a distance from neighbors, the children were taught at home. When several families had settled within a radius of a few miles, a town was incorporated, and a school was established which was usually taught by the minister, the best schoolmaster that could be found. As these schools were wholly voluntary, receiving their support from the parents of the pupils, there was great danger that many children might not receive any education. But in 1642, seven years after the establishment of the Boston School, the General Court, recognizing and sanctioning the public schools, passed an order compelling the people to educate their children, and subsequently in 1647 enacted a school law which contains the entire substance of the American common-school and industrial education.

The law of 1642 as revised in 1658 reads: " Forasmuch as the good education of children is of singular behoof and benefit to any commonwealth, and whereas many parents and masters are too indulgent and negligent of their duty in that kind : It is ordered by this court and the authority thereof that the selectmen of every town, in the several precincts and quarters where they dwell shall have a vigilant eye over their brethren and neighbors, to see, first, that none of them should suffer so much barbarism in any of their families as not to endeavor to teach, by themselves or others, their children and apprentices so much learning as may enable them to read the English tongue, and knowledge of the capital laws, upon penalty of 20 shillings for each neglect therein. Also that all masters of families do once a week at the least, catechise their children and servants in the grounds and principles of religion, and if any be unable to do so much, that then at the least, they procure such children and apprentices to learn some short catechism without book, that they may be able to answer unto the questions that shall be propounded to them out of such catechism by their parents or masters or any of the selectmen when they shall call them to a trial of what they have learned in this kind. And further, that all parents and masters do breed and bring up their children and apprentices in some honest, lawful calling, labor, or employment, either in husbandry or some other trade, profitable for themselves and the commonwealth, if they will not or cannot train them up in learning to fit them for higher employments. And if any of the selectmen after admonition by them given to such masters of families shall find them still negligent of their duty in the particulars aforementioned, whereby children and servants become rude, stubborn, and unruly, the said selectmen with the help of two magistrates, or the next county court for that shire, shall take such children or apprentices from them, and place them with some masters for years (boys until they come to twenty-one, and girls eighteen years of age complete), which will more strictly look unto and force them to submit unto government, according to the rules of this order, if by fair means and former instructions they will not be drawn unto it."

The school law of 1647 reads : " It being one chief project of that old deluder, Satan, to keep men from the knowledge of the scriptures, as in former times by keeping them in an unknown tongue, so in these latter times by persuading from the use of tongues, that so at least the true sense and meaning of the original might be clouded by false glosses of saint-seeming deceivers, that learning may not be buried in the grave of our fathers in church and commonwealth, the Lord assisting our endeavors; it is therefore ordered that every township in this jurisdiction, after the Lord hath increased them to the number of fifty householders, shall then forthwith appoint one within their town to teach all such children as shall resort to him to write and read, whose wages shall be paid either by the parents or masters of such children, or by the inhabitants in general, by way of supply, as the major part of those that order the prudentials of the town shall appoint; provided, those that send their children be not oppressed by paying much more than they can have them taught for in other towns; and it is further ordered, that where any town shall increase to the number of 100 families or householders they shall set up a grammar school, the master thereof being able to instruct youth so far as they may be fitted for the university, provided that if any town neglect the performance hereof above one year, that every such town shall pay five pounds to the next school till they shall perform this order."

Here is the foundation of the common-school system, including the elementary, secondary, and higher moral, religious, and industrial training. There is no reference in these statutes to the church or minister. The education of the young was taken in hand by the people themselves, through officials elected by the people. Here was the origin of the town school, which could be found scattered all over New England for more than two hundred years after the passage of these statutes.

Rev. A. D. Mayo, D.D., says: "The more we look for the innermost hiding-place of this marvellous genius for republican civilization, we find it not in the policy of church or state, in the habits of society, or the methods of industry, though all these were the outcome of the radical conviction silently and persistently at work below. It was the conviction that every child born into this world is the child of God, capable of becoming a vital and useful member of society : and the corresponding obligation of the community to give to it the opportunity of that training at home, in the church, and in the school, which would send it forth at early manhood and womanhood a self-directing, competent person and a respectable citizen of a self-governed state.

" This conviction was the corner-stone of every respectable New England home, and explains the domestic life of that people as nothing else can. And out of the New England home, not from the church or state, but out of the very heart of the fatherhood, and motherhood, and childhood, and youth of the home was born the early New England school. It undoubtedly took on the form of the old English organization of education. It was largely under the influence of the church. But beneath these it was the firstborn child out of the deepest heart of Puritan New England. It first appeared at home, where the instruction was given by parents or relatives, often specially competent to teach in letters as in morals and manners. Gradually, in the neighborhood, it grew into the primitive country district school. Step by step it expanded into the grammar school and college. Before the first generation had passed away the colony of Massachusetts Bay virtually had on the ground, for the first time in history, a system of public education over which neither state, nor church, nor municipality, nor corporation, nor the despotic personal control of private beneficence had full domination, where every responsible citizen was a working partner in the community or state that had burdened itself with the heavy responsibility of educating every child for worthy manhood and womanhood and competent citizenship by the combined agencies of private and public wealth. Here was the beginning of the American common school, the most precious and permanent gift to the Republic from the genius of New England, the stone for two hundred and fifty years so persistently rejected by builders of other commonwealths, but in these later days now recognized as the ' head of the corner,' the corner-stone of the new Republic that ' cannot be broken,' but ' upon whomsoever it shall fall it shall grind him to powder.'

" Here at the outset is laid the broadest foundation for the education of the whole people by private and public coöperation in the establishment of the elementary, secondary, and higher departments. The country district school with its meager fare of the three R's; the grammar school with its narrow curriculum of classics and mathematics; the college, at first little more than a nursery for ministers, because the ministers were virtually the ' men of all work,' who were expected to attend to everything that everybody else had no time for, were equally a part of the new scheme of universal education. About all that any country school could give were the most simple lessons of reading, writing, and ' figuring,' as a help in working out the profound problems of civilization with which he was soon to be confronted. Thousands of brave boys and girls were sprouted in these country schools and worked their way up to an education through privations, toils, and sacrifices only next to perpetual martyrdom.

" And the most hopeful feature of the revival of the new education in the new South, is that these great States are now swarming with brave boys and girls who are going through the same process of working out an education in a meager country school, through labors and experiences well known to multitudes of the best New England men and women, recalling their own experience in the good fight for manhood and womanhood out of which is woven the warp and woof of our splendid American life."

Hon. Joseph White, formerly Secretary of the Board of Education of Massachusetts, says: " This notable law, giving voice, as it did, to the convictions and the experiences of the people, was everywhere cheerfully obeyed. On every side, as the ancient forests gave way before the hardy pioneers, in their slow but sure advance from seaboard into the interior, the meeting-house and the schoolhouse rose side by side with the log huts of the settlers, thus converting the desolate places of the wilderness into the homes of a Christian people, — the seed-plots of a higher and purer life for ages yet to come.

" No grander spectacle is presented in the history of any people than that of these ancient men, thus struggling for a scanty subsistence amid the privations and dangers of border life, and often for itself against the attacks of a stealthy and relentless foe, and yet, as if with a prophetic prevision of the future, sparing no effort in their deep poverty, shrinking from no sacrifice of time and money, needful to plant the pillars of the new commonwealth — their beloved ' New England,' as they were wont to call it — on the everlasting foundations of universal intelligence and virtue.

" Thus within a single score of years from the landing on the shores of the bay, the new State is successfully launched, fully equipped for the voyage, we trust, of all ages, with a good array of towns, each with a government wisely adapted to its needs, and all bound together by the strong bonds of a vigorous central government of their own creation, and administered for the common good, while the meeting-house and the school-house, in every township, and the University at Cambridge, were all working together for the building up of youthful youths in way of learning for the service of the Country in future times."

Notwithstanding the school law of 1647, which provided for preparatory and grammar schools, Boston had only one school, the Latin Grammar school, until 1684, when a writing school was established. In 1785 there were two Latin schools and four writing schools. In the Latin schools children were not admitted until they had arrived at the age of seven. In the writing schools they had been received at an earlier age, but at this time a rule was adopted by the school committee forbidding the admission of children under seven years of age.

In the early days, therefore, the younger children were instructed at home or in private schools. As early as 1666 Mr. Jones kept a private school in Boston. In 1667 Will Howard, and in 1668 Robert Cannon, were licensed " to keep a writing school to teach children to write and to keep accounts." Girls were not admitted to the public schools until 1789, and then only from April to October. As they were not expected to go to the university, the Latin school was not open to them.

In 1790 the Legislature passed a law providing that "no youth shall be sent to the Grammar Schools unless they shall have learned in some other school, or in some other way, to read the English language, by spelling the same," and also provided for the establishment of preparatory schools where grammar is not taught. Until 1818, however, there were no public schools in Boston where children could be prepared for the grammar schools. The age at which they were eligible having been fixed at seven, it was necessary for parents to send their children to private schools, where they could be taught the rudiments of reading and writing preparatory to admission to the grammar school. In 1817 there were 164 private schools, 135 of which were taught by women, the number of pupils being 4,132, of which 2,218 were girls.

In 1818, notwithstanding the opposition of the selectmen, the school committee, and the persuasive eloquence of Hon. Harrison Gray Otis, the people voted almost unanimously to provide instruction for children between four and seven years of age, the schools to be taught by women. This was the beginning of the present system of primary schools.

Outside of Boston in all the towns it was possible for the children to begin their education at a very early age, almost the only conditions being that they could stand up and keep their places. In 1658 Ichabod Wiswell contracted with the selectmen " to instruct and teach in a free school in Dorchester all such children as by the inhabitants shall be committed unto his care in English, Latin, and Greek, as from time to time the children shall be capable, and also instruct them in writing as he shall be able; which is to be understood such children as are so far entered all ready to know their letters and to spell somewhat." Also " that the Selectmen of Dorchester shall from year to year, every year pay or cause to be paid unto Ichabod the full sum of twenty-five pounds, two thirds in wheat, peas, or barley, merchantable, and one third in Indian, at price current, which is to be understood the price which the General Court shall from time to time appoint."

In 1668 Master John Prudden made an agreement with feoffees of the Roxbury Grammar School in which he " promised and engaged to use his best endeavour, both by precept and example, to instruct in all scholasticall, morall, and theological discipline, the children soe far as they are or shall be capable, of the signers, all A B C darians excepted."

The following extracts from the " rules and orders concerning the school" established by the town of Dorchester at the March meeting in 1645 show how this school was managed and may be considered as a model of all the other grammar schools.

" First. It is ordered that three able and efficient men of the plantation shall be chosen to be wardens or overseers of the school who shall have charge, oversight, and ordering thereof, and of all things concerning the same in such manner as is hereafter expressed, and shall continue in their office and place for term of their lives respectively.

" Second. The said wardens shall take care and do their utmost and best endeavor that the said school may from time to time be supplied with an able and sufficient schoolmaster.

" Third. The said wardens shall from time to time see that the school-house be kept in good sufficient repair, and if necessary shall repair to the seven men of the town for the time being, who shall have power to tax the town with such sums as shall be requested for the repairing of the school-house.

" Fourth. The said wardens shall take care that every year at or before the end of the ninth month there be brought to the school-house twelve sufficient cart loads of wood for fuel . . . the cost and charge of which said wood to be borne by the scholars for time being, who shall be taxed for the purpose at the direction of the said wardens.

" Fifth. The said wardens shall take care that the school-master for the time being do faithfully perform his duty in his place as schoolmaster ought to do, as well in other things as in these which are hereinafter expressed, viz:

" First. That the schoolmaster shall diligently attend his school and do his utmost endeavor for benefiting his scholars according to his best discretion.

" Second. That from the beginning of the first month until the end of the seventh, he shall every day begin to teach at seven of the clock in the morning and dismiss his school at five in the afternoon. And for the other five months, that is, from the beginning of the eighth to the end of the twelfth month he shall every day begin at eight of the clock in the morning and end at four in the afternoon.

" Thirdly. Every day in the year the usual time of dismissing at noon shall be at eleven and to begin again at one, except that

"Fourthly. Every second day in the week he shall call his scholars together between twelve and one of the clock to examine them what they have learned on the sabbath day preceding, at which time he shall take notice of any misdemeanor or outrage that any of his scholars shall have committed on the sabbath to the end that at some convenient time due admonition and correction may be administered.

"Fifthly. He shall equally and impartially receive and instruct such as shall be sent and committed to him for that end whether their parents be poor or rich, not refusing any who have right and interest in the school.

"Sixthly. Such as shall be committed to him he shall diligently instruct, as they shall be able to learn, both in humane learning and good literature, and likewise in point of good manners and dutiful behaviour towards all, especially their superiors as they shall have occasion to be in their presence whether by meeting them in the street or otherwise.

"Seventhly. Every sixth day in the week at two of the clock in the afternoon he shall catechise his scholars in the principles of Christian religion, either in some Catechism which the wardens shall provide and present, or in defect thereof in some other.

"Eighthly. And because all man's endeavors without the blessing of God needs be fruitless and unsuccessful, therefore it is a chief part of the schoolmaster's religious care to commend his scholars and his labors amongst them unto God by prayer morning and evening, taking care that his scholars do reverently attend during the same.

"Ninthly. And because the rod of correction is an ordinance of God necessary sometimes to be dispensed unto children, but such as may easily be abused by overmuch severity and rigor on one hand, or by overmuch indulgence and lenity on the other, it is therefore ordered and agreed that the schoolmaster for the time being shall have full power to administer correction to all or any of his scholars without respect of persons, according as the nature and quality of the offence shall require." The rule further requires that the parents "shall not hinder the master therein" but if aggrieved they can complain to the wardens "who shall hear and impartially decide between them."

Such were the rules adopted by the town of Dorchester in 1645, for the management of this school established in 1639, and it is very probable that all the schools established previous to 1647 were managed in a similar manner.

These earlier schools, however, were grammar schools, the masters of which "must be able to teach English, Latin, and other tongues" and fit boys for the university, where they were to be educated for the ministry. Nothing is said about the age at which they were admitted, but they were not received until they had at least learned their letters and were able to spell somewhat. Indeed, the law of 1642 required "all masters of families to teach their children so much learning as may enable them to read the English tongue," which necessitated their being taught at home sufficient to admit them to the grammar school.

There were, however, many children who from various reasons would never attend the grammar schools, and there was danger that children would grow up in ignorance; therefore, the stringent law of 1647 was passed establishing common schools in towns of fifty householders "to teach all such children as resort to them to read and write," and in towns of one hundred householders grammar schools. In the common schools children of both sexes were admitted at a very early age and continued until thirteen or fourteen years of age, when the boys were old enough to be apprenticed to a trade. If, however, their parents wished them to receive the higher education, at about seven years of age, in later years at ten, they entered the grammar schools.

It will therefore be seen that the country lads had better facilities for receiving an education than the Boston boys. The country lads were taught at the public expense from the earliest age ; while the Boston boy until seven years of age was taught either in a private school, or must be content with what education his parents were able to give him.

Country girls also fared better than Boston girls, for in the common schools there was no distinction of sex, although the girls were not considered strong enough to attend the schools in the winter season. Their education, however, was limited to the common school. The grammar school was closed to them until 1784, when " such girls as could read the Psalter " were permitted to attend the grammar school from the first of June to the first of October.

The education of the girl was not considered to be so important as that of the boy. The means of communication between the various towns were so slight that the women made few acquaintances outside of their own town, and there being no need of correspondence it was not essential that girls should learn to write : business affairs being conducted by the men, there was no necessity for the girls to learn more of arithmetic than the four fundamental rules by which they might count the eggs, or the stitches in the stockings they were knitting. It was to the interest of the Church, however, that they should know something about the Bible, therefore they were taught to read the Catechism and Testament. They were expected to marry young, and were brought up not only to the wheel and sewing, but were very proficient in the dairy and the management of the home, making cloth out of their wool and flax.

Happily other ideas now prevail, and the girl of to-day receives an education equal and similar to the boy. In fact, in addition to such institutions as Radcliffe, Smith, Wellesley, Vassar, and Bryn Mawr, which are attended only by girls, throughout the States hardly can we find an institution wherein the so-called co-education system does not prevail. There is no privilege accorded to young men that is not extended to the gentler sex in the acquisition of knowledge in all its branches. No distinction is made between the sexes in the subjects taught or in the standard of curriculum. The degrees given to the young women at Radcliffe are equal to the degrees given to the young men at Harvard, and are presented by President Eliot. America leads the world in female education.

The teacher of the schools in early days was always a man, frequently the minister, or a candidate for the ministry. It is only within recent years that a woman has been considered competent to preside over a grammar school, a high school, or a college. It was many years before she could teach a common school, and then only during the summer term. Hundreds of the ablest and most devoted clergymen have done their part in the work of instruction in the public schools. But there gradually grew up a class of professional schoolmasters who devoted their whole time to education and who were respected by the people equally with the minister, lawyer, and physician. It is recorded that " his wife was to be accommodated with a pew next to the wives of the magistrates." Many young men while studying at the university spent their vacations in teaching, their vacation being extended for that purpose. Rev. John Woodbridge, afterwards the minister at Newbury, taught the school at Boston in 1643; Rev. John Fiske taught in Salem in 1637. Rev. Thomas Waterhouse taught in Dorchester in 1639, and Rev. John Norton had as pupils Nathaniel and Increase Mather. In modern times John Adams taught school in Worcester, Daniel Webster in Salisbury, N. H., and

Fryeburg, Maine, and Hannibal Hamlin in Paris, Maine. The profession of a schoolmaster has always been a respectable one, and many a public official owes his success to the experience he obtained while governing a town school.

The early schools were held first in the house of the master and later in the meeting-house. When our ancestors began to build schoolhouses, they naturally copied the architecture of the schools they had attended in England. Hon. Frank A. Hill, late Secretary of the State Board of Education of Massachusetts, says: "The English schoolroom was long, high, and narrow. The floor rose by steps at the sides and ends from a spacious area, and on these were the benches, wooden benches, plain, hard, back-breaking as any you ever sat upon. The windows were high up and out of reach. Between them and the floor was the wooden wainscot where the English boys wrote, cut, and printed their names, a species of vandalism from which time often removed the stigma, since the name for whose writing the young rogue may have merited a flogging was likely to become a thing of secret, if not open, pride to the school authorities when it became famous. Now the old New England schoolhouse often repeated the English interior only in a small and rude way, the same raised platforms, the same plank seats, the same wooden wainscot, and the same high windows above it: and everything about it, too, was usually whittled and cut in the ruthless English way. In the little room the master's desk often loomed up like a pulpit. Just why so exalted a throne was reared in a room often not much larger than a dry goods box it would be difficult to guess, if one did not look into an ancient English schoolroom and see there its undoubted prototype. And so in a score of things pertaining to our old schoolhouses the dominating influence of the mother country is seen."

A few years ago, while driving in the Dalton Hills, N. H., with a party of ladies from the Mountain View House, Whitefield, such a queer-looking schoolhouse attracted our attention that our curiosity was awakened to stop and examine it.

The structure had never been painted by man, but the clouds of many years had stained it with their own hue. The nails were starting from their fastnesses, and fellow clapboards were becoming less closely and warmly intimate. There were three windows through which the passage of light was occasionally stopped by fractures, patches, and seams of putty. These windows were guarded by board shutters, which, owing to the loss of buttons and to being blown about by the shifting winds, probably occasioned more damage than the small boy who was suspected to be ready at all times to throw stones through the panes of glass. The shingles had been battered apart by a thousand rains and were dingy with the mould and moss of time. The bricks of the little chimney were losing their cement, and it looked as though it needed only a strong wind to send them rattling upon the roof. The doorstep was a broad, unhewn rock brought from the neighboring pasture. The surface was so uneven that in icy weather it became a matter of skilful manœuvring to enter or leave in safety.

Passing over the doorstep, we found ourselves in a small entry, where was kept a stock of dry pine kindlings to be used in making a fire with the wet and green logs outside, and on the sides of which were pegs on which the children hung their hats and coats, while their lunch baskets were placed on a small shelf lower down. A door opened into the schoolroom, which was twenty-five feet wide by twenty-five feet deep. In front was a space twenty-five feet wide by ten in depth, where the classes were paraded to read and spell. At the right of this space near a window was the home-made magisterial desk, an excellent specimen of old school furniture, raised upon a platform a foot from the floor. About in the centre of the parade, but near the front wall, was an old-fashioned, long-bodied, air-tight stove, resting on four slender iron supports looking like a giant grass-hopper ready to spring at the children. An aisle two feet and a half wide ran up an inclined plane from near the stove to the opposite wall of the room fifteen feet in length. On each side of the aisle were four or five long seats and writing-benches for the accommodation of the school at their studies. The seats and benches were made of planks at least two inches thick. On these, pupils of several generations of the same family had engraved their names in letters which would never wear out, so deeply were they cut.

On the front of the first bench was another seat, low down, which was usually occupied by abecedarians and others near that rank. These could use the bench for a back, but had no bench for themselves. In general the older the scholar, the farther from the front was his location. The walls of the room were unpainted and destitute of all decoration, no pictures, maps, or even a blackboard. Through the front and side windows the scholars were able to see the occasional passer-by on that lonely road, — an event as interesting to the teacher as to the children.

The ladies of the party were extremely interested in this home of learning, but were pained to think that the children of that neighborhood were compelled to put up with such poor accommodations. A week later I passed that way again, and, missing the quaint schoolhouse, was informed upon inquiring that it had been struck by lightning during a heavy rainstorm and wholly destroyed by fire, nothing being left to mark the spot but a few field stones which had formed the underpinning, and the old air-tight stove, which occupied the same position amid the ruins that it did in the schoolhouse, and, standing upon its supports, was apparently wondering what had happened, as its fire had been heretofore on the inside and not on the outside. I was also in-formed that there was great sorrow for several miles around at the loss of the old schoolhouse, which had stood there for nearly one hundred years and in which several generations of children had received all the schooling they had ever had. The schoolhouse has never been rebuilt, as under the new system of graded schools there is no longer any use for the district school.

This old Dalton schoolhouse was a fair sample of the buildings in which our ancestors struggled with the three R's, and occasionally enlivened and abridged the school term by putting an unpopular master through the window.

To show that this description of the Dalton schoolhouse is not a fancy picture, we present the plan of the palatial building which the town of Boston, in 1704, erected for its Latin School, called by Rev. Mr. Prince " the principal school of the British colonies, if not in all America."

" July 24th, 1704. Agreed with Mr. John Bernard as followeth ; he to build a new schoolhouse of forty foot long, twenty-five foot wide, and eleven foot stud, with eight windows below and five in the roofe, with wooden casements to the eight windows, to lay the lower floor with sleepers and double boards so far as needful, and the chamber floor with single boards ; to board below the plate inside, and inside and out, to clapboard the outside and shingle the roofe, to make a place to hang the bell in, to make a pair of stairs up to the chamber, and from thence a ladder to the bell ; to make one door next the street and a partition across the house below and to make three rows of benches for the boys on each side of the room ; to find all timbers, boards, clapboards, shingles, nails, hinges."

" In consideration whereof the said Mr. John Barnerd is to be paid one hundred pounds and to have the timber, boards, and iron work of the old schoolhouse.

" Oct. 30, 1704. Ordered that Mr. John Barnerd do make house convenient for the laying of wood at the easterly end of the schoolhouse."

From the Records of the Roxbury Grammar School we learn

that on the 25th of the 9th month, 1652, the feoffees agreed with Mr. Daniel Welde "that he provide convenient benches with forms, with tables for the scholars, a convenient seat for the schoolmaster, a deske to put the Dictionary on and shelves to lay up bookes, and keepe the house and windows and doores with chimney sufficient and proper." The hard usage this schoolhouse received is shown by a letter, which the master wrote to the trustees in 1681. He says : " Of inconveniences, I shall instance no other, but that of the schoolhouse the confused and shattered and nastie posture that it is in, not fitting for to reside in, the glass broken and thereupon very raw and cold, the floor very much broken and torn up to kindle fires, the hearth spoiled, the seats some burnt and others out of kelter, that one had as well nigh as goods keep school in a hogstie as in it."

The course of instruction in these early town schools was very meagre, including little besides reading, spelling, writing, and the little ciphering necessary to the ordinary business of life.

John Locke, in his *Thoughts concerning Education*, written in 1690, says that the method of teaching children in England at that time " was the ordinary road of Hornbook, Primer, Psalter, Testament, and Bible."

William Webster, in *An Attempt towards rendering the Education of Youth more easy and effectual*, the fourteenth edition of which was published in 1765, says : " The present method is, as soon as he can stammer over a chapter in the Bible and before he hath well lost the uncouth tone of pronunciation, which he has perhaps learnt of his mistress, immediately to send the boy to the Latin-school, where, instead of studying his own language, and improving in the necessary qualifications of reading it distinctly and with proper emphasis, he is unreasonably entered upon a Latin grammar, and not only perplexed with abstruse terms of art, but confounded with rules wrote in a language he is altogether a stranger to." He then proceeds to advocate the teaching of those children who do not intend to be scholars, but rather clerks and traders, English Grammar, Arithmetic, Writing, Book-keeping, Drawing, Geography, Chronology, and History.

The New England schools were close copies of the English schools, and it was not until after the American Revolution that the curriculum was enlarged. To learn to read and write appears to have been the sum of good education in the seventeenth century. Dekker, a dramatist of that period, makes a man of substance who is asked, " Can you read and write, then? " reply : " As most of your gentlemen do — my bond has been taken with my mark at it." Sir Matthew Hale, in his *Counsels of a Father*, left the following course of instruction for sons : " Till eight, English reading only : from eight to sixteen, the grammar-school ; after sixteen, the university."

We have seen that in the Dorchester school during the winter months the school hours were from eight in the morning to four in the afternoon ; in the summer months from seven to five ; with an intermission from eleven to one. As the schoolhouses were not provided with clocks, and as few teachers possessed watches, a good deal of guessing had to be done about the passage of time. Some teachers carried hour-glasses to school, others constructed a sun dial in the yard, while each school was sure to have a noon mark on a southern window sill, it being noon when the shadow of the middle window frame crept into the little furrow cut in the wooden sill with a jack-knife.

The master opened the school with prayer, and then there was reading from the Testament, the scholars taking turns in reading the verses. The older scholars now settled down to study, while the youngest children were called up to say their letters. Then the older classes took their turn in reading and spelling. About the middle of the forenoon other tasks were laid aside, and the remainder of the session was devoted to writing and arithmetic, considerable time being spent by the master in making and mending quill pens. No more of history, geography, or grammar was taught than was found in the Primer or in later years in the Speller or Reader. The studies of the afternoon were a repetition of those of the morning, the master closing the exercises with prayer. A certain day in the week was devoted to studying the Catechism, which was to be committed to memory, and on which the children were to be examined by the minister.

The pupils who attended the grammar schools were to be prepared for the college, and their instruction was confined largely to the classics and mathematics. Admission to Harvard College required the ability of the applicant to read any classical author in English, to readily make and speak true Latin and write it in *verse* as well as *prose*, and to decline perfectly the paradigms of nouns and verbs in the Greek tongue.

In 1740 there was published a small volume of two hundred and twenty-two pages, the object of which is fully explained by its facsimile titlepage. Mr. Clarke was not only a famous master of his day, but also the author of many school-books which met with large sales both in Old and New England. In this *Essay* Mr. Clarke tells us something about the faults of the old plan of education and of the school-books that had been used previously, among which he mentions Lily's *Latin Grammar*, *Dictionaries*, *Nomenclatures*, Hoole's *Corderius*, Æsop's *Fables*, Erasmus, Galtrucius's *Heathen Gods*, *Pantheon*, Ovid, Virgil, Horace, Homer, *Greek Grammar*, *Sententiæ Pueriles*, and Hoole's *Construing Book to the Latin Grammar*. He also outlines a new system, names the school-books to be used, and describes the character of the ideal schoolmaster. As his *Essay* was received with great favor in England, and as many of his school-books were used in the New England schools, it is probable that some of his recommendations were adopted, and that a few extracts from

A N

E S S A Y

UPON THE

E D U C A T I O N

OF

Y O U T H

I N

*Grammar-*S C H O O L S.

In which the *Vulgar Method of Teaching* is
examined, and a *New* one propofed, for the more
Eafy and Speedy Training up of *Youth* to the
Knowledge of the *Learned Languages,* together
with *Hiftory, Chronology, Geography,* &c.

By JOHN CLARKE, *late Mafter of the*
Publick GRAMMAR-SCHOOL *in* Hull.

𝔗𝔥𝔢 𝔗𝔥𝔦𝔯𝔡 𝔈𝔡𝔦𝔱𝔦𝔬𝔫.
With very Large ADDITIONS.

Quod Munus Reipublicæ afferre majus, meliufvè pof-
fumus quàm fi docemus atque erudimus juventutem.
Cic. de Div. l. 2. Sect. 2.

L O N D O N:

Printed for CHARLES HITCH, at the *Red*
Lion in *Pater-Nofter-Row.* MDCCXL.

his *Essay* will give us a fair idea of the school-books and school-masters of the New England Grammar School in the eighteenth century. He says: "The great, and I think, I may say, the only end propounded both by Parents and Masters in the common method is the instruction of youth in the languages of *Latin* and *Greek*. This their whole time is spent in at school and if a boy can but shew a very moderate skill in the *Latin* by a copy of verses and a theme, and make a shift to construe an easy Greek author indifferently, the master thinks he has played his part sufficiently, and the father is very well satisfied with his son's proficiency. But how far short this is of what boys might be brought to by the age of sixteen or seventeen will appear I hope by the sequel of this discourse. . . . It is not therefore bare *Latin* and *Greek* a boy should spend his whole time in at school. These must of necessity go to the making of a scholar, but then there are other things as necessary, which school-boys are not only capable of but may be easily taught without any hindrance to their proficiency in the tongues; I mean History and Geography, both ancient and modern, with Chronology, and the most necessary and useful things in Divinity."

Having shown the faults and demolished the old system, he proceeds " to the erecting of one more regular, beautiful, and convenient." At one point in the new plan he advocates the use of newspapers as follows: "By that time boys are fit to be entered in *Greek* or sooner, it may be convenient to bring them acquainted with the *Public News*, by making them read the *Evening Post* or some other *newspaper* constantly. These the master may at first read along with them, explaining, as occasion offers, the Terms of War, and whatever else he apprehends they do not understand. . . . For this I think there can be no reasonable objection against, since it will be both diverting and useful, without being any hindrance at all to their other business, will give them manly thoughts, and a relish for the company and conversation of men, amongst whom news always makes one head of discourse."

After recommending a Latin and Greek Grammar, the *Geographies* of Cellarius and Sansom, Kennett's *Antiquities, Medulla Historiæ Anglicanæ*, and Echard's *Roman History*, he mentions the various Latin and Greek authors to be read, concluding the chapter as follows: "That the reader may still the better judge of this matter I shall here present him in one view with all the authors I think requisite to be read, in order to qualify boys with a competent skill in the languages for an academy. Those for the *Latin* tongue are, *Cæsar's Seven* Books of the Gallick War, twelve Books at least in *Justin*. All *Eutropius Nepos, Florus, Terence, Sallust, Suetonius* entire. Seven or eight Books in *Ovid's Metamorphoses*, the *Eclogues* and *Æneid* of *Virgil* entire, with all *Horace* and *Juvenal*. For the *Greek*, the Gospels and Acts in the *Greek Testament*, twelve Books in *Homer's Iliad*, all *Theocritus, Herodian*, and *Zosinus* entire. I am by long experience convinced that the reading these several authors, or others equivalent to them, more than once over, is absolutely necessary to give boys any tolerable knowledge of the two languages, such as they ought to have, before they go off to a College." If this list is compared with the list of books used in the Boston Latin School in 1790 it will be seen that there is but little difference. The Boston school committee even recommended that " newspapers were to be introduced occasionally at the discretion of the masters."

What Mr. Clarke has to say concerning the qualifications requisite in a schoolmaster is briefly as follows: "The great end of education is to instil into the minds of youth a love of virtue and knowledge, and to give them such an insight into the learned languages, geography, history, chronology, &c., as may enable them to proceed therein by themselves, with ease and pleasure. From hence it follows that a Schoolmaster ought to be, First; a man of virtue. Second; he ought to have a pretty large acquaintance with the Latin tongue. Third; he should be able to talk the Latin tongue pretty readily and properly. Fourth; he should be able to read the Greek Testament, Homer's *Iliad*, and other authors that are commonly read at school. Fifth; he should be a philosopher. Sixth; he should be a good master of his own language, or mother-tongue. Seventh; He should be well acquainted with the old and new geography and know something of chronology."

How many of the New England schoolmasters of that period possessed these qualifications? Although written in 1740, Mr. Clarke's *Essay* deserves to be well read and considered by every schoolmaster of to-day, for there are in it many ideas of which a prudent master may take advantage.

Notwithstanding the early schoolhouses were unattractive, the education meagre, and text-books few, yet the graduates of Harvard College were able to compete with and even to surpass the graduates of Oxford and Cambridge ; and the graduates of the common schools, when they had become farmers, mechanics, mariners, and merchants, soon made the influence of New England felt in the markets of the world and were able to contend for the world's prizes on equal terms. When the nations of Europe after bloody wars sought to make treaties with one another, the American question had to be considered, and peace was not assured unless the consent of the American colonies was secured. As England disregarded the consent of the governed, many of her American colonies revolted, cast off her authority, and became their own governors. The Free School of New England had resulted in the establishment of the Free Republic of the United States of America.

Early School-Books of New England

EARLY SCHOOL-BOOKS OF NEW ENGLAND

𝕳istorical 𝕾ketch and 𝕭ibliography

OF the twenty thousand Englishmen who came to New England between 1620 and 1640 a large number had received at least a common-school education. Out of every two hundred and fifty, one had been a graduate of an English university. Having received the benefits of an education, it was natural that they should desire that their children should be educated, and we have seen that very shortly after their arrival schools were established. Naturally the schools were modelled after the schools in which they had received their own education, but, making a new start, they were able to introduce some important changes, notably the addition of elementary schooling and the compulsory education of all the children at the public expense. These changes were far reaching in their effects and are still exerting a mighty influence. The magnificent system of public education in the United States to-day is proof of how firmly and broadly our ancestors laid the foundations. Education in the early days of the Colony was very simple, and it has required over two hundred and fifty years of careful nursing and ceaseless vigilance to produce the present elaborate system.

In the preceding pages an attempt has been made to give a brief sketch of the New England school previous to the American Revolution. From a little book published by Warren Burton in 1833, entitled *The District School as it Was*, we are able to continue the sketch about fifty years later. The author gives a very full account of the steps necessary for a child to take in order to acquire a common-school education from the time of entering the school as an abecedarian until he leaves to enter upon a business life. He says : " Entering the summer school at the age of three and a half he was put into the A B C class, and at the age of four and a half was able to read the ' Reading Lessons,' that is, little words arranged in little sentences, and spell somewhat. At the age of seven and a half he commenced the study of grammar. When at nine years of age he began to write. At twelve he entered upon the study of arithmetic. At fourteen he had ciphered through the Rule of Three and was supposed to have had enough of arithmetic for the common purposes of life. At fifteen he was taught composition, which closed his district school life. The spelling-book was the first manual of instruction used in school, and kept in the child's hands for many years. He generally passed directly from the spelling-book to the reading-book."

The spelling-book used by Mr. Burton in his school-days was Perry's *Only Sure Guide to the English Tongue*, and the reading-book, Adams' *Understanding Reader*. Although Perry's *Only Sure Guide* contained a few moral tales and fables, it was practically a spelling-book with long lists of words of from one to seven syllables. Easy lessons in reading, consisting mostly of words of one syllable, were scattered at intervals among the numerous spelling columns, and it took the child three or four years to arrive at the more manly and dignified reading of the *Moral Tales* and *Fables*.

The generations of children preceding Mr. Burton were not so fortunate in their reading-book. They had only the Primer, Speller, Psalter, Testament, and Bible. The primer and speller were the most important books in the earlier schools, the speller eventually driving out the primer. A spelling-book published in 1701, entitled, *The Country-man's Conductor in Reading and Writing True English. By John White*, contains selections in reading and an arithmetic. Dilworth's *Speller*, published in 1740, contains also *A Practical English Grammar, Sentences in Prose and Verse*, and *Fables*. A spelling-book written by A. Fisher, the seventeenth edition of which was published in 1778, entitled, *A Practical Grammar, with Exercises in bad English ; or an Easy Guide to Speaking and Writing the English Language Properly and Correctly*, treats not only of Orthography or True Spelling, but also of Prosody, Etymology, and Syntax, with Exercises in Reading and a small Dictionary.

The early speller therefore was hornbook, primer, speller, reader, arithmetic, and sometimes geography, combined in one book. For more advanced reading resort was had to the Psalter and Bible.

Of the text-books used in the schools during the first century after their establishment we have but little knowledge. The books themselves have disappeared, and their titles have not been recorded. We are well informed in regard to the foundation of the school, and possess lives of many of the early schoolmasters, but the historians paid very little attention to the text-books. The references made by the earlier writers of New England history to text-books relate almost wholly to the Latin, Greek, and Hebrew books used by the boys preparing for college. Of the books used in the elementary schools there is very little mention.

It is not the intention of the writer to give a list of all the books used in the elementary or secondary schools. Such a list would be not only almost impossible, but also very tiresome, and would exceed the limits proposed for this essay.   It is our purpose to mention a few of the earlier books which may be considered the foundation-stones upon which the later ones were built, and then to notice a few of the more prominent books which were used by the pupils in the colonial and provincial schools, many of which are either in the possession of the writer or have been kindly loaned by members of the Club.

In 1766 there was published in London " A Complete Catalogue of Modern Books published from the Beginning of this Century to the Present Time, with the Prices Affixed.   To which is added A Catalogue of the School Books now in general use." If this catalogue was carefully examined, as well as the catalogues printed at the end of many of the books hereinafter mentioned, there would be found the titles of many other textbooks which undoubtedly were used in the early New England schools.

The Catechism

THE first book used in New England in the education of the children, even before the establishment of the common school, was the Catechism, which remained in use until within the memory of people now living. In their contract with the Massachusetts Bay Company the ministers agree " to teach and catechize the Company's servants and their children, as also the savages and their children." At a meeting of the Company on the 16th of April, 1629, it was voted to spend three shillings for two dozen and ten catechisms to be used by the ministers in teaching the children.

It is not known which catechism it was, but it is generally believed to have been the one composed by Rev. William Perkins and published as early as 1590. The titlepage of this edition reads, *The Foundation of Christian Religion gathered into sixe Principles. And it is to be learned of ignorant people, that they may be fit to heare Sermons with profit, and to receive the Lord's Supper with comfort. Psal. 119. 30. The entrance into thy words sheweth light, and giveth understanding to the simple.* [*London:*] *Printed by Thomas Orwin for John Porter, 1590.* It is an octavo containing twenty leaves, and the title is enclosed within a pictorial border. Rev. John Robinson, the pastor of the Pilgrims, republished this Catechism for the benefit of the youth of his congregation, to which he added an appendix of questions and answers " touching the more solemn fellowship of Christians." The earliest-known copy of this appendix, printed probably at London in 1636, contains sixteen pages.

It is very probable that it was an edition of Perkins' *Six Principles* with Robinson's Appendix that Mr. Skelton recommended to be bought by the Massachusetts Bay Company.

To catechise is to sound a thing into one's ears, to impress it upon one by word of mouth. Teaching by catechising is certainly as old as the Greek philosophers of Athens, for Socrates is said to have introduced a catechetical method of arguing.

In order to propagate the gospel and to perpetuate to posterity the principles of the Christian religion, the primitive Church established schools and instructed the pupils by asking questions, receiving answers, and offering explanations and corrections concerning the points of the new religious faith. The pupil who was receiving rudimentary instruction in the doctrine of Christianity was called a catechumen.

A catechism is a book containing a summary of principles reduced to the form of question and answer, and when we speak of a catechism, from its universal employment by the Christian Church, we are understood to refer to a religious catechism, although there are many others, such as legal, medical, geographical, and botanical catechisms. Catechisms with the A B C prefixed were very common.

Teaching by catechising was a favorite system with the Roman Catholic Church, and has been very popular with the Church of England, and the Pilgrim and Puritan churches of New England. Increase Mather, in speaking of catechisms, says : " These last ages have abounded in labours of this kind ; one speaketh of no less than five hundred Catechisms extant." Hugh Peters, in *A Dying Father's Last Legacy to an onely Child, or Mr. Hugh Peters Advice to his Daughter, London, 1661*, says : " Though there are near an hundred several Catechisms in this Nation, yet (if sound), they must speak one thing, viz ; Man lost in himself, redeemed only through Christ." As this *Legacy* was addressed to his daughter, it shows not only the great vogue of catechisms, but also that girls as well as boys were instructed by them.

Under date of the 2d of June, 1641, the Records of the Colony of the Massachusetts Bay in New England read: "It is desired that the elders would make a catechisme for the instruction of youth in the ground of religion." This request was readily responded to, and nearly every minister tried his hand at making a catechism. The most popular were two by John Cotton, one for adults and the other for children. The title of the first reads: *The Doctrine of the Church, to which is committed the Keys of the Kingdom of Heaven. Wherein is demonstrated by way of Question and Answer, what a visible Church is according to the order of the Gospel: and what Officers, Members, Worship and Government, Christ hath ordained in the New Testament. By that Reverend and learned Divine, Mr. John Cotton, B.D. and Teacher of the Church at Boston, in New England. London, 1642.* It is a small quarto of thirteen pages.

Cotton's catechism for children was published as early as 1646, and is spoken of by Cotton Mather as "that incomparable Catechism." The titlepage of the oldest known edition printed in New England, of which only a single copy has come down to us, reads: *Spiritual Milk for Boston Babes in either England Drawn out of the Breasts of both Testaments for their soul's nourishment But may be of like use to any Children. By John Cotton, B.D. late Teacher to the Church of Boston in New England. Cambridge. Printed by S. G. for Hezekiah Usher at Boston in New England, 1656.* It is an octavo of fifteen pages. Both of these books were reprinted many times.

Mr. Shattuck, in his *History of Concord*, says that catechising was one of the constant exercises of the Sabbath. "All the unmarried people were required to answer questions, after which expositions and applications were made by Mr. Bulkeley to the whole congregation."

Rev. John Fiske, while a minister at Chelmsford, prepared a catechism for the use of children which was printed in 1657 at the expense of the town. The following extract is taken from Mr. Fiske's Note-Book : —

" 6 of 12, '64. A Church meeting Catechizing. Agreed by the Church that the said course of Catechizing of all under sixteen years old, be attended at the house of the pastor, viz., for mayds the day after the Lecture & for youths the 2.^{d} day of the weeke following the lecture.

" Item. That for all young men above sixteen years old, unmarried. That it be moved who will voluntarily appear to give in their names to Answer in publick: & for such as shall decline; if Children of the Church, that the Church shall see that they attend to be catechized by the pastor in his House upon the 2^d day of the week monthly after the lecture at the usual time of meeting (viz. aboute 3 of the clock in the afternoone) & if they shall neglect to come on one day, to bring as much the next time, as may proportion the Time. This voted."

The first publication in the Indian language of Massachusetts was a short catechism compiled by John Eliot as early as 1651. It was issued in manuscript for several years, but in 1654 was printed at Cambridge by Samuel Green at the expense of the Corporation for the Propagation of the Gospel in New England. Although two editions of this book were printed, one of one thousand and the other of fifteen hundred copies, yet not a single copy has come down to us.

Perhaps the largest catechism ever published was the ponderous volume compiled " By the Reverend and Learned Samuel Willard, M. A., Late President of Harvard College in Cambridge, in New England. Boston, 1726." It was a folio volume of nine hundred and twenty-seven pages, and in the list of subscribers were the names of about four hundred and fifty of the then men of learning of New England.

No common catechism was adopted until the Westminster Assembly formulated the Shorter Catechism, which was first printed for official use in London in 1647, and which in course of time took the place of nearly every other catechism in New England.

It will thus be seen that the Catechism was a universal school-book, being taught in its simplest form by the parents by word of mouth to children that perhaps had not been taught their letters. In a somewhat enlarged form it was studied and committed to memory by the youths and maidens; and in its highest development it was read by the adults and held in a reverence equalled only by the Bible.

Hornbooks

THE first book used exclusively in the tuition of a child and from which the letters were taught was the Hornbook.

The Hornbook, or tablet, is supposed to have originated with some tired scribe, who sought to preserve his parchment by fastening it to a slab of wood and covering it with horn. The first hornbooks contained only the alphabet, which was sometimes written and sometimes carved in the wood. Devotional booklets for children, opening with the A B C, followed, the earliest examples being in Latin and emanating from the Church of Rome. The earliest record of hornbooks found is 1450, at which time they were printed in black letter, although this was changed to Roman soon after the introduction of the latter in 1457.

The Hornbook in English appeared about the time of the Reformation; and there is in existence a specimen, printed in black letter, of the time of Queen Elizabeth. Parchment or paper, about four or five inches long by two inches wide, on which were printed the letters of the alphabet, vowels, etc., mounted on wood, having the front covered with transparent horn to protect it from constant thumbing, and the whole inserted in a frame resembling a hand-mirror, constituted an English hornbook. In the handle was a hole through which was passed a leather lacing by which the Hornbook was hung around the neck or tied to the girdle of the child. Running across the top of the parchment were the letters of the alphabet, both small and capital, or Christ cross-row, so called from a large + placed at the beginning of the alphabet " as a charm,"

HORNBOOK OF THE EIGHTEENTH CENTURY

so it is said, "against the devil who might be in the letters."
The vowels followed next, and their combinations with conso-
nants ; the invocation ; Lord's Prayer ; and the Roman numerals.
Shakespeare thus refers to the cross-row of the Hornbook :

> " He hearkens after prophecies and dreams ;
> And from the cross-row plucks the letter G ;
> And says a wizard told him that by G
> His issue disinherited should be."
>
> RICHARD III.

Cowper thus describes the Hornbook of his time : —

> " Neatly secured from being soiled or torn
> Beneath a pane of thin translucent horn,
> A book (to please us at a tender age
> 'T is called a book, though but a single page,)
> Presents the prayer the Saviour deigned to teach,
> Which children use, and parsons — when they preach."

These hornbooks were used by the parents at home and in
the petty schools.   When the children were to recite they came
up before the teacher, who pointed out the letters on the hornbook with his quill.   In *Specimens of West Country Dialect* the
use of the hornbook is humorously depicted : —

" Commether, *Billy* Chubb, and breng the horner book.
Gee ma the vester in the windor, you *Pat Came!* — What ! be
a sleepid — I 'll wake ye.   Now, *Billy*, there 's a good bway !
Ston still there, and mind I da za to ye, an whaur I da point.
Now ; cris-cross, girt A, little a—b—c—d.   That 's right,
Billy ; you 'll zoon lorn the criss-cross-lain — you 'll zoon au-
vergit Bobby Jiffry — you 'll zoon be *a scholard*.   A's a pirty
chubby bway — Lord love 'n."

In England the Hornbook went out of use in the early part
of the nineteenth century, a large wholesale dealer in London
being quoted as having received his last order in 1799, the previous sales of himself and his business predecessors having been

several million hornbooks in sixty years. Notwithstanding the great number of copies printed, at the Loan Exhibition of the "Worshipful Company of Horners" held at the London Mansion House in October, 1882, after a special effort had been made to bring together as many as possible, only eight copies could be shown. For several years Mr. Andrew W. Tuer was engaged in collecting material for a *History of the Horn Book*. After searching carefully in Great Britain and America, it was with great difficulty that, in his second edition published in 1898, he was able to mention and illustrate one hundred and fifty copies in various states of preservation.

These little printed scraps of paper are much sought for and highly prized, book collectors being willing to pay high prices for them, a copy having been sold in London a few years ago for £65, its original cost having been one penny.

In New England the Hornbook was contemporary with the Catechism. The famous Thomas Morton, Master of Revels at Merry-Mount, in his *New English Canaan* printed in 1632, says: "A silenced Minister out of courteousness, came over into new Canaan to play the spie: Hee pretended out of a zealous intent to doe the Salvages good, and to teach them. Hee brought a great Bundell of Horne books with him, and carefull hee was (good man) to blott out all the crosses of them for feare least the people of the land should become Idolaters." Reference probably is made to the Rev. Francis Bright, who is termed on the Records of the Company of Massachusetts Bay "minister to the Company's servants." He arrived in June, 1629, but returned in July, 1630.

In the Inventory of the estate of Michael Perry, a Boston bookseller, which was taken in 1700, is an itemized list of his stock in trade, on which appears the following record : —

> " 16 doz. gilt horne bookes 16*s.*
> 38 doz. plain "   "   19*s.*"

The Hornbook was not always mounted on a board ; many were pasted on the back of the horn only, and from the valuation probably Mr. Perry's stock was of this kind. Hornbooks were advertised for sale in the *New York Gazette* in 1753 and in the *Pennsylvania Gazette* in 1760. The Primer and Speller eventually superseded the Hornbook, and at the present time an American hornbook is of the greatest rarity, three copies only being known in the United States. At the Probasco sale in New York, Jan. 16, 1899, a copy of a hornbook described as one sheet mounted on a worm-eaten wooden tablet, covered with horn fastened down with brass border (in a morocco case), brought $147. It was claimed to have been the only example of a hornbook ever sold at auction in this country.

The Hornbook of which a facsimile is given was found in the stock of an English bookseller in 1850. Its dimensions are nine by five inches. The text is printed on white paper which is laid upon a thin piece of oak, and is covered with a sheet of horn, secured in its place by eight tacks, driven through a border or mounting of brass.

The Hornbook was followed by the Battledore, so named from the instrument used to strike the shuttlecock in the old game of battledore and shuttlecock. It was similar to a hand mirror, having a long handle and a flat part covered with parchment, and is familiar to us in the modern game of ping-pong. Upon the face of the parchment was painted or printed the alphabet, and it thus served the double purpose of bat and book. A later form of the battledore, said to have been invented by Benjamin Collins of Salisbury, and sold by John Newbery of London, the well-known publisher of children's books in the middle of the eighteenth century, was a single card, folded and printed on the inside pages, with a flap lapping over like a pocket-book on which was printed the title. Sometimes the outside pages were decorated with simple lines or vines and the

The Uncle's Present,
A NEW BATTLEDOOR

Published by Jacob Johnson, 147. Market-Street Philadelphia.

A a	B b	G g	H h
Almanack, will you buy an Almanack	Buy a Broom; Mop, Bruſh, or hair broom;	Great News, in the London Gazette;	Hot fine ginger bread, all hot.

C c	D d	I i	K k
Chairs to mend old chairs to mend?	Duſt ho; bring out your duſt;	Images, very fine, very pretty.	Knives to grind, or ſciſſors to grind?

E e	F f	L l	M m
Eels, live eels; large ſilver eels;	Fowls, live fowl or fat Chicken	Lobſter; buy my live lobſter;	Milk below maids, Milk from the cow

[115]

title was printed on the inside of the flap. One of those sold by Newbery bears the title, *The Royal Battledore: Being the first Introductory Part of the Circle of the Sciences.* The price was two pennies. On one side of the inside pages was printed the alphabet, small and large, the vowels, syllabarium, invocation, blessing, and Lord's Prayer. On the other a picture alphabet, each letter being illustrated by a small engraving. In the British Museum is a booklet of six pages, dated 1835, containing A B C, Arabic and Roman numerals, and words of two or three syllables entitled *The Battledore or First Book for Children.* The writer possesses a similar six-page battledore, printed possibly a few years earlier in Philadelphia. It consists of a single card, folded, enclosing a single leaf, with a flap. On each of the outside pages is a picture, two alphabets, and numerals, the first page carrying the imprint of the bookseller. On the inside of the flap is printed *The Uncle's Present. A New Battledoor*, with the imprint of the publisher. The four inside pages are devoted to the alphabets, small and large, each letter being illustrated by a picture representing street-hawkers, under which are printed their cries. The pages measure 6½ by 3½ in. and each picture 2 by 1¾ in. It is evidently a reprint of an English booklet. The battledore lingered until about 1850, when it was superseded by the various forms of *Reading Made Easy.*

The Hornbook undoubtedly was the prototype of the sampler worked by our great-grandmothers, who learned letters and stitches at the same time. These were pieces of canvas of various sizes, a large one measuring twenty by fourteen inches, in which the stitches were taken in colored silks. They all followed a general plan. First, the alphabet in small letters was worked across the top; next, the capitals followed by the numerals; then a verse from the Bible, the Lord's Prayer, an original composition, or perhaps a few lines writter. by the

ABCDEFGHIJKLMNOPQR
1234567
89010

ABCDEFGHIJKLM
NOPQRSTUVWZ

Jesus permit thy gracious name to stand
As the first effort of an infant hand or
And while her fingers oer this canvas m
Engage her tender heart to seek thy love

Wrought by
Eunice Goodridge
Aet 16 yrs
Fitchburg
1828

minister, and below all the name and age of the worker with the year and day of the month on which it was ended. The embellishment was left entirely to the fancy of the child, and after the date in many samplers will be found wonderful ornamental pieces representing red brick houses, sugar-loaf trees, flowers and flower-pots, with birds, lambs, dogs, and lions, all of one size. Frequently the whole was surrounded with a checkered or floriated border, in which were worked flourishes, vines, pens, dolphins, and swans.

The sampler was used in the colonial homes and dame schools, where the little girls were taught to sew, spin, weave, embroider, and knit. As the girls were allowed to attend school only in the summer-time, they were taught their letters largely at home, and the sampler served the purpose of the Hornbook.

Great pride was taken in the artistic appearance of these samplers, and they were shown with a great deal of satisfaction. Many of them were framed and handed down as heirlooms. At the present day they are held in great esteem, and are regarded by their possessors almost as a patent of nobility.

The sampler of which a facsimile is given was worked by a relative of the wife of the writer.

In Pilgrim Hall, Plymouth, Massachusetts, is exhibited a sampler supposed to have been wrought by Lorea Standish, daughter of Capt. Miles Standish. It bears the following verses: —

> " Lorea Standish is my name,
>   Lord guide my heart that I may do Thy will;
>   Also fill my hands with such convenient skill
>   As will conduce to virtue void of shame,
>   And I will give the glory to thy name."

The Speller

FOLLOWING the Hornbook as a manual of instruction in the schools was the Speller. Who was the author and what was the character of the first speller used in the New England schools there is no record. We only know that among the books printed by Stephen Day, at Cambridge, Mass., between 1642 and 1645, was "The Spelling Books." No copy of it has come down to us, but probably it was a reprint of some English speller of the day and may have been an exact copy of Coote's *English Schoolmaster*, a very popular speller of the seventeenth century which was first published in 1590, and was extensively used in the petty schools of England more than one hundred years. John Brinsley, in his *Ludus Literarius*, the first edition of which was published in 1612, expresses the opinion that no one ought to enter the grammar school until they are able to read English, and suggests that there might be some other schools for the little ones. "To teach them would help some poor man or woman who knew not how to live otherwise." These petty schools, as they were called, were frequently in the hands of poor women or other necessitous persons; and it was largely for such persons that Edmund Coote, Master of the Free School in St. Edmunds Bury, wrote his little manual. In his Preface he says: "The learned sort are able to understand my purpose. I am now to direct my speech to the unskilful, which desire to make use of it for their own private benefit, and to such men and women of trade, as Tailors, Weavers, Shopkeepers, Seamsters; and such others as have undertaken the charge of teaching others.

. . . If peradventure for 2 or 3 days at the first it may seem somewhat hard and strange unto thee, yet be not discouraged, neither cast it from thee, for if thou take but diligent pains in it but 4 days, thou shalt learn many very profitable things that thou never knewest, yea, thou shalt learn more of the English tongue than any man of thy calling (not being a Grammarian) in England knoweth : thou shalt teach thy scholars with better commendation and profit than any other (not following this order) teacheth, and thou mayest sit on thy shop-board, at thy looms, or thy needle, and never hinder any work to hear thy scholars, after thou hast once made this little book familiar to thee.''

This little manual was well known to John Winthrop and his associates of the Massachusetts Bay Company, and its peculiar character would strongly recommend it as a book very well adapted not only for the parents and teachers of the town schools in the new colony in training the younger children, but also for the children themselves in learning their letters, as the first thirty-two pages are given up to the Alphabet and Spelling. It would seem to be very probable that in selecting a speller to reprint, our forefathers would choose Coote's *English Schoolmaster*, which was recommended by Brinsley, and which was the speller most in vogue in the petty schools of England.

Whether this conjecture be true or false, as this little manual was extensively used in the New England schools of the seventeenth century, a copy of the titlepage would seem to be proper. Copies of the book are extremely scarce, and the writer has not been able to secure a specimen of any edition. As the titlepage of the fortieth edition, printed in 1680, does not differ from the titlepage of the twenty-sixth edition, printed in 1656, excepting in date, it is probable that in the successive editions there was no change in the text. The following titlepage is taken from a copy formerly in the possession of Francis

Brinley, of Hartford, Conn. It reads: "The English School-master, teaching all his Scholars, of what age soever, the most easie, short, and perfect order of distinct Reading and true Writing our English tongue, that hath ever yet been known or published by any. And further also, teacheth a direct Course, how many unskilful persons may easily both understand any hard English words which they shall in Scriptures, Sermons, or elsewhere hear or read; and also be made able to use the same aptly themselves; and generally whatsoever is necessary to be known for the *English* speech: so that he who hath this book only, needeth to buy no other to make him fit from his Letters unto the *Grammar-School* for an *Apprentice*, or any other private use, so far as concerneth *English*. And therefore is made not only for Children, though the first book be meer childish for them, but also for all other; especially for those that are igno-rant in the *Latin* Tongue. In the next Page the *Schoolmaster* hangeth forth his Table to the view of all beholders, setting forth some of the chief Commodities of his profession. Devised for thy sake that wantest any part of this skill: by Edward Coote, Master of the Free-school in Saint Edmund's-Bury. *Perused and approved by public Authority: and now for the 40 time Imprinted; with certain Copies to write by, at the end of this Book, added.* Printed by A. M. and R. R. for the Company of *Stationers*, 1680." The price of the book was one shilling. It was a small octavo of seventy-nine pages. Nearly thirty-two are given to the Alphabet and Spelling, about eighteen to a Short Catechism, necessary observations of a Christian, prayers, and psalms, five to chronology, two to writing copies, and the remainder of the book contains a list of hard words, "alphabetically arranged and sensibly explained."

In the latter part of the seventeenth century other English spelling-books were also used in the New England schools, for we find in the inventory of Michael Perry's stock taken in

1700, " 12 Strongs Spelling bookes" and " 20 Youngs Spelling bookes" appraised at about one shilling each. Sixty-six years later these titles appear on a London bookseller's catalogue among " School Books now in general use."

Miss Alice Morse Earle, in *Child Life in Colonial Days*, describes the manner in which the child was taught to spell as follows : " The teaching of spelling in many schools was peculiar. The master gave out the word, with a blow of his strap on the desk as a signal for all to start together, and the whole class spelled out the word in syllables in chorus. The teacher's ear was so trained and acute that he at once detected any misspelling. If this happened he demanded the name of the scholar who made the mistake. If there was any hesitation or refusal in acknowledgment, he kept the whole class, until by repeated trials of long words, accuracy was obtained. The roar of the many voices of the large school, all pitched in different keys, could be heard on summer days for a long distance. In many country schools the scholars not only spelled aloud but studied all their lessons aloud as children in Oriental countries do to-day, and the teacher was quick to detect any lowering of the volume of sound and reprove any child who was studying silently. Sometimes the combined roar of voices became offensive to the neighbors of the school and restraining votes were passed at town-meetings."

The titlepage of a spelling-book, on one of the fly-leaves of which is written, " Noah Gruchy his book 1718," reads *The Country-Man's Conductor in Reading and Writing True English, containing such Rules as the Author, by near Forty Years Practice in Teaching, hath found Necessary and Useful to that end. By John White, sometime Master of Mr. Chilcot's English-Free-School in Tiverton, and now Master of a Boarding School in Butterly, near Tiverton aforesaid. Exeter, 1701.* It is a small duodecimo of one hundred and fifty-eight pages, the last fifteen containing,

THE
Country-Man's
CONDUCTOR
In READING and WRITING
TRUE ENGLISH,

Containing fuch 𝕽𝖚𝖑𝖊𝖘 as the AUTHOR, by
near Forty Years Practice in Teaching, hath
found Neceffary and Ufeful to that end.

Printed chiefly for the Ufe of the Author's own
School, and may alfo be ufeful to all Teachers, Parents, Mafters of Families, and Single-Perfons, to
improve themfelves, their Children and Families,
in good Englifh.

To which are Added,

Some EXAMPLES of the Englifh of our Ho-
nourable Anceftors, and alfo of our Weftern Dialoct
And fome Arithmetical RULES to be learnt by
Children, before or as foon as they are put to Writing.

By *JOHN WHITE,* fometime Mafter of
Mr. *Chilcot*s Englifh-Free-School in *Tiverton,* and
now Mafter of a Boarding-School in *Butterly,* near
Tiverton aforefaid.

EXETER : Printed by *Sam. Farley,* for the Author ;
and fold by Mr. *Humphry Burton* in *Tiverton,* Mr.
Philip Bifhop in *Exon,* Mr. *Taylor* at the *Ship* in
St. Paul's *Church-Yard* in *London,* Mr. *Rich. Gravett*
at the *Tolzey* in *Briftol,* 1701.

"Some Rules of Arithmetic fitted for Children to read and learn by Heart, by that time they have come capable of Writing and Cyphering." There are also several pages of sentences containing words of like sound but different signification, the first of which reads, "My Neighbour *Abel* was not *able* to find one *Acorn* in an *Acre* of Wood," and the last, "*You* that were present at the writing hereof, know that I wrote it under the shadow of a *Yew*-Tree, not far from some *Ewe*-sheep, *July* 1700."

On the seventy-second page are given instructions for playing a game which will be recognized as a very popular entertainment at the present day. They read: "Directions for the Use of the following Alphabets in Schools and private Families. — In Schools, let half an Hour be set apart three or four Days every Week, for Spelling these Alphabets; let the Learner have his Book home with him, and get ready his Lesson for the Morning, and the Words for the Evening. Then half an Hour before you dismiss them in the Evening, take as many of your School as are near of equal Capacities, and set them before you; having the Book in your hand, put them a Word of that Letter you are to spell on; suppose *A*, put them the first Word *All*; let him next your Right-hand spell it, and so on one to another, 'till the Word has passed all; such as miss, let them go down towards your Left-hand, and they that spell it right, come above them towards your Right-hand. This way I have found, by thirty Years Experience, to be very useful in bringing Youth to spell well. The same Order may be observed in private Families, where are three or more children; and if Parents would take a little Pains with their own Children in Winter-Evenings, or other spare Hours, or order some Servants to do it (that is capable) they would make their Children to out-doe their Fellows at School, and love both the School and Learning."

In 1731 there was printed in Boston an edition of a well-known English spelling-book. The author was Henry Dixon,

Frontispiece to Dilworth's New Guide.

A New GUIDE

TO THE

English Tongue:

In FIVE PARTS.

CONTAINING,

I. Words both *common* and *proper*; from *one* to *six Syllables*: The several Sorts of *Monosyllables* in the common Words being distinguished by Tables into Words of *two*, *three*, and *four Letters*, &c. with *six* short Lessons at the End of each Table, not exceeding the Order of Syllables in the foregoing Tables.——— The several Sorts of *Polysyllables* also, being ranged in proper Tables, have their Syllables divided, and Directions placed at the Head of each Table for the *Accent*, to prevent *false Pronunciation*; together with the like Number of Lessons on the foregoing Tables, placed at the End of each Table, as far as to Words of *four* Syllables, for the easier and more speedy Way of teaching Children to read.

II. A large and useful Table of Words, that are the same in *Sound*, but different in *Signification*; very necessary to prevent the writing one Word for another of the same *Sound*.

III. A short but comprehensive GRAMMAR of the *English Tongue*, delivered in the most familiar and instructive Method of *Question* and *Answer*; necessary for all such Persons as have the advantage only of an *English* Education.

IV. An useful Collection of *Sentences*, in *Prose* and *Verse*, *Divine*, *Moral* and *Historical*; together with a Select Number of *Fables*, &c. &c. adorned with proper Sculptures, for the better Improvement of the young Beginner. And,

V. *Forms* of *Prayer* for Children, on several Occasions.

The *Whole* being recommended by several *Clergymen*, and eminent *School-Masters*.

By THOMAS DILWORTH.

[*A New Edition*, *with some Improvements*.]

BOSTON: Printed by T. and J. FLEET, at the *Bible* and *Heart* in Cornhill, 1786.

and there were at least nine editions during the following twenty years. In 1750 Thomas Fleet printed an edition for Daniel Henchman with the title, *The Youth's Instructor in the English Tongue: or the Art of Spelling improved. Being a more plain, easy and regular Method of teaching young Children, with a greater Variety of Useful Collections than any other Book of this Kind and Bigness extant. For the Use of Schools. Collected from Dixon, Bailey, Watts, Owen and Strong. Ninth edition.* It is a small octavo of one hundred and thirty-four pages. The frontispiece is a woodcut, signed J. T. (J. Turner), of "The Old Brick Meeting-House in Cornhill" over against D. Henchman's shop.

The writer possesses a copy printed at Boston in 1757, enlarged to one hundred and fifty-nine pages, which formerly belonged to "Richard Critchett, 1768." It is in three parts. The first part treats of spelling and moral lessons. The second part treats of letters in general with an account of the points, stops, etc., by way of question and answer. The third part contains rules in arithmetic with forms of bills, bonds, and releases, concluding with stories from the Bible, Lord's Prayer, Creed, and Ten Commandments.

A spelling-book which became a great favorite was, *A New Guide to the English Tongue. By Thomas Dilworth.* The first edition was published in 1740. It was reprinted in New England and remained in use until after 1800. The copy in the possession of the writer was printed in Boston "by T. and J. Fleet at the *Bible* and *Heart* in Cornhill, 1786." In addition to lessons in spelling it contains a short grammar of the English tongue; a collection of sentences in prose and verse, divine, moral, and historical; together with a select number of fables, adorned with proper sculptures; and forms of prayers for children. Among the illustrations is the well-known one "of the boy that stole apples."

Among the other spelling-books used in New England in the eighteenth century, all by English authors, were *Spelling Dictionary. By Thomas Dyche, 1750; A Spelling-Dictionary of the English Language, on a new Plan. For the Use of Young Gentlemen, Ladies, and Foreigners. By John Newberry*, the seventh edition of which was published at London in 1760; *British Instructor, 1768;* and Henry's *Universal Spelling Book, 1769.*

A spelling-book which was very popular with the Society of Friends was, *Instructions for Right Spelling and Plain Directions for Reading and Writing True English. With several other Things, very useful and necessary both for Young and Old, to read and learn. By G. Fox.* George Fox was born in Leicestershire, England, in 1624. When about twenty-three years of age he joined the Society of Friends, of which he became one of the leaders. In 1672 and 1673 he visited America, where he made many converts to his peculiar religious faith. He died at Swarthmore, England, in January, 1691. Although deprived of the benefit of an early education, he was a friend of learning and took a great interest in establishing schools, and spent considerable time in acquiring a knowledge of one or more of the ancient languages. As early as 1673, assisted by Ellis Hookes, he published *Instructions for Right Spelling, etc.*, which was so well received that a second edition, with additions, was published in the same year. Between 1673 and 1706, seven editions had been printed in London. The third Dublin edition was published in 1726. It was reprinted in Boston by Rogers and Fowle in 1743, and again in Newport in 1769, by S. Southwick. This little manual, which was written for the Friend schools, in addition to Lessons in Spelling, contained a Catechism, Proverbs, Selections from the Scriptures, and an Arithmetic.

Dilworth's *New Guide to the English Tongue*, after holding the field for forty years, was superseded by *The Only Sure Guide*

INSTRUCTIONS

FOR

Right Spelling,

AND

PLAIN DIRECTIONS

FOR

Reading and Writing

True Englifh.

With feveral other Things, very ufeful and neceffary, both for Young and Old, to read and learn.

By *G. FOX.*

Newport : Printed by S. SOUTHWICK, M,DCC,LXIX.

to the English Tongue, or New Pronouncing Spelling Book. By William Perry, the first Worcester edition of which was published by Isaiah Thomas in 1785. The author, William Perry, was Lecturer on the English Language in the Academy of Edinburgh and the author of several valuable school-books, more especially an English Dictionary. So popular was this spelling-book that the publisher, Isaiah Thomas, announced in 1804 that he had sold more than three hundred thousand copies. It was revised and corrected in 1804, and in 1817 the twenty-second *Improved Edition* was published. *A New Improved Edition* was published in 1820. Notwithstanding the *Improvements* and the extensive advertising of Isaiah Thomas, Perry's *Sure Guide* was compelled to yield the field to Webster's *Standard of Pronunciation*.

In 1783 the first spelling-book by an American author was published in Hartford, Conn. Its title reads, *A Grammatical Institute of the English Language, comprising an easy, concise, and systematic method of education, designed for the use of English Schools in America. Part I. Containing a new and accurate standard of Pronunciation. By Noah Webster Hartford: Hudson and Goodwin, 1783*. It was the first volume of a series of school-books for the instruction of youth, the second, published in 1784, being a grammar, and the third, published in 1785, being a compilation for reading. Concerning these books Mr. Webster himself said : " In the year 1782, while the American army was lying on the bank of the Hudson, I kept a classical school in Goshen, Orange County, New York. I there compiled two small elementary books for teaching the English language. The country was then impoverished, intercourse with Great Britain was interrupted, school-books were scarce and hardly attainable, and there was no certain prospect of peace."

These books were gradually introduced into most of the schools of the country. The success of the first part was im-

Frontispiece to Perry's Only Sure Guide.

THE
ONLY SURE GUIDE
TO THE
English Tongue,
OR,
NEW PRONOUNCING
Spelling Book.

Upon the fame Plan as *Perry's* Royal STANDARD ENGLISH DICTIONARY, now madeUfe of in all the celebrated Schools in *Greatbritain* and *America.*

TO WHICH IS ADDED, A LARGE COLLECTION OF

MORAL TALES AND FABLES.
For the INSTRUCTION of YOUTH.
With an APPENDIX :

Containing, An Eafy Introduction to Englifh Grammar—Of Orthography—Of Punctuation—Directions concerning the Capitals ; alfo, Directions for the different Sounds of the Confonants before all the Vowels, with every Exception that is to be met with in our Language, from fuch general Rules : Alfo, a complete Lift of thofe Words in the English Language, which, though written differently have a Similarity of Sound ——Of thofe Subftantives and Verbs.of the fame Orthography, but of a different Accent. ——Of thofe Subftantives and Verbs, which vary in their Sound, either by a different Confonant, or by changing the hard Sound of that Confonant into the foft Sound. ——Of thofe Adjectives and Verbs alike in Orthography, but differently accented.——Of thofe Subftantives and Adjectives changing the Seat of the Accent.

By WILLIAM PERRY,
Lecturer on the Englifh Language, in the Academy of EDINBURGH, and AUTHOR of feveral Valuable SCHOOLBOCKS.

Tenth Improved Edition.
Carefully REVISED, CORRECTED, and Illuftrated with feveral new CUTS.

PRINTED AT *WORCESTER*, MASSACHUSETTS, By ISAIAH THOMAS JUN [Proprietor of the Improvements, according to Law.] Sold WHOLESALE and RETAIL by him at his BOOKSTORES in *Bofton* and *Worcefter*, and by THOMAS & WHIPPLE, in *Newburyport* and by various other Bookfellers.——*November* 1809,

[131]

mediate and unparalleled. The third edition was published in 1787, the frontispiece of which was a portrait of George Washington. In later editions the portrait of Noah Webster was substituted for Washington. In 1790 Isaiah Thomas and Ebenezer T. Andrews secured the copyright and changed the title to *The American Spelling Book*, and still later to *The Elementary Spelling Book*. The illustrations for the edition of 1795 were engraved by A. Anderson. During the twenty years 1807–24, in which Mr. Webster was employed in compiling his American Dictionary, the entire support of his family was derived from the profits of this work at a premium of less than a cent a copy. It is stated that more than eighty million copies had been sold previous to 1880, and that in 1900 it was selling at the rate of hundreds of thousands annually, being the most generally used of all school text-books.

Webster's Speller was the most popular school-book ever published in America, and Dr. Goodrich says: " To the influence of the old Blue-back spelling-book probably more than to any other cause we are indebted for that remarkable uniformity of pronunciation in our country which is so often spoken of with surprise by English travelers."

The following sketch of Noah Webster is taken from a memoir of his life by Chauncey A. Goodrich, D.D. : —

" Noah Webster was born in Hartford, Conn., Oct. 16th, 1758. He commenced the study of the classics in 1772 under the instruction of the Rev. Nathan Perkins, D.D., and in 1774 was admitted a member of Yale College, from whence he graduated in 1778. His intention of pursuing the practice of the law was in a great measure set aside by the War of the Revolution. Upon his return from the Commencement when he graduated his father gave him an eight-dollar bill of the Continental currency (then worth about four dollars in silver), and told him that he must thenceforth rely on his own exertions for support.

THE

A M E R I C A N

𝕾pelling 𝕭ook :

CONTAINING AN EASY

STANDARD of PRONUNCIATION

BEING THE

F I R S T   P A R T

OF A

GRAMMATICAL INSTITUTE

OF THE

ENGLISH LANGUAGE

TO WHICH IS ADDED,

An APPENDIX, containing a MORAL CAT
ECHISM and a FEDERAL CATECHISM.

By NOAH WEBSTER, JUN. ESQUIRE,
AUTHOR of "DISSERTATIONS ON the ENGLISH LANGUAGE,"
,,COLLECTION OF ESSAYS and FUGITIVE WRITINGS," &c.

Thomas & *Andrews'* *TWENTY-FOURTH* EDITION.
With many CORRECTIONS and IMPROVEMENTS, by the AUTHOR.

PRINTED AT *BOSTON*,
BY ISAIAH THOMAS AND EBENEZER T. ANDREWS,
FAUST'S STATUE, NO. 45, NEWBURY STREET,
Sold, Wholesale and Retail, at their Bookstore; by said THOMAS,
in *Worcester* ; by THOMAS, ANDREWS & PENNIMAN,
in *Albany;* and by THOMAS, ANDREWS &
BUTLER, in *Baltimore.*——1802.

[133]

Frontispiece to Webster's Reader.

See page 154.

As a means of immediate subsistence he resorted to the instruction of a school, and during the summer of 1779 resided at Hartford, Conn. Not having the means of obtaining a regular education for the bar, Mr. Webster at the suggestion of a distinguished counselor of his acquaintance, determined to pursue the study of the law in the intervals of his regular employment, without the aid of an instructor; and having presented himself for examination, at the expiration of two years was admitted to practice in the year 1781. As he had no encouragement to open an office in the existing state of the country he resumed the business of instructor and taught a classical school in 1782 at Goshen, Orange County, New York. Here in a desponding state of mind created by the unsettled condition of the country at the close of the war, and the gloomy prospects for business, he undertook an employment which gave a complexion to his whole future life. This was the compilation of books for the instruction of youth in the schools. Having prepared the first draught of an elementary treatise of this kind, he made a journey to Philadelphia in the autumn of the same year, and after exhibiting a specimen to several members of Congress, and to Rev. S. S. Smith, Professor at Princeton College, he was encouraged by their approbation to prosecute his design. Accordingly, in the winter following, he revised what he had written; and leaving Goshen in 1783, he returned to Hartford, where he published his *First Part of a Grammatical Institute of the English Language.* The second and third parts were published in the year immediately following. These works, comprising a spelling-book, an English grammar, and a compilation for reading, were the first books of the kind published in the United States.

" Besides the Dictionary, which was the leading employment of his life, Mr. Webster published several books and papers on political, literary, and moral subjects. He died at New Haven, May 28, 1843.

" In conclusion it may be said that the name of Noah Webster from the wide circulation of his books is known familiarly to a greater number of the inhabitants of the United States than the name, probably, of any other individual except the Father of his Country. Whatever influence he thus acquired was used at all times to promote the best interests of his fellow-men. His books, though read by millions, have made no man worse. To multitudes they have been of lasting benefit, not only by the course of early training they have furnished, but by those precepts of wisdom and virtue with which almost every page is stored."

Readers

THE object which our ancestors had in view in teaching the art of reading was very different from that of the present day. From very early times the Church had recognized the duty of teaching children the Catholic faith and the Lord's Prayer, and this was the subject-matter of the early reading-books. The school was the handmaid of the Church, and it was in the church schools that was obtained all the education the children received. The *Enschede Abecedarium*, which is claimed to be the first book printed with movable type, contained the Alphabet, Pater Noster, Ave Maria, Credo, and two prayers. It was the elementary book of the Romish Church, which children were expected to learn to recite without book, or if they had no book, they were to be taught orally.

The adults had a larger book, the well-known *Book of Hours*. Previous to printing, these *Books of Hours* were in manuscript. As only a few of the people, other than the clergy, could read, they were written, ornamented, and bound by the monks, and presented or sold to dignitaries of Church or State, or wealthy nobles and tradesmen. Naturally they are now very scarce, and fine copies have sold for $10,000. They were translated into English, and printed as early as 1490. One of them is known as *The Primer of Salisbury Use.*

The Reformation caused a study of the Bible and stimulated a desire among the people that their children should be taught to read in order that they might read the Bible for themselves. It was a distinguished maxim with the Reformers that the

Scriptures were the great repository, the storehouse of religious truth, and that all doctrines essential to salvation were to be deduced from the Bible and to be supported by its authority. It was always, therefore, their anxious wish that the people at large should have the power of reading and consulting the Scriptures in their vernacular, or common tongue. With this view the Bible had been translated into English by Wickliffe about 1380. This version was made from the Vulgate, the Latin translation in common use. This translation was very instrumental in preparing the people for the reformation of the Church of England, which was carried into effect about one hundred and fifty years afterwards.

The first printed English version of the Scriptures was the New Testament, translated from the Greek into English by William Tyndal. It was printed either at Antwerp or Hamburg in 1526. The whole Bible, translated into English by Miles Coverdale, was printed in London in 1535; and in 1536 one of the Injunctions to the Clergy by the king's authority required that " every parson or proprietary of any parish church within this realm, should, before the first of August, provide a book of the whole Bible, both in Latin and English, and lay it in the choir, for every man that would to look and read therein."

In 1537 another edition of the English Bible was printed by Grafton and Whitechurch in Germany. It bore the name of Thomas Mathews, which is presumed to be fictitious, and that the real editor was John Rogers, the martyr. " It was wonderful," says Stype, the historian, " to see with what joy, not only among the more learned, and those who were noted lovers of the Reformation, but generally all over England, among all the common people ; and with what avidity God's Word was read, and what resort there was to the places appointed for reading it. Every one that could, bought the book and busily read it or heard it read, and many elderly persons learned to read on purpose."

To be able to read the Bible therefore appears to have been the main object in teaching children to read, and as late as 1690 John Locke in his *Thoughts on Education* says that the method of teaching children in England at that time was "the ordinary road of Hornbook, Primer, Psalter, Testament, and Bible."

Little manuals were prepared very similar to the Catholic A B C and primers. The first Protestant Primer was published by Philip Melanchthon. It was first printed in Latin and later translated into German. Its title in German reads: *Philipps Melanchthons Handbuchlin wie man die Kinder zu der geschrifft und lese halten soll Wittenberg, MDXIX*. It contains the alphabet, syllabarium, Lord's Prayer, Ave Maria, Creed, portions of Psalms, and Ten Commandments. Then follow the Sermon on the Mount, selections from the Bible, and sayings of the wise men of Greece.

The Child's Little Primer by Martin Luther contained the Lord's Prayer, the Commandments, the Creed, and the Catechism.

There were many editions of these little Protestant manuals, and Henry VIII., in order to keep his people true to Catholicism, issued proclamations against them. But he himself soon renounced his allegiance to the Pope and allowed to be printed in 1534 what is known as the *Reform Primer*. He was not, however, quite ready to break wholly with the Church of Rome, and in 1535 he caused to be printed another primer beginning, *A Goodly Prymer in English*. Later he received more light and marked out a new path to heaven for his subjects by causing to be published, *The Primer set furth by the kinges majestie and his Clergie, to be taught, lerned and red: and none other to be used thorowout all his Dominions*, the titlepage

Frontispiece to King Henry VIII. Primer. 1700 Ed

[140]

of which forms the frontispiece of this book. By the kind permission of Mr. D. F. Appleton of New York his copy of this Primer was used in securing the facsimile. The book is excessively rare, if not unique. It is a small octavo of one hundred and sixty-eight pages, and its contents are the " Kalendre, Kynges Highness injunction, Praire of our Lorde, Salutation of the Angel, Crede or Article of Faith, ten Commandments, Certain Graces, Matyns, Evensong, Complin, Seven Psalmes, Letany, Dirige, Commendations, Psalmes of the Passion, Passion of our Lorde, Certain godly Praiers for sundry purposes." The writer has in his possession a copy, reprinted in 1700, the frontispiece of which is a portrait of Henry VIII., engraved by J. Nutting.

As the Roman Catholic Church had a preliminary book to its Primer, so Henry had his *A B C*, which contained the Alphabet, Lord's Prayer, Hail Mary, Creed, various Graces for before and after dinner and for fish days, and the Ten Commandments. The *A B C* and the *Primer* were the primary manuals of church service and the forerunners of the Book of Common Prayer. That the *A B C* and the *Primer* were to serve as an elementary reading-book and as a first book of religious instruction for children and of ordinary prayers for adults, is set forth in the royal injunction attached to the *Primer*, which reads : —

"An Injunction geven by the King our souveraigne lordes most excellent maiestie for the autorising and establishing the use of this *Primer*.

"Henry the VIII. by the grace of God kyng of Englande, France, and Ireland, defendour of the faith, and of the church of Englande and also of Irelande in yerth the supreme hedde. To all and singuler subiectes, aswel Archbishops, Byshoppes, Deanes, Archedeacons, Prouostes, persons, vicars, curates, priestes and all other of the Clergie : as also all estates and degrees of the laye see, and teachers of youth within any our realmes, dominions, and countries gretyng.

"Emong the manyfold busines, and most weightie affaires appertayning to our regall authoritie and office, we much tenderyng the youth of our realmes, (whose good education and vertuous bringyng up redouneth most highly to the honoure and prayse of Almightie God) for diuers good considerations, and speciallye for that the youthe by diuers persons are taught the Pater noster, the Aue maria, Crede, and x. Commaundementes al in Latin and not in Englyshe, by meanes wherof the same are not brought up in the knowledge of their fayeth, dutie and obedience, wherein no Christen person ought to be ignoraunt. And for that our people and subjectes which haue no understanding in the Latin tong and yet haue the knowledge of readyng may praye in their vulgar tong, which is to them best knowne; that bi the meane therof thei should be more prouoked to true deuotion, and the better set theyr hertes upon those thinges that thei pray for. And finallye, for the auoyding of the aduersitie of primer bokes that are nowe abrode, whereof are almost innumerable sortes, which minister occasion of contentious and vaine disputations rather than edyfy, and to haue one uniforme ordre of al suche bokes throughout all our dominions, both to be taught unto children, and also to be used for ordinary praiers of al our people not learned in the Latin tong : haue set furth this Primer or boke of praiers in Englyshe to be frequented and used in and throughoute all places of our sayde realmes and dominions as well of the eldre people, as also of the youth for their common and ordinary praiers, willing commaundyng, and streightlye chargyng, that for the better bringing up of youth in the knowledge of their dutie towardes God, their prince, and al other in their degree, euery scole mayster and brynger up of yong beginners in learning next after their A. B. C. now by us also set furth do teach this Primer or boke of ordinary prayers unto them in Englyshe, and that the youth customably and ordinarily use the same untyll thei be of competent understandyng and knowledge to perceiue it in Latin. At what tyme thei maye at their libertie ether use this Prymer in Englyshe, or that which is by our autoritie like wyse made in the Latin tong, in al poyntes correspondent unto this in Englysh. And furthermore we streightly charge and commaund aswel all and singuler our subjectes and sellers of bokes as also al scholemasters and teachers of young children within this our realme and other our dominions as they entende to haue our fauoure and auoyde our displesure by the contrary, that immediately after this our sayed Prymer is publyshed and imprinted, that they ne any of them bye, sell, occupye, use, nor teache preuely or apertly any other primer ether in Englyshe or Latin then this, nowe by us published, which with no smal study, trauayl, and labor, we haue purposely made to the high honor and glory of almightie god, and to the commoditie of our louing and obedient subiectes, and edefiyng of the same in godly contemplation and vertuouse exercise of prayer.

" Geuen at our palayce of Westminster the VI daye of Maye in the XXXVII yere of our reigne."

Notwithstanding that Henry commanded that these books alone should be used in all his dominions, many declined to use them, but purchased unauthorized manuals, which accorded more with their religious convictions, of which numberless editions were published, differing in details according as their authors were more or less inclined to depart from the old formularies or doctrines. We have reproduced in facsimile the first and last pages of the earliest-known copy of the unauthorized A B C, which is supposed to have been printed in 1538. The only copy known to be in existence is in the library of the British Museum.

℗ The . B A C bothe in latyn
and in Englysshe.

✠ A a b c d e f g h j k l m n o p
q r z ſ s t v u x y z ꝫ ⁊ est Amen.

a e i o u   a e i o u
ab eb `ib ob ub   ba be bi bo bu
ac ec ic oc uc   ca ce ci co cu
ad ed id od ud   da de di do du
af ef if of uf   fa fe fi fo fu
ag. eg ig og ug   ga ge gi go gu

In nomine patris ⁊ filii ⁊ spiriteus
sancti. Amen. ℗ In the name of
the . Father and of the Sone and of
the holy ghost. . Amen.

Pater noster qui es in celis
sanctificetur. nomen tuū:
Adueniat regnum tuum
Fiat. voluntas tua sicut
in celo et in terra. Panem nostrum
quotidianum da nobis hodie.   Et
dimitte nobis debita nostra/ sicut et

First page of A B C 1538.

And to correcte with charyte
To suffer in all aduersyte
My neyghbors trespas to forgyue
And to pray for grace whyle I lyue
℧The. vij. Capitall synnes.
Good lorde graunt me pryde to for
And not to syn in couetous   (sake
Nor slouth / but in good workes to
wake
Nor to be wrath nor furyous
Nor byscoaynous nor enuyous
Nor for to synne in glotony
Nor in no carnall Lechery.

Thus endeth the. A B C transla
ted out of Laten to toEnglysshe
with other deuoute Prayers.

℧ Imprynted at Londõ mPaules
Chyrche yarde at the sygne of the
maydens heed by thomas Pctyt.

Last page of A B C 1538.

THE
Indian Primer;

O R,

The way of training up of our
Indian Youth in the good
knowledge of God, in the
knowledge of the Scriptures
and in an ability to Reade.

Composed by J. E.

J'un. 3 14, 15. *Qut ken nag-
wutteaush ni h nahtunt.mani h
k h pohkoat.manish, wah.adt
nob sahtuhtakoaadt
15, Kah wutch kummukki suix-
neat h owabteo wunneetupaca
tamwe wuffxkwhorgish. &c.*

Cambridge, Printed 1669.

The authorized editions of the *A B C* and the *Primer* were monopolies, and could be printed only by printers who had received the royal license. They were sold separately and were costly. The unauthorized editions, such as the Independent and Separatist manuals, could be published by any printer. By uniting both manuals in one volume and selling at a low price, large sales and great profits were made, and very quickly there were published many editions of these unauthorized manuals which have retained the name of primers, while the authorized manuals are known as the Book of Common Prayer.

Which one of these unauthorized primers was used in teaching the children of the New England colonists is unknown, but it is very probable it was the one in vogue in England among the Puritans previous to their leaving the mother country. From the Plymouth Colony Records we learn that in 1655 Rev. John Eliot imported " common primers " and hornbooks for use among the Indians. No copies have come down to us, and its identification is impossible. In 1668 Marmaduke Johnson and Samuel Green, the Cambridge printers, were summoned to appear before the Council sitting at Boston to give an account of what books they had lately printed and by what authority. They both appeared before the Council on the 3d of September, and Johnson answered that besides other books of which he gave the titles, he had " printed the primer and ye psalter," for which he had license by Mr. Chauncey and Mr. Mitchell.

As no primer other than a Puritan primer would be salable, it is very probable it was one of that nature that he printed, and possibly a copy of the one that had been in use just previously. In 1669 Samuel Green and Marmaduke Johnson printed, *The Indian Primer*, a 32mo containing sixty-four unnumbered leaves. This primer was " composed " by Rev. John Eliot, and it is a fair inference that it was simply a translation into the Indian language of the primer printed by Johnson in 1668. If this conjecture be true, an examination of the contents of *The Indian Primer* will give a clear idea of the contents of the primer used in the early days of the New England colonies. One copy only is known to be in existence, the one in the library of the University of Edinburgh. Its contents are the two alphabets, small and capital, the five vowels, nine diphthongs, spelling lessons, reading lessons, Lord's Prayer, ancient creed, creed expounded, degrees of Christian duties, the Large Catechism, the Ten Commandments, the Short Catechism, the numerical letters and figures, and names and order of the books of the Old and New Testaments. If in place of the Large and Short Catechisms we substitute Perkins' *Six Principles*, we shall approximate the primer of the Pilgrims and Puritans.

This primer was the reading-book of the elementary schools and remained in use until the advent of *The New England Primer* in 1690. The arrival of Benjamin Harris in Boston marked the beginning of a new era in publishing and bookselling. Having been obliged to leave England on account of his anti-Popery principles, Boston and New England were great gainers in receiving the benefit of his intelligence and enterprise. Having secured the most prominent business corner in Boston, he not only stocked his shop with books, but also added a counter for the sale of temperance drinks. At his shop was delivered the mail by incoming shipmasters, and the last visit made by outgoing shipmasters was at his shop to secure the return mail. It was the most frequented shop in all the town and was the place of meeting for all the literary lights of the period. Having been a publisher of prominence in England, almost immediately upon his arrival in Boston he began to print, and was soon the leading publisher of New England, during his short stay of eight years having published

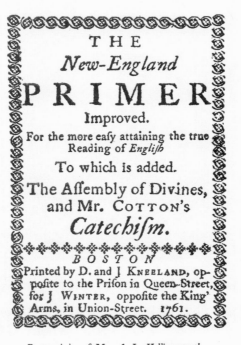

THE
New-England
PRIMER
Improved.

For the more eafy attaining the true
Reading of *Englifh*

To which is added.

The Affembly of Divines,
and Mr. COTTON's
Catechifm.

BOSTON
Printed by D. and J KNEELAND, oppofite to the Prifon in Queen-Street,
for J WINTER, oppofite the King'
Arms, in Union-Street. 1761.

By permission of Mr. A. L. Hollingsworth.

King GEORGE the Third Crown'd
September 22*d*, 1761, whom *GOD*
long Preferve.

By permission of Mr. A. L. Hollingsworth.

THE
ROYAL PRIMER.

OR,

An EASY and PLEASANT GUIDE
To the ART of READING :

Authorized by His
MAJESTY King GEORGE II.

TO BE USED THROUGHOUT

His *Majesty's* DOMINIONS.

(Adorned with CUTS.)

B O S T O N,

Printed and Sold by WILLIAM McALPINE,
in *Marlborough*-Street; where may be
had a Variety of entertaining and inftruc-
tive Books for Children. MDCC LXXIII.

By permission of Mr. A. L. Hollingsworth.

more than fifty books. He attracted a great deal of attention by attempting to establish a newspaper in Boston which was suppressed by the government after the issue of the first number. His fame, however, will rest probably upon the fact that he composed and published the most popular text-book of colonial or provincial times ; namely, *The New England Primer*. Having published several children's books in England, he saw that there was a crying need of a good reading-book in the elementary schools. After studying the situation carefully, assisted no doubt by Cotton Mather, Samuel Sewall, and Samuel Willard, well-known frequenters of his shop, he finally produced the book to which he gave the very appropriate title *The New England Primer*. From its extensive use in teaching the Catechism, it has been called *The Little Bible of New England*, which would seem to convey the idea that it is only a church book. Although the Catechism and the moral and religious ideas which it inculcated peculiarly adapted it to the use of the Church, yet it was intended to be a child's text-book, to give children their first instruction in reading, and to imbue their minds with a thirst for knowledge. By introducing pictures it was an attempt to teach by the eye as well as by the ear ; and by including in the text matter not strictly spiritual, it was a step in the direction of secularizing the previous primers.

Using the old Primer as a basis, he added several new features, some of which he had used in other publications in London, and some of which he took from various books which had been very popular in England. The illustrating each letter of the alphabet with a picture, and having single lines for each letter, the first word of the line being the letter itself, was as old as the A B C of Marens Schultz of 1532. Doggerel verses which associated rhymes with each of the letters were common in sixteenth-century primers. The *Orbis Pictus* of Comenius, a Latin Grammar illustrated with pictures, first published in 1657, and which has been called the first child's picture-book, furnished Harris with many ideas. *A Dialogue between Christ, Youth, and the Devil* was adopted from Benjamin Keach's *War with the Devil*, a popular publication of John Dunton.

All of these features, owing to their great popularity, Harris used in his scheme, having rewritten them to suit his own ideas, and adding *Cotton's Spiritual Milk for Babes*, offered his book for sale probably in the latter part of 1690. It was an immediate success, and a second edition was shortly announced to which he added the *Prayer of King Edward VI.*, the great patron of education, and *Verses made by Mr. Rogers, the Martyr*, which were really written by Robert Smith, also a martyr. These *Verses* were first printed in 1559, and proved so popular that they were reprinted many times.

By the addition of these new features its success was so materially increased that it entirely superseded the old primers. The popularity of *The New England Primer* continued until well into the nineteenth century, and its sales have been numbered by millions. Although it is still published, it is more as a curiosity than as a text-book, its place as a school-book in the elementary schools having been taken first by Webster's Speller and later by other spellers and readers.

Besides the various primers the children used for readers the Psalter, which contained the Psalms, Proverbs, and Nicene Creed. As they grew older, the Testament and Bible were substituted.

The first school reader in the modern sense of the term published in America was *An* American *Selection of Lessons in Reading and Speaking, calculated to improve the Minds and refine the Taste of Youth. And also to instruct them in the Geography, History, and Politics of the United States. To which is prefixed Rules in Elocution, and Directions for expressing the principal Passions of the Mind. Being the Third Part of a Grammatical Insti-*

HIS EXCEL: G:WASHINGTON ESQ.

Frontispiece to Webster's Reader.   Third Ed.

By permission of Mr. Z. T. Hollingsworth.   See page 156.

[154]

An AMERICAN

SELECTION

OF

Leſſons in Reading and Speaking.

CALCULATED

To improve the MINDS and refine the TASTE of YOUTH.

AND ALSO

To inſtruct them in the GEOGRAPHY, HISTORY, and POLITICS of the UNITED STATES.

To which is prefixed,

RULES in ELOCUTION, and DIRECTIONS for expreſſing the principal PASSIONS of the Mind.

BEING

The THIRD PART of a Grammatical Inſtitute of the Engliſh Language.

BY NOAH WEBSTER, jun. ESQ.

THE THIRD EDITION,
GREATLY ENLARGED.

Begin with the Infant in his Cradle: Let the firſt Word he liſps be Waſhington.
MIRABEAU.

PHILADELPHIA:

Printed and ſold by YOUNG and M'CULLOCH, at the Corner of *Second* and *Chefnut-ſtreets.*

M.DCC.LXXXVII.

By permiſſion of Mr. Z. T. Hollingsworth.

tute of the English Language. By Noah Webster, Jun., Esquire, Hartford; Printed and Sold by Hudson and Goodwin. [*With the Privilege of Copy-Right.*] *MDCCLXXXV.*"

The third edition, printed in 1787, has as a frontispiece the portrait of George Washington, a metal-faced engraving by Trenchard. Copies of this edition are very scarce. Mr. Z. T. Hollingsworth has very generously allowed the use of his copy to secure facsimiles of the titlepage and portrait. In 1790 Isaiah Thomas and Ebenezer T. Andrews bought the copyright and substituted the portrait of Noah Webster, a crude woodcut, engraved possibly by Paul Revere, who is known to have done considerable engraving for Thomas and Andrews.

Webster's Reader was not so successful as his Speller, as it met with formidable competitors in *The American Preceptor*, published in 1794, and *The Columbian Orator*, published in 1797, both written by Caleb Bingham. In 1832 more than six hundred and forty thousand copies of *The American Preceptor* had been printed, and of *The Columbian Orator* more than two hundred thousand. *The American Preceptor* displaced Webster's Third Part and *The Columbian Orator* displaced the Bible, which was now read by the master as a religious exercise at the opening of the school in the morning and at its close in the afternoon. The dialogues in *The Columbian Orator* were written by David Everett, a graduate of Dartmouth College who came to Boston and established the *Boston Patriot* some years afterwards. He also wrote the well-known "lines spoken at a School Exhibition by a little boy seven years old," beginning, —

> " You'd scarce expect one of my age
> To speak in public, on the stage;
> And if I chance to fall below
> Demosthenes or Cicero,
> Don't view me with a critic's eye,
> But pass my imperfections by."

THE

AMERICAN PRECEPTOR ;

BEING A NEW

SELECTION of LESSONS

FOR

READING and SPEAKING.

DESIGNED FOR THE USE OF SCHOOLS.

By CALEB BINGHAM, A. M.

Author of the Young Lady's Accidence, and Child's Companion.

" TRAIN UP A CHILD IN THE WAY HE SHOULD GO —"

The *Third* Edition.

Published according to Act of Congress.

Boston :

PRINTED BY MANNING AND LORING,

For the *AUTHOR;* and sold at his Book-Store, No. 44,
Cornhill ; sold also by THOMAS & ANDREWS, S. HALL.
D. WEST, J. WEST, J. BOYLE, B. LARKIN, E. LAR-
KIN. W. P. BLAKE, J. WHITE, &c. &c.

1796.

[157]

Caleb Bingham, whose school-books made him known more extensively than any contemporary teacher in the United States, Noah Webster excepted, was born in Salisbury, Conn., April 15, 1757. Having been prepared for college by Rev. Dr. Salter, he entered Dartmouth College in 1779 and graduated in 1782. After serving two years as Master of Moor's Charity School, he removed in 1784 to Boston, where he opened a school for girls, the first that had ever been kept in the town, in which he taught not only writing and arithmetic, but reading, spelling, and English grammar. His success was so great that the town established schools to which girls were admitted, and in 1789 employed Mr. Bingham to teach one of them. In 1796 he gave up teaching and opened a bookstore at 44 Cornhill, where he remained until his death, April 6, 1817. Mr. W. B. Fowle gives the following description of his personal appearance : " His height was about six feet and his frame well proportioned and well developed. His face was pleasant, but rather short. His eyes were light blue, his nose short and rather sharp, his hair was dressed with earlocks, powdered and braided behind, exactly in the style of Washington. He wore almost to the last a cocked hat, black coat and small clothes, with a white vest and stock, and black silk hose. In winter he wore white topped boots, and in summer shoes with silver buckles. His appearance and manners were those of a gentleman; he was respectful to all ; affable, gentle, and free from any of the traits which are apt to cling to the successful pedagogue."

In 1793 he was the chief agent in establishing the Boston Library, which is still in existence, having recently removed to Newbury Street. The initiatory meetings were held at his house, and he officiated gratuitously as librarian for about two years.

𝔄𝔯𝔦𝔱𝔥𝔪𝔢𝔱𝔦𝔠𝔰

THE early colonial schools had but very few arithmetics. Usually only the teacher owned a book, and very frequently even this was a manuscript "ciphering-book," made by himself or procured from some other teacher. Printed arithmetics were rarities, and many scholars never saw one.

Lemuel Shattuck, the well-known historian, relates a conversation which he held in 1830 with an intelligent farmer who was then sixty-eight years old. On being asked how arithmetic was taught when he was a youth, he replied, " they had a kind of a Hodder to teach arithmetic, but what it was, whether a book or something else, he could not tell." When informed that THAT was probably the name of the author of the book, he observed, it was the first time he had heard of it.

The method of teaching arithmetic was very similar to that pursued in teaching writing. The example to be performed was given out by the teacher from his " ciphering-book," which the scholar worked out upon a separate sheet of paper. When pronounced correct, it was copied neatly into a blank book, similar to the writing-book, which was known as a " ciphering-book," and which very seldom went beyond the " Rule of Three."

The style of the sixteenth-century arithmetic was so obscure and the rules so involved in symbols that they were difficult to be understood. " From that time the science of arithmetic has been perfected in many ways. Since the days of Oughtred more authors in England and America have written on this

Records Arithmetick:

OR,

THE GROUND
OF ARTS:

TEACHING

The perfect work and practice of Arithmetick,
both in whole Numbers and Fractions, after a more
easie and exact form then in former time hath been set forth:
Made by M. *Robert Record*, D. in Physick.

Afterward, augmented by M. John Dee.

And since enlarged with a third part of Rules of Practice, abridged into a briefer method then hitherto hath been
published, with divers necessary Rules incident to the
Trade of Merchandise : with Tables of the valuation of all Coyns, as they are currant
at this present time.

By JOHN MELLIS.

And now diligently perused, corrected, illustrated and enlarged ;
with an *Appendix* of figurative Numbers, and the extraction of
their Roots, according to the method of *Christian Urstitius:* with
Tables of Board and Timber measure; and new Tables of Interest, after 10. and 8. *per* 100; with the true value of Annuities
to be bought or sold present, Respited, or in Reversion: the first
calculated by *R. C.* but corrected, and the latter diligently calculated by *Ro. Hartwell, Philomathemat*

Scientia non habet inimicum nisi ignorantem.
Fide ——— sed ——— Vide.

LONDON,

Printed by *J. Flesher*, for *John Harrison* ; and are to be
sold by *Edw. Dod* and *Nath. Ekins* in Ivy-lane at the
sign of the Gun. 1652.

Arithmetics

subject than on any other with the exception perhaps of English Grammar," says J. M. Greenwood, LL.D., Superintendent of Schools, Kansas City, Missouri. During the seventeenth century all the arithmetics used in the colonial schools were imported from England. In the selection of the book to be used, each school was a law unto itself, and the master for the time being usually chose the book. All the arithmetics hereafter mentioned were used in some one or other of the schools of New England, and many of those in possession of the writer have the autographs of the boys who used them.

The first arithmetic printed in English was published in 1540. It was written by Robert Record, the physician, who was born about 1500, a Fellow of All Souls College, Oxford, 1531, and died in 1558. Its title reads : *The Ground of Arts : Teaching the perfect work and practice of Arithmetic, both in whole Numbers and Fractions, after a more easie and exact form then in former time hath been set forth : Made by Robert Record, D. in Physick, London, 1540.* It was written in the form of " A Dialogue betweene the Master and the Scholar ; teaching the Art and use of Arithmetick with Pen." It was very popular and passed through many editions, the writer possessing an edition published in 1652, " augmented by John Dee and enlarged by John Mellis," octavo in size and containing six hundred and fifty-four pages. On a leaf is written, " Thomas Hardinges his Booke given him by Mr. Francis Grosvener the 22d of September Ano. 1652."

John Timbs, in speaking of Robert Record, says : " He was a man whose memory deserves a much larger portion of fame than it has met with. He was the first who wrote on Arithmetic and the first who wrote on Geometry in English ; the first who introduced Algebra into England ; the first who wrote on Astronomy and the doctrine of the Sphere in England ; and, finally, the first Englishman (in all probability) who adopted

Guilelmi Oughtred

AETONENSIS,

quondam Collegii Regalis
in CANTABRIGIA Socii,

CLAVIS MATHEMATICÆ
DENVO LIMATA,

Sive potius
FABRICATA.

Cum aliis quibufdam ejufdem
Commentationibus, quæ in fe-
quenti pagina recenfentur.

Editio tertia auctior & emendatior.

OXONIÆ,
Excudebat LEON. LICHFIELD, Veneunt
apud THO. ROBINSON. 1652.

Oughtred's Arithmetic.

See page 166.

the system of Copernicus. Record was also the inventor of the sign of equality ; and the inventor of the method of extracting the square-root of multinomial algebraic quantities."

Humphrey Baker, a citizen of London in the time of Queen Elizabeth, and a mathematician, was the author of a very popular work on arithmetic, entitled, *The Well Spring of Sciences ; which teacheth the perfect worke and practise of Arithmetic.* The first edition was published in 1562, and it continued to be constantly reprinted until 1687. " Of all the works on arithmetic prior to the publication of Cockers celebrated work on the same subject (1668), this of Baker's approaches nearest to the masterpiece of that celebrated mathematician."

Edmund Wingate was the author of a very popular arithmetic which was frequently reprinted. He was born in Yorkshire in 1593, educated at Queen's College, Oxford, and after taking his degree in arts, removed to Gray's Inn, where he studied the law. His chief inclination, however, was to the mathematics, which he studied with much success at college. He went to France in 1624, and while there gave instruction in the English language to the Princess Henrietta Maria (afterwards consort of Charles I.). After his return to England he became a bencher of Gray's Inn, and on the breaking out of the Rebellion joined the popular party and was made justice of the peace of the county of Bedford. In 1650 he was elected to Parliament for Bedford, and was also appointed one of the commissioners for that county to eject from their situations those loyal clergymen and schoolmasters, who were accused of being scandalous and ignorant. He died in 1656 and was buried in the church of St. Andrews, Holborn. He wrote several mathematical and legal works, the best known of which is, *Of Natural and Artificial Arithmetic, or Arithmetic made easy. London, 1630.* The edition, printed in London in 1753, edited by James Dodson, is considered the best edition. A copy of

ke Kings arithmetic

Hee that more of thine Excellence would Know
On this thy Book let him some thoughts bestow;
Deep Questions in Arithmetick here are
Demonstrated by Rules so plaine so Rare,
Envy it Selfe must needs confess thus much
Read all y Book's i'th World youl find nonsuch
T.H.

Frontispiece of Hodder's Arithmetic.

See page 167.

HODDER's ARITHMETICK:

OR, THAT
NECESSARY ART

Made moſt eaſie.

Being explained in a way familiar to the *Capacity* of any that deſire to learn in a little Time.

By James Hodder, *Writing-Maſter.*

The Twentieth Edition revifed, augmented, and above a thouſand Faults amended, by Henry Moſe, *late Servant and Succeſſor to the Author.*

LONDON,

Printed for *Ric. Chiſwell,* at the *Reſe* and *Crown* in St. *Paul's* Church-yard, and *Geo. Sawbridge* at the *Three Flower-de-luces* in *Little Britain.* MDCXCVII.

the first edition is now in existence, which was used in the Winslow family of Massachusetts for over one hundred years.

In 1631 William Oughtred, an eminent divine and a distinguished mathematician, published *Clavis Mathematicæ*, in which he introduced the sign × (of multiplication), St. Andrew's Cross. A third edition was published in 1652. It is an octavo volume of two hundred and sixty pages, and written in Latin.

William Oughtred, the first mathematician of his time and one of the ablest England has ever produced, was born at Eton in 1573, was educated on the foundation of the college, and became a Kingsman in 1592. Aubrey, in his memoir of Oughtred, says : " His father taught to write at Eaton and was a scrivener; and understood common arithmetique, and 't was no small help and furtherance to his son to be instructed in it when a school-boy." Although he improved his opportunities to acquire a classical and philosophical education, he was more inclined to mathematics, and spent the greater part of his boyhood, manhood, and old age in what he fondly termed " the more than Elysian fields of the mathematical sciences." At the age of twenty-three he wrote a treatise on geometrical dialling, entitled *Horologiographia Geometrica*, which was first published in 1647. In 1600 he projected the instrument now known as the Sliding Rule, by which the processes of addition and subtraction are performed mechanically. In 1631 appeared *Arithmeticæ in Numero et Speciebus Institutio*, or, as it was speedily and generally called, his *Clavis*. This work soon became the text-book for mathematical students at Cambridge, and passed through many editions. During his life he published other works of high merit and reputation on mathematical subjects. About 1600 he became rector of the parish of Albury in Surrey, which he held for more than half a century. He resided at his living, and his house was frequented by scientific men of all nations, who came to consult him and do him honor, and it was continually filled with pupils who sought the benefit of his teaching. Fuller says he was unanimously acknowledged the prince of mathematicians, and his fame was so great that during the troubles of the civil wars in England the Duke of Florence invited him to Italy, offering him a salary of £500 a year, which he declined on account of his religion. He died Jan. 30, 1660, universally esteemed and beloved for the exemplary discharge of his pastoral duties.

In 1661, the first edition of Hodder's *Arithmetic* was published in London, a small duodecimo of two hundred and sixteen pages. It met with such success that in 1697 the twentieth edition was published in London, and in 1719 the twenty-fifth edition was printed in Boston, New England, by James Franklin. A copy of this edition with the boyish autograph of Samuel Seabury brought $32.50 at the sale of the Brinley library in 1886.

James Hodder, the author, was the master of a writing-school in London, to whom Charles Hoole sent his grammar-school scholars to learn writing and arithmetic. In the Preface Hodder says: " Having for sundry Years kept a Writing-School in this City and having gained some Experience in that commendable Art, I thought good heretofore to publish somewhat thereof. And now for the better compleating of Youth as to Clerkship and Trades, I am induced to publish this small Treatise of Arithmetic."

Charles Hoole, in his *New Discovery of the Old Art of Teaching School*, published in 1660, says: " In London it is ordinary for scholars at eleven and five o'clock to go to the Writing-Schools, and there to benefit themselves in writing. In that City, having the opportunity of the neighbourhood of my singular loving friend, Mr. James Hodder (whose copy-books of late printed, do sufficiently testify his ability for the profession he hath undertaken, and of whose cares and pains I have had abun-

Ingenious *Cocker*. now to Reſt thou'rt gone,

No *Art* can ſhew thee fully, but thine own.

Thy rare *Arithmetick*, alone can, ſhow

Th' vaſt *Sums* of *Thanks*, we for thy *Labours* owe

Frontispiece to Cocker's Arithmetic.

COCKER's
Arithmetick.

BEING,

A Plain and Familiar Method, suitable to the meaneft Capacity, for the full Underftanding of that incomparable Art, as it is now taught by the ableft School-Mafters in CITY and COUNTRY.

By EDWARD COCKER, late Practitioner in the Arts of Writing, Arithmetick, and Engraving: Being that fo long fince promifed to the World.

Perufed and publifhed

By JOHN HAWKINS Writing-Mafter, near St. *George*'s Church in *Southwark*, by the Author's correct Copy, and commended to the World by many eminent Mathematicians and Writing-Mafters in and near *London*.

The FIFTY-FOURTH EDITION, carefully Corrected, and Amended

By GEORGE FISHER, *Accomptant.*
Licenfed *Sept.* 3, 1677. *Roger L'Eftrange.*

L O N D O N:

Printed for R. *Ware* at the *Bible* and *Sun* on *Ludgate-Hill*; C. *Hitch*, at the *Red Lion* in *Paternofter-Row*; and J. *Hodges*, at the *Looking Glafs* over-againft S. *Magnus* Church, *London-Bridge.* 1753.

dant trial by his profiting of my scholars for twelve years together; who had most of them learned of him to write a very fair hand; not to speak of Arithmetic or Merchants Accounts, which they gained also by his teaching at spare times); in the Token-house Garden in Lothbury, somewhat near to the Old-Exchange, I so ordered the business with him that all my lower scholars had their little paper-books ruled, wherein they writ their lessons fair, and then their translations and other exercises in loose papers in his sight, until they were able to do everything of themselves in a handsome manner. And afterwards, it is not to be expressed, what pleasure they took in writing and flourishing their exercises, all the while they continued with me in the school."

In 1677, John Hawkins, writing-master, published Cocker's *Arithmetic*, which has served as the model of almost all school-treatises subsequent to its publication. The expression " according to Cocker " is owing to its frequent use on the titlepages of the treatises following his method. This celebrated arithmetic was used both in England and America for more than one hundred years, an edition having been published in Philadelphia in 1779. Upon a bookseller's catalogue published in London in 1766 containing " A Catalogue of the School Books now in general use," Cocker's *Decimal Arithmetic* is listed at 3s. and his *Vulgar Arithmetic* at 1s. 6d.

It has been stated that Cocker had nothing to do with writing this arithmetic, and that its real author was John Hawkins. On the titlepage, however, Hawkins says he perused the author's correct copy; in the " Introduction to the Reader " he says he had often solicited Mr. Cocker in his lifetime to publish his arithmetic, but he refused, and after his death his copy fell into his hands. John Collins, a well-known mathematician, in a " Letter to the Reader " says he was well acquainted with Cocker and found him " knowing and studious in the Mysteries of

Numbers and Algebra, of which he had some choice Manu-
scripts, and a great Collection of printed Authors in several
Languages" and did not doubt "but he hath writ his Arithmetic suitable to his own Preface and worthy Acceptance;"
the names of several eminent mathematicians and writing-masters, commending the book, are also printed. It would seem,
if it was a forgery, it was a very bold one.

Augustus De Morgan, in his *Arithmetical Books*, devotes
seven pages to an examination of this question. He says: " I
am perfectly satisfied that Cocker's Arithmetic is a forgery of
Hawkins, with some assistance, it may be, from Cocker's
papers : that is to say, there has certainly been more or less
of forgery, without any evidence being left as to whether it
was more or less. I could easily believe that all was forged,"
and his reasons are given at full length.

Edward Cocker was born in London about 1631, and died
about 1675. He was not only a mathematician, but also an
accomplished penman and a skilful engraver, all of which he
taught in his school. Before 1660 he had published ten books
on penmanship, all of which were engraved by himself. So
successful was he in his profession that in 1661 a warrant was
issued to pay Edward Cocker, scrivener and engraver, the sum
of £161 as a gift.

Joseph Moxon, the celebrated hydrographer and bookseller
of London, published in 1679, *Mathematics made Easie; or a
Mathematical Dictionary explaining the Terms of Art and Difficult
Phrases used in Arithmetic, and other Mathematical Sciences.*
He was born in Wakefield, Yorkshire, in 1627, and died in
London in 1700. He wrote several books on Mathematics,
Astronomy, and Navigation, and for several years taught
mathematics in Warwick-lane in London, where he constructed
globes and maps. In 1679 he was keeping a bookshop
for the sale of " All manner of Maps, Sea-Plats, Drafts,

Mathematicks made Eafie :

Or, a Mathematical

DICTIONARY,

EXPLAINING *Jn.º Busack*

The Terms of Art, and Diffi-
cult Phrafes ufed in *Arithmetick*, *Geometry*, *Aftronomy*, *Aftrology*, and
other Mathematical Sciences.

Wherein the true Meaning of the
Word is Rendred, the Nature of
Things fignified Difcuffed, and (where
Need requires) Illuftrated with
apt Figures and Diagrams.

With an *APPENDIX*, exactly con-
taining the Quantities of all forts of
Weights and Meafures: The Characters and
Meaning of the Marks, Symbols, or
Abreviations commonly ufed in *Algebra*.
And fundry other Obfervables.

By *Jofeph Moxon*, a Member of the Royal Society,
and *Hydrographer* to the King's moft Excellent Majefty

LONDON.
Printed for *Jofeph Moxon*, at the Sign of *Atlas*
on *Ludgate-Hill*. M. DC. LXXIX.

Mathematical Books, Instruments, &c." He published in 1697 *A Catalogue of Globes, Celestial and Terrestrial, Spheres, Maps, Sea-Plats, Mathematical Instruments and Books, made and sold by Joseph Moxon on Ludgate-Hill at the Sign of Atlas.* Among the maps advertised was " A Map of the English Empire in America describing all Places inhabited there by the English Nation, as well on the Islands as on the Continent. Price 15*s*.''

Another popular arithmetic, which was indorsed by more than fifty English schoolmasters, was " The School-master's Assistant. Being a Compendium of Arithmetic, both Practical and Theoretical. By Thomas Dilworth." The first edition was published in 1743 and the nineteenth in 1776. The copy in the possession of the writer bears the autograph " Charles Taylor. 1778," and was used in the Boston schools during the Revolution. Following the Preface is " An Essay on the Education of Youth," in which he pleads very strongly for the education of the girls. He says in part, " It is a general remark that they are so unhappy as seldom to be found either to spell, write, or cipher well. . . . Girls therefore ought to be put to the writing-school as early as boys, and continued in it as long, and then it may reasonably be expected that both sexes should be alike ready at their pen."

Dilworth's *Spelling Book, Bookkeeper's Assistant, Schoolmaster's Assistant,* and *Miscellaneous Arithmetic,* were long used and very popular.

Thomas Dilworth was for some time engaged at Stratford-le-Bow with Dyche, but later set up a school for himself at Wapping. He died in 1780.

Dilworth's Schoolmaster's Assistant was much esteemed in America, an edition called the "Twenty-third" being published at Hartford in 1785. It was also published at Wilmington, " Printed and Sold by Peter Brynberg, 1796," and

Tho. Dilworth
Schoolmaster

H. Burgh Sculp.

Frontispiece to Dilworth's Arithmetic.

.[174]

THE
Schoolmasters Assistant.
BEING A
Compendium of ARITHMETIC,
BOTH
Practical and Theoretical.

In Five PARTS.

CONTAINING

I. Arithmetic in whole Numbers, wherein all the common Rules, having each of them a sufficient Number of Questions, with their Answers, are methodically and briefly handled.

II. Vulgar Fractions, wherein several Things, not commonly met with, are there distinctly treated of, and laid down in the most plain and easy Manner.

III. Decimals, in which, among other Things, are considered the Extraction of Roots; Interest, both Simple and Compound; Annuities; Rebate, and Equation of Payments.

IV. A large Collection of Questions with their Answers, serving to exercise the foregoing Rules, together with a few others, both pleasant and diverting.

V. Duodecimals, commonly called Cross Multiplication; wherein that Sort of Arithmetic is thoroughly considered, and rendered very plain and easy; together with the Method of proving all the foregoing Operations at once by Division of several Denominations, without reducing them into the lowest Terms mentioned.

The Whole being delivered in the most familiar Way of *Question* and *Answer*, is recommended by several eminent *Mathematicians, Accomptants*, and *Schoolmasters*, is necessary to be used in *Schools* by all Teachers, who would have their *Scholars* thoroughly understand, and make a quick Progress in ARITHMETIC.

To which is prefixt, An ESSAY on the *Education* of YOUTH ; humbly offer'd to the Consideration of PARENTS.

The Nineteenth Edition.

By THOMAS DILWORTH,
Author of the *New Guide* to the *English* Tongue ; *Young Bookkeeper's Assistant*, &c. &c. and *Schoolmaster* in *Wapping.*

All Things, which from the very first Original Being of Things, have been framed and made, do appear to be framed by the Reason of Number ; for this was the principal Example or Pattern in the Mind of the CREATOR.   Anitius Boetius.

Thou [O LORD] hast ordered all Things in Measure, Number, and Weight.   Wisdom xi. 20.

LONDON:

Printed and Sold by RICHARD and HENRY CAUSTON (Successors to the late Mr. HENRY KENT) at the Printing-Office, No. 21, in *Finch-Lane*, near the *Royal Exchange.* M DCC LXXVI.

[175]

another edition, styled, "The latest Edition," was printed at New London, Connecticut, "by Samuel Green for Naphthali Judah, New York, 1797."

The first arithmetic by an American author was written by Isaac Greenwood and published in 1729. Its title reads: *Arithmetick Vulgar and Decimal: with the Application therof, to a variety of Cases in Trade and Commerce. Boston: N. E. Printed by S. Kneeland and T. Green, for T. Hancock at the Sign of the Bible and Three Crowns in Ann street. MDCCXXIX.* It is a small duodecimo of one hundred and sixty-two pages, exclusive of four pages of advertisement prefixed. Three copies only are known to be in existence, two in the library of Harvard College, and one in the library of Congress.

In the advertisement Mr. Greenwood says that "the Author's Design in the following Treatise is to give a very concise Account of such Rules as are of the easiest Practice in all the Parts of Vulgar and Decimal Arithmetick; and to illustrate each with such Examples as may be sufficient to lead the Learner to the full Use thereof in all other Instances. . . . He has had his mind all along upon Persons of some Education and Curiosity. . . . He has thought it improper to go into an elaborate Explanation of the Rules in the lower Parts of Arithmetick, as most authors have done and has been very cautious of multiplying Examples under the same Rules, consulting such a method as should encourage the Reader rather to the true Sense and Use of each particular Rule, than the useless Practice of Multiplication, Division, and the like. . . . The Reader will observe, that the Author has inserted under all those Rules, where it was proper, Examples with Blanks for his Practice. This was a Principal End to the Undertaking; that such Persons as were desirous thereof might have a comprehensive Collection of all the best Rules in the Art of Numbring, with Examples wrought by themselves. And that

ARITHMETICK
Vulgar and *Decimal* ;

WITH THE

APPLICATION
THEREOF TO

A VARIETY of CASES

IN

Trade, and *Commerce.*

By: Isaac Greenwood M.A et P.M:

BOSTON: N. E.

Printed by S. KNEELAND and T. GREEN, for T. HANCOCK at the Sign of the Bible and Three Crowns in *Annſtreet.* MDCCXXIX.

nothing might be wanting to favour this Design, the Impression is made upon several of the best Sorts of Paper. This Method is entirely new."

The method followed was to give the rule in each subject, then examples illustrating the rule, then examples for the student, and finally the proof. Each example has a "blank" beneath it for the student's "practice."

Isaac Greenwood, the author, was born May 7, 1702, and was graduated at Harvard College in 1721. For several years Thomas Hollis of London, England, had been meditating the establishment of a professorship of Mathematics and Natural Philosophy at Harvard College, and in 1727 carried this intention into effect, at the same time sending to the college a philosophical apparatus, several boxes of valuable books, and Hebrew and Greek types. The selection of the professor was left to the Corporation. "All eyes were turned on Isaac Greenwood, as the most promising candidate for this office, and a visit to England about this time, enabled him to qualify himself more perfectly for the expected appointment. Mr. Hollis saw him frequently while abroad, and afforded him all the facilities in his power." Mr. Hollis, however, was not entirely satisfied, and suggested another candidate whom he had himself assisted in pursuing his studies on the Continent, and who could bring the most flattering testimonials from the first scholars in Europe. But he was a Baptist, of the same denomination with Mr. Hollis himself, and this was an insuperable objection. His proposal was rejected. Mr. Greenwood was elected in May, 1727, was accepted by Mr. Hollis, and was inaugurated Feb. 13, 1728, as "Hollisian Professor of Mathematics and Natural and Experimental Philosophy." In May, 1737, he was a candidate for the Presidency of the college, and divided the votes of the Corporation equally with Edward Holyoke. At a meeting of the Corporation May 20, Rev. William

Cooper of Boston was elected, but declined to serve. At the next meeting Edward Holyoke was elected by unanimous vote.

On the 7th of December, 1737, the Corporation voted to remove Professor Greenwood from his office. Professor Peirce, in his *History of Harvard University*, says: "From a spirit, however, of extreme forbearance, the Overseers deferred their decision till July 13, 1738, when they passed their final vote, confirming the act of the Corporation. He held his office ten years and five months, and might have continued to hold it, with credit to himself and benefit to the College, had his wisdom and firmness been equal to his acknowledged abilities." He went to Charleston, South Carolina, and there died Oct. 22, 1745.

Nearly sixty years elapsed before the second American arithmetic was published. The English favorites, Hodder, Cocker, and Dilworth, were superseded by *A New and Complete System of Arithmetic*, composed for the use of the citizens of the United States by Nicholas Pike, the first edition of which was published in Newburyport in 1788. It was a handsome octavo volume of five hundred and twelve pages. Before publication the author submitted his manuscript to several gentlemen interested in education, who wrote him letters approving the system and recommending its publication. Among the more prominent were J. Wheelock, President of Dartmouth College, Joseph Willard, President of Harvard College, and Ezra Stiles, President of Yale College.

In acknowledging the receipt of a copy sent as a present, George Washington wrote the following interesting letter:

MOUNT VERNON, June 20, 1788.

SIR: I request you will accept my best thanks for your polite letter of the 1st of January (which did not get to my hand 'till

A NEW

AND

COMPLETE SYSTEM

OF

ARITHMETIC,

COMPOSED FOR THE

USE OF THE CITIZENS

OF THE

UNITED STATES

By NICOLAS PIKE, *A. M.*

QUID MUNUS REIPUBLICÆ MAJUS MELIUSVE AFFERRE POS-
SUMUS, QUAM SI JUVENTUTEM DOCEMUS, ET BENE ERU-
DIMUS?
——E VARIIS SUMENDUM EST OPTIMUM.

Cicero.

NEWBURY-PORT:

PRINTED AND SOLD BY JOHN MYCALL.
MDCCLXXXVIII.

yesterday) — and also for the copy of your *System of Arithmetic* which you were pleased to present to me.

The handsome manner in which that work is printed, and the elegant manner in which it is bound are pleasing proofs of the progress which the arts are making in this Country. But I should do violence to my own feelings, if I suppressed an acknowledgement of the belief that the work itself is calculated to be equally useful and honorable to the United States.

It is but right, however, to apprise you, that, diffident of my own decision, the favourable opinion I entertain of your performance is founded rather on the explicit and ample testimonies of Gentlemen confessedly possessed of great mathematical knowledge, than on the partial and incompetent attention I have been able to pay to it myself. But I must be permitted to remark that the subject, in my estimation, holds a higher rank in the literary scale than you are disposed to allow. The science of figures, to a certain degree, is not only indispensably requisite in every walk of civilised life, but the investigation of mathematical truths accustoms the mind to method and correctness in reasoning, and is an employm. peculiarly worthy of rational beings. In a cloudy state of existence, where so many things appear precarious to the bewildered research, it is here that the rational faculties find a firm foundation to rest upon. From the high ground of Mathematical & Philosophical demonstration, we are insensibly led to far nobler speculations & sublime meditations.

I hope and trust that the work will ultimately prove not less profitable than reputable to yourself. It seems to have been conceded, on all hands, that such a system was much wanted. Its merits being established by the approbation of competent judges, I flatter myself that the idea of its being an American production, and the first of the kind which has appeared; will induce every patriotic and liberal character to give it all the

countenance & patronage in his power.   In all events, you may
rest assured, that, as no person takes more interest in the encouragement of American genius, so no one will be more highly
gratified with the success of your ingenious, arduous & useful
undertaking than he, who has the unfeigned pleasure to sub-
scribe himself with esteem & regard

   Sir Your Most Obed.^t and Very H^{ble} Servant,

                      G:° WASHINGTON

NICHOLAS PIKE, Esqr

With such high recommendations it is not surprising that it
was immediately adopted by the public schools of New England
and kept its place for more than fifty years.   In 1832, an edition
edited by Chester Dewey was published at Troy, N. Y.

Nicholas Pike, the author, was the son of Rev. James Pike,
was born at Somersworth, N. H., Oct. 6, 1743, and died at
Newburyport, Mass., Dec. 9, 1819.   He was graduated from
Harvard College in 1766, and for many years was the principal of the grammar school in Newburyport.   When the news
was received in Newburyport that the Continental Congress
had declared the United States free and independent, he was
the Town Clerk.   The Declaration of Independence was read
in all the meeting-houses, August 11, and the Town Clerk
evinced his satisfaction at the measure, by recording, under
date of Sept. 2, 1776, this indorsement to the call for the
meeting :

" This meeting was illegal, because the *venire* for calling it was
in the name of the British tyrant, whose name all America justly
execrates.

                      NICHOLAS PIKE."

He was also for many years a justice of the peace, and " the
rigid discipline he had exercised in the schoolroom, prepared
him to visit with severity, the petty trespasses subjected to his

decisions." The biographer Knapp says : " He was ready in the classics and seldom took a book to hear his pupils recite. He could boast of many excellent scholars, who had received the rudiments of a classical education under his care, a proof that he was himself well grounded in the same branches of learning."

Self-Instructors

BESIDES the separate treatises on reading, writing, and arithmetic, there were numerous miniature encyclopædias, which contained compends of nearly all the sciences and were known as "companions," "assistants," and "self-instructors." They were used not only in the schools, but were also very much in demand by young men and women who had not received a school education or whose school-days had been of short duration. They were nearly all by English authors and were either imported or reprinted. The various chapters contained plain directions for reading, writing, and arithmetic, how to write letters of compliment, friendship, and business; forms of notes, bills, leases, wills, and receipts; method of shop and bookkeeping; the art of mensuration; a family companion or book of recipes; geography; astronomy; etc. They were advertised to be "written in a plain and easy style, that a young man may both readily and easily improve and qualify himself for business without the help of a master." *Hill's Manual* and *Gaskell's Compendium*, very popular books of the present day, of which many thousand copies are sold annually, are similar books and are used for the same purpose.

One of the earliest of these encyclopædias of universal information was *The Young Secretary's Guide: or A speedy help to Learning*, one of the chapters being "A Short English Dictionary, explaining hard Words." It was a small duodecimo, containing one hundred and twenty pages. It was a very popular book in England, the seventh edition being published in 1696 and the twenty-seventh in 1764, in each of which the

THE
Young Secretary's Guide :
OR,
A speedy help to Learning.

In Two Parts.

Part I. Containing the moſt curious Art of
Inditing familiar Letters, relating to Bu-
ſineſs in Merchandize, Trade, Correſpon-
dence, Familiarity, Friendſhip, and on all
occaſions : alſo Inſtructions for Directing,
Superſcribing and Subſcribing of Letters
with due reſpect to the Titles of Perſons
of Quality and others : Rules for Point-
ing and Capitalling in Writing, *&c.*
Likewiſe a ſhort *Engliſh* Dictionary, Explaining hard Words.

Part II. Containing the nature of Writings
Obligatory, *&c* With Examples of Bonds:
Bills, Letters of Attorney, Deeds of Sale, of
Mortgage, Releaſes, Acquittances, Warrant
of Attorney, Deeds of Gift, Aſſignments
Counter Security, Bills of Sale, Letters of
Licenſe, Apprentices Indentures, Bills of
Exchange, & many other Writings made by
Scriveneis, *&c.* With a Table of Intereſt
Made ſuitable to th· People of *New-England*

The Sixth Edition.

With large and uſeful Additions.

By *Thomas Hill.* Gent.

BOSTON Reprinted for *Nicholas Boone*
at the BIBLE in *Cornhill,* 1727.

author's name is given as J. Hill. From 1694 to 1700 it was imported and offered for sale by Michael Perry "at his shop in Boston under the stairs at the West end of the Exchange." It was reprinted in Boston in 1708 under the title *The Young Clerk's Guide*. The name of the author is not given. The title of the fourth Boston edition reads: *The Young Secretary's Guide; or a speedy help to Learning. Made suitable to the people of New England. By Thomas Hill. Boston. Printed by T. Fleet, 1713*. In the twenty-fourth edition, printed by Thomas Fleet in 1750, the author's name is given as J. Hill. The name of the author is probably a pseudonym.

This little manual may have been introduced to the American public by John Allen, a London printer, who arrived in Boston in 1686, having come over by invitation of his uncle, Rev. James Allen, pastor of the First Church. The writer has in his possession a copy of the sixth edition, on the verso of the titlepage of which is printed a letter from " The Printer to the Reader" signed by J(ohn) A(llen). In it he says: " Since Epistles to all sorts of Books are fully in Fashion I suppose it will not be Impertinent to trouble you with a word or two here, to acquaint you That this is not an Imposition on the World, like the greatest part of Books of this kind now-a-days ; (of which there are more than a good many) but a Book stored with so great a variety of necessary Expedients as cannot in my Opinion but meet with a general Acceptation. It is impossible for me here to enumerate the Particulars of what this Book is composed, so I shall decline it, the Title page having done it already. As for my own part, this much I can say in its Praise, That a more useful Book on this Subject never came to my Hands ; so that it is needless to trouble you with a long and tedious Epistle in its Favour, it having sufficiently Recommended itself to the World already by the Sale of five large Impressions all of which were sold in a short Time and were found too few to furnish this large and daily increasing Country; which has of late occasioned very sad Complaints for want of so useful and necessary a Companion. This and a desire to serve the Publick, has encouraged the Booksellers to present the World with a sixth Impression of it."

In the twenty-fourth edition, the imprint of which reads: " Boston : Printed and sold by *Thomas Fleet*, at the *Heart & Crown* in Cornhill, 1750 " this letter of John Allen is omitted and in its place is " The Epistle to the Reader " signed " J. Hill," who claims the authorship. The text has been entirely rewritten and the number of pages increased to 178.

In 1731 there was reprinted in Boston *The Poor Man's Help and Young Man's Guide. By William Burkitt*, the celebrated commentator on the New Testament, who was born in Northamptonshire in 1650 and died in 1703. An edition called the thirty-first was printed in New York in 1795. The price of the book was one shilling.

The first edition of an English *vade-mecum* which obtained an enormous popularity was published in London in 1681. It was entitled, *The Young Man's Companion : or, The several Branches of Useful Learning made perfectly easy. Written by W. Mather, in a plain and easy Style, that a Young Man may both readily and easily improve and qualify himself for Business, without the Help of a Master.* The writer's copy is styled *The Twenty-fourth Edition, with large Additions and Improvements, by J. Barrow, London, 1775.* It is a duodecimo containing four hundred and seventeen pages.

In the library of the State Department at Washington are several copy-books in the handwriting of George Washington. They are mostly mathematical books, but one of them contains one hundred and ten maxims of civility and good behavior which biographers have asserted Washington coined and wrote out for his own use. In a lecture on " George Washington at

Happy the YOUTH, *who are* betimes *set right,*
And taught *the* Rules *of* VIRTUE *with* delight!
By ſoft Endearments *Generous Minds* are won,
By rigid Doctrines *very* Few *or* None: ——
The CYNIC TUTOR ſruitleſs Lectures *reads,*
HE *who* gilds *o're his* Precepts *beſt* SUCCEEDS

Frontiſpiece to Mather's Young Man's Companion, 1775.

George Washington 1742

THE
Young Man's Companion:
OR,
Arithemetick made Easy
WITH

Plain Directions for a Young Man to attain to
Read and Write true *English*, with Copies in Verfe
for a Writing School, Indicting of Letters to Friends,
Forms for making Bills, Bonds, Releafes Wills, &c.

LIKEWISE,

Eafy Rules for the Meafuring of Board and
Timber, by the Carpenter's Plain-Rule, and by Fractions; with Tables for fuch as have not learned
Arithmetick: And to compute the Charge of Building a Houfe or any Part thereof.

Alfo Directions for Meafuring, Guaging, and
Plotting of Land by *Gunter's* Chain; and taking heights
and diftances by the Quadrant and Triangle. The Ufe
of *Gunter's* Line in Meafuring Globes, Bullets, Walls,
Cones, Spire Steeples, and Barrels: With the Art of
Dialling, and Colouring of Work within and without Doors. Directions for Dying of Stuffs, &c.

Together with a Map of the Globe of the Earth
and Water; and *Copernicus's* Defcription of the vifible
World. Alfo a Map of *England*; and to know which
are Cities, and their Diftance from *London*.

Choice Monthly Obfervations for Gardening
Planting, Grafting, Inoculating Fruit-Trees, and the
beft Time to Prune them; and the making Wine
of Fruit: With experienc'd Medicines for the Poor.

An Account of *Curiofities* in London *and* Weftminfter.

Written by *W. Mather*, in a plain an eafy Stile, that a
a young Man may attain the fame without a Tutor.

The Thirteenth Edition; *With many Additions and Alterations, efpecially of the* Arithmetick, *to the Modern Method.*

London: Printed for *S. Clarke*, the Corner of *Exchange*.
Alley, next *Birchin Lane*, 1727.

See page 191.

School," Rev. A. D. Mayo, LL.D., said : " Notwithstanding the fact that the majority of the distinguished public men of the Revolutionary epoch in civic life were graduates of the higher institutions of learning of the time, the four men to whom perhaps the country was most vitally indebted, Washington, Franklin, Marshall, and Roger Sherman, had never enjoyed what a Massachusetts school-boy of any class, rank, or nationality would now regard a fair outfit for life ; and not one in a score of the mothers of the Revolution could boast the opportunity of the high-school girl of to-day.

" Yet these men were in the most enlarged sense educated in the university of the colonial life of a hundred and fifty years ago. Washington never went to what to-day we call a good school, and at thirteen he wrote out a dozen manuscript school-books and began life as a young engineer in the vast wilderness of the Old Dominion. During the twenty-seven years before he appears in history as the commander-in-chief of the Revolutionary American armies, he had become educated : first, in making his own school-books ; second, in forcing everybody he knew to teach him ; third, in doing everything in the best way possible ; and, fourth, in becoming the nation's foremost man in manhood by appropriating the best and having no use for the worst of everybody he knew."

The natural inference from these statements is that Washington's early education was very meagre, and in default of printed text-books was obliged to write them or go without. The statements in regard to his education and school-books are not borne out by facts.

As to education. Washington was born at Wakefield, Virginia, Feb. 22, 1732 ; in 1735 his parents moved to " Washington," so called before it was named Mount Vernon by Lawrence Washington, in honor of Admiral Vernon, with whom he had served. In 1739, owing to the burning of the homestead, another remove was made to an estate on the Rappahannock, nearly opposite Fredericksburg. It was while living here that he learned to write, for in a volume of sermons by the Bishop of Exeter now in the library of the Boston Athenæum his name is written. On a fly-leaf a note in the handwriting of G. C. Washington, a relative who inherited Washington's library, states that "This autograph of Gen'l Washington's name is believed to be the earliest specimen of his writing when he was probably not more than eight or nine years of age."

On the death of his father, April 23, 1743, Washington, then eleven years old, went to live with his brother Augustine, who lived at Wakefield, and attended the school of which a Mr. Williams was master, who kept what was known as a "field school," — a voluntary organization, where a group of neighbors united for a school, supported by a tuition fee paid by its patrons. After a time he returned to his mother and attended a school kept by the Rev. James Marye, in Fredericksburg, which was a school of higher grade, in which he probably wrote the copy-books, and where he studied Latin, as there is in the possession of Prof. Charles Eliot Norton, Cambridge, a book by Samuel Patrick entitled, *Clavis Homerica sive Lexicon vocabulorum omnium quæ continentur in Homeri Iliade et potissima parte Odyssæ. Londini 1742.*

On a fly-leaf is written, —

Hunc mihi quaeso (bone Vir) Libellum
Redde, si forsan tenues repertum
Ut scias qui sum sine fraude scriptum

Est mihi nomen
Georgio Washington
George Washington
Fredericksburg
Virginia.

On the inside of the cover is written, " Busred Washington's Book, given him by G. Washing."

Here is positive proof that George Washington had some knowledge of at least one language other than the English.

In 1745, at the age of thirteen, the same age at which Edward Everett entered Harvard College, his school-days came to an end. It was necessary for him to earn his living. He wished to go to sea, but as his mother would not give her consent he turned his attention to surveying. From a book of which we will speak later he had learned the use of Gunter's Line and its application to surveying, and also the use of the quadrant. He now completed his knowledge of surveying by entering the office of James Genn, a licensed surveyor of Westmoreland County, with whom he remained two years, and in 1747 started out as a surveyor on his own account. He followed the profession until 1752, when by the death of his brother Lawrence he came into possession of Mount Vernon.

Washington's social education was due to his spending much of his time with his brothers Lawrence and Augustine, both of whom had been educated at Appleby School in England and were of some colonial importance, and Lord Fairfax, by whom he was employed as clerk and surveyor, and whose great establishment offered a fine " object lesson " of British high life in the colonies, which he studied with all his might. Although the death of his father prevented his receiving a college education, he did receive very nearly the equal of a New England grammar-school education.

As to books. The fact that Washington wrote several arithmetical copy-books is not in itself proof that he possessed no printed text-books. This method of teaching arithmetic was very old. Isaac Greenwood, who compiled the first American arithmetic in 1729, " inserted under all the Rules, where it was proper, Examples with Blanks for Practice," and in 1801 Daniel

Adams followed the general custom by leaving blanks in his *Scholar's Arithmetic* for the pupil to write his solution in. That Washington did possess printed text-books we have already shown by his possession of a Homeric Lexicon. But in addition to other text-books which he possessed, such as James Greenwood's *Royal English Grammar* and *Leybourn's Surveying*, he owned a copy of the book with which we began this discussion; namely, *Mather's Young Man's Companion*, printed in 1727. When he first began to use this book is unknown, but it is very probable it was while living on the Rappahannock with his father and mother from 1735 to 1743; and it was from the "copy" sheets in this book that his handwriting was modelled. This book presumably was used by Washington all through the remainder of his school-days, and undoubtedly exerted a tremendous influence on his life. The mastering of this book was in itself a grammar-school education, and it was from this book that Washington transcribed that pile of copy-books in the library of the State Department. They are just what their name implies, — namely, copy-books, — and were used for no other purpose. The writer possesses several similar copy-books made by New England scholars.

An examination of the titlepage of this book will give a very clear idea of its contents, and a perusal of the book itself will show that this was the book from which Washington learned to "spell, read, and write True English," to write letters, and to draw legal forms. It also taught the rules of Arithmetic, Merchants Accounts, Mensuration, Surveying, and Astronomy. It contained twenty-one pages of maxims to be used as "Copies in Prose" in the writing lessons, and which undoubtedly was the source from which Washington compiled those one hundred and ten maxims which he wrote in his copy-book and to which he gave the title *Rules of Civility & Decent Behaviour In Company and Conversation.*

Tis to ỷ Press & Pen we Mortals owe | All hail ye great Preservers of these Arts
All we believe & almost all we know . | That raise our thoughts & Cultivate our P.

Frontispiece to Fisher's Instructor.

THE
INSTRUCTOR:
OR,
Young Man's Best Companion.
CONTAINING,

Spelling, Reading, Writing, and Arithmetic, in an easier Way than any yet published ; and how to qualify any Person for Business, without the Help of a Master.

Instructions to write Variety of Hands, with Copies both in Prose and Verse. How to write Letters on Business or Friendship. Forms of Indentures, Bonds, Bills of Sale, Receipts, Wills, Leases, Releases, &c.

Also Merchants Accompts, and a short and easy Method of Shop and Book-keeping ; with a Description of the Product, Counties and Market-Towns in *England* and *Wales* ; with a List of FAIRS according to the New Stile.

Together with the METHOD of measuring *Carpenters, Joiners, Sawyers, Bricklayers, Plasterers, Plumbers, Masons, Glasiers,* and *Painters* Work. How to undertake each Work, and at what Price ; the Rates of each Commodity, and the common Wages of Journeymen ; with the Description of *Gunter's* Line, and *Coggeshall's* Sliding-Rule.

Likewise the PRACTICAL GAUGER made Easy ; the Art of *Dialling,* and how to erect and fix *Dials* ; with Instructions for *Dying, Colouring,* and making *Colours* ; and some General Observations for *Gardening* every Month in the Year.

To which is added,
The FAMILY'S BEST COMPANION :

With Instructions for *Marking* on *Linen* ; how to *Pickle* and *Preserve* ; to make divers Sorts of Wine ; and many *excellent Plasters,* and *Medicines,* necessary in all *Families :*

And
A COMPENDIUM of the SCIENCES of GEOGRAPHY and ASTRONOMY;
Containing
A brief Description of the different Parts of the Earth, and a Survey of the CELESTIAL BODIES.

Also some useful INTEREST-TABLES.

By *GEORGE FISHER*, Accomptant.
The Twenty-fifth Edition, Corrected and Improved.

LONDON: Printed for J. RIVINGTON and SONS ; J. BUCKLAND; T. LONGMAN, B. LAW, J. JOHNSON, G G. J. and J. ROBINSON, R. BALDWIN, T. VERNOR, W. GOLDSMITH, W. WOODFALL, J. BEW, T. LOWNDES, and C. STALKER. M DCC.LXXXIX.
[Price bound 2s. 6d.]

Washington's copy of this book is now in the possession of Mr. Abner C. Goodale of Salem, Massachusetts, who has very generously allowed a facsimile of the titlepage to be made. In reply to a letter asking permission Mr. Goodale says, —

"You are quite welcome to use the book as you propose, and I will aid you in any manner you may suggest."

The book not only bears the autograph "George Washington, 1742," but, scattered here and there on the blank spaces among the problems and legal forms, are crude drawings of birds, faces, and other typical school-boy attempts.

The date 1742, the striking similarity between Washington's signature and the copy sheets in *The Young Man's Companion*, and the improvement in the formation of the letters in this signature over the signature said to have been written two years earlier on the titlepage of the Bishop of Exeter's Sermons, would seem to prove conclusively not only that this was the book from which he had learned to write but also that it had been in his possession two or three years at least before he ventured to place his signature upon the titlepage in 1742. The close resemblance of this signature to the signature engraved on his bookplate may help to decide the date when that bookplate was first engraved, as there is a considerable difference between these early signatures and his signatures several years later.

Perhaps the most popular of these compends was *The Instructor: or, Young Man's Best Companion, By George Fisher*, the twenty-fifth edition of which was published in London in 1789, price bound, two shillings and sixpence. It was a duodecimo of three hundred and forty-eight pages, containing several illustrations. The writer's copy has the autograph of "Sion Heath." It was frequently reprinted in America, the titlepage of one edition reading *The American Instructor: or, Young Man's Best Companion*. Containing Spelling, Reading, Writing, Arithmetic, etc. To which is added *The Poor Planter's Physician . . . and also Prudent Advice to Young Tradesmen and Dealers. By George Fisher. Ninth Edition. Philadelphia: Printed by B. Franklin and D. Hall 1748.* As late as 1794 an edition was published by Isaiah Thomas at Worcester, Mass.

Higher Mathematics

THE manuals of Algebra, Geometry, Trigonometry, Navigation, Astronomy, etc., were used in the higher classes of the grammar schools and in the college. There was no difficulty in procuring the desired books, but there were necessarily fewer copies of manuals in these branches of study used, as only a small proportion of the young men went to the college. As these young men were old enough to know the value of text-books, these manuals were used more carefully and are now more common than the manuals used by the younger boys. We mention only a few titles, as it is our intention to consider only primary and secondary schools, but as all the books bear the autographs of boys who used them, it has been thought proper to include them.

The titlepage of the oldest manual reads in part, *Euclidis Elementorum Libri XV, Graecé & Latiné. Parisiis apud Viduam Guileelmi Cavellat, sub Pellicano, monte D. Hilarii 1598.* It is an interleaved copy of the Elements of Euclid, with Greek and Latin text and contains three hundred and fifty printed pages. The titlepage carries the autograph, " Winslow Taylor."

Another edition of Euclid is entitled, *Euclide's Elements ; the whole Fifteen Books, compendiously Demonstrated : with Archimedes's Theorems of the Sphere and Cylinder. By Isaac Barrow, D.D., late Master of Trinity College in Cambridge. To which is added an Appendix containing the Nature, Construction, and Application of Logarithms. By J. Barrow, Author of Navigatio Britannica, &c. London, 1751.* It is an octavo of three hundred and

EVCLIDIS

ELEMENTORVM

LIBRI XV Grae-
cè & Latine,

Quibus, cum ad omnem Mathematicæ scientiæ
partem, tùm ad quamlibet Geometriæ tractatio-
nem, facilis comparatur aditus.

Επίγραμμα παλαιόν.

Σχήματα πέντε Πλάτωνος, ἃ Πυθαγόρας σοφὸς
εὗρε.

Πυθαγόρας σοφὸς εὗρε, Πλάτων δ' ἀείδηλ' ἐδί-
δαξεν,

Εὐκλείδης ἐπὶ τοισι κλέος περικαλλὲς ἔτευξεν.

IN ME MORS, IN ME VITA.

PARISIIS,

Apud Viduam Guilielmi Cavellat,
sub Pellicano, monte D. Hilarij.

1598.

Frontispiece to Barrow's Euclid.

EUCLIDE's ELEMENTS;

The whole

FIFTEEN BOOKS,

compendiously Demonstrated:

WITH

ARCHIMEDES's Theorems of the

Sphere and Cylinder, Investigated by the
Method of Indivisibles.

ALSO,

EUCLIDE's DATA,

and a brief

Treatise of REGULAR SOLIDS.

By ISAAC BARROW, D.D. *late Master of*
Trinity *College in* Cambridge.

The whole carefully Corrected, and Illustrated
with Copper Plates.

To which is now added an

APPENDIX,

Containing,

The Nature, Construction, and Application of
Logarithms.

By J. BARROW, Author of *Navigatio Britannica*, &c.

LONDON: Printed for W. and J. MOUNT, and T. PAGE
on *Tower-Hill*; and C. HITCH and L. HAWES in *Pater-noster-
Row*; R. MANBY and S. COX on *Ludgate-Hill*; E. COMYNS
under the *Royal-Exchange*; J. and J. RIVINGTON in St. *Paul's
Church-Yard*; and J. WARD in *Cornhill*, opposing the *Royal-
Exchange*, 1751.

THE
MARINER'S
NEW CALENDAR.

Containing

The Principles of Arithmetic and Practical Geometry;
with the Extraction of the Square and Cube Roots :
Also Rules for finding the Prime, Epact, Moon's
Age, Time of High-Water, with Tables for the same.

Together with

Exact Tables of the Sun's Place, Declination, and Right-Ascension : Of the Right Ascension and Declination of the
Principal Fixed Stars : Of the Latitude and Longitude of
Places : A large Table of Difference of Latitude and Departure, for the exact Working a Traverse.

ALSO

The Description and Use of the Sea-Quadrant, Fore-Staff
and Nocturnal : Necessary Problems in Plane-Sailing and
Astronomy, wrought by the Logarithms, and by *Gunter's*
Scale: A Tide Table: The Courses and Distances on the
Coast of *Great Britain*, *Ireland*, *France*, &c. And the
Soundings at coming into the Channel : With Directions for
sailing into some Principal Harbours.

BY
NATHANIEL COLSON, *Student in the Mathematics.*

The whole revis'd, and adjusted to the NEW STILE,
By WILLIAM MOUNTAINE, *F.R.S.*

London : Printed for *W.* and *J. Mount*, *T.* and *T. Page*,
on *Tower-Hill*, 1754.
Where you may have all Sorts of Mathematical Books.

William THE Taylor
of Boston, N.E. 1754

Mariner's Compafs
RECTIFIED.

Containing TABLES, fhewing the True Hour of the Day, the Sun being upon any Point of the Compafs : With the true Time of the *Rifing* and *Setting* of the *Sun* and *Stars*, and the Points of the *Compafs*, upon which they *Rife* and *Set :* With Tables of *Amplitudes.* Which Tables of Sun-Dials, Semidiurnal-Arches, and Amplitudes are calculated from the *Equator* to 60 Degrees of Latitude, either North or South.

With the Defcription and Ufe of thofe Inftruments moft in Ufe in the Art of NAVIGATION.

Alfo a TABLE of the LATITUDE and LONGITUDE of Places.

By ANDREW WAKELY, *Mathematician.*

Enlarged with many ufeful Additions, by *J. Atkinfon.*

The Whole revifed, and carefully correſted, with Accurate Tables of the *Sun's Declination,* adjuſted to the *New-Stile.*

By WILLIAM MOUNTAINE, F.R.S.

LONDON:
Printed for W. and J. MOUNT, T. and T. PAGE, on *Tower-Hill*, where you may have all forts of Sea-Books, 1754.

[203]

eighty-four pages, and bears the autograph of "Joseph Taylor, 1762."

A manual for those who wished to study navigation is entitled, *The Mariner's New Calendar. Containing the Principles of Arithmetic and Practical Geometry. . . . Rules for finding the Prime, Epact, Moon's Age, Time of High Water . . . the Latitude and Longitude of Places. . . . A large Table of Difference of Latitude and Departure, for the Working a Traverse : also the Description and Use of the Sea-Quadrant, Fore-Staff, and Nocturnal, etc. By Nathaniel Colson, Student in the Mathematics. The whole revised and adjusted to the New Stile by William Mountaine, F.R.S. London, 1754.* It is a small quarto of one hundred and thirty-six pages, and the titlepage carries the autograph, " Winslow Taylor."

Another book for the use of students in navigation is entitled, *The Mariner's Compass rectified . . . with the Description and Use of those Instruments most in Use in the Art of Navigation. By Andrew Wakely, Mathematician. Enlarged by J. Atkinson. The Whole Revised by William Mountaine, F.R.S. London, 1754.* In his Preface Mr. Mountaine signs as, " Teacher of the Mathematics, in Shad-Thames, Southwark. Young Gentlemen Boarded." It is a small octavo of two hundred and seventy-two pages. It came to Boston in the same year in which it was published, as on the titlepage is written, " William Taylor of Boston, N.E. 1754."

What may be considered a complete treatise upon the three branches of Mathematics, Arithmetic, Algebra, and Geometry is entitled, *The Young Mathematician's Guide ; being a Plain and Easy Introduction to the Mathematics. In Five Parts, viz. I. Arithmetic. II. Algebra. III. The Elements of Geometry. IV. Conick Sections. V. The Arithmetic of Infinities. By John Ward. The Tenth Edition, carefully corrected. London, 1758.* It is an octavo of four hundred and ninety-five pages, and its published price was £3 10s. 0d. On the fly-leaf in a bold hand is written, " John Marrett's Book 1763." John Marrett was a graduate of Harvard College in the Class of 1763

A handsomely printed manual is entitled, *The Elements of Plain and Spherical Trigonometry. Also a Short Treatise of the Nature and Arithmetick of Logarithms. By Doctor John Keil, F.R.S. and late Professor of Astronomy in Oxford. The Third Edition, Translated by Samuel Cunn. And carefully Corrected by S. Fuller. Dublin: 1726.* It is a small octavo of one hundred and forty-three pages, illustrated with diagrams. On the fly-leaf is the autograph, " Timothy Pitkin, Owner."

In the Preface to the *Nature of Logarithms*, Dr. Keil says : " The wonderful Invention of Logarithms we owe to the Lord Neper, who was the first that constructed and published a Canon thereof at Edinburgh, in the Year, 1614." Following the dedication are four pages containing a list of " Mathematical Books, Sold by Samuel Fuller, at the Globe in Meath-Street. 1726." As this list contains the names of about three hundred authors of mathematical books printed before 1726, some of which were undoubtedly used in the New England schools, we have reproduced these pages, as showing that in these branches of study the necessary books could be procured without much trouble, and that it was the fault of the school committees if the children were not provided with books. It will be noticed that Mr. Fuller had " Also ready Money for old Libraries."

THE
ELEMENTS.
Of PLAIN and SPHERICAL
TRIGONOMETRY.
Alſo a Short
TREATISE
OF THE
NATURE and ARITHMETICK
OF
LOGARITHMS.

By Doctor John Keil, F. R. S. And late Profeſſor of Aſtronomy in Oxford.

The Third Edition, Tranſlated by Samuel Cunn. And carefully Corrected by S. Fuller.

DUBLIN:

Printed by W. Wilmot on the Blind-Key, for Samuel Fuller, at the Globe in Meath-Street, and Sold by the Book-Sellers, MDCCXXVI.

MATHEMATICAL Books, Sold by SAMUEL FULLER, at the GLOBE in MEATH-STREET. 1726.

ARITHMETICK	MERCHANTS ACC.	GEOMETRY, OR MENSURATION
by	by	by
A Lingham Ayres	C Ollins Dafforne	A Lingham Alphonsus
Baker	Gentleman-Account.	Anderson
Cocker	Hatton	Barrow
Collins	Hawkins	Bonnel
Cunn	King	Cogshal
Foster	Author of Lex Mer catoria.	Cohorn
Hallyman		Dechales
Hatton	Malcolm	Euclid
Hewit	Nevel	Hawney
Hill	Scarlet	Leybourn
Johnson	Snell	Moor
Jordan	Vernon	Pardie
Leybourn	Wilson.	Record
Lydal		Rudd
Author of Mercantile, Arith.	CHRONOLOGY	Tacquet
		Vauban
Moor		Wallis
Moreland		Wells
Newton	by	Whiston
Parsons		GAGING
Pascal Record		by
Richardson	B Ucholcherus Nisbet	A Nderson Brown
Shelley		
Speidal	Petavius	Clayton
Tacquet	Strauchius	Collins
Wells	Swan	Cumpsty
Wilson	Usher	Davis
Wingate.	Wells	Everard
		Eyers

Gaging	Navigation	Astronomy
Eyers	Hodgson	Goad
Hunt	Jones	Goclenius
Jones	Kelly	Gregory
Light-body	Newhouse	Greenwood
Smith	Newton	Halley
Wibrand.	Norwood	Haly. Hanna.
	Perkins	Harris
Trigonome-	Phillips	Hues
try.	Seller	Huigens
by	Sturmy	Keil
	Wilson	Kepler
Foster	Wright	Lamb
Gellibrand		Lansbergius
Harris	Astronomy	Leybourn
Hawney		Lilly
Heins	or	Mastlin
Keil		Manilius
Napier	Astrology	Mercator
Newhouse		Middleton
Newton	by	Morden
Norwood		Morinus
Pitiscus	Alphonsus	Moxon
Sherwin.	Argol	Newton
	Baker	Partridge
Navigation	Ball	Proclus
	Bishop	Ptolomy
by	Blagrave. Blacu.	Ramsay
	Blundevil	Saunders
Atkinson	Cattan	Spark
Blackborow	Colon	Street
Bond	Culpepper	Ubaldus
Collins	Edlin	Wells
Colson	Gadbury	Wharton
Gellibrand	Galileo	Whiston
Hardingham	Gassendus	Wing
Hawney	Gemma Frisius	Wright Geo-

GEOGRAPHY	ALGEBRA	ARCHITECTURE
by	by	by
BLome	**A**Lexander	**B**Rown
Cambden	Baker	Evelin
Carpenter	Branker	Halfpenny
Clark	Cotes	Le-Clerk
Cluverius	Ditton	Leybourn
Echard	Gibson	Neve
Fer	Harris	Palladio
Gordon	Jones	Scamozzi
Gregory	Kersey	
Mead	Newton	MECHANICKS
Meriton	Oughtred	by
Moll	Parsons	
Morden	Record	**D**Erham
Newton	Ronayne	Mandy
Senex	Sault	Mariot
Speed	Sturmy	Moxon
Varenius	Wallis	Rohault
Wells	Ward	Wats
	Wells	

SURVEYING	DIALLING	PERSP.
by	by	or
BUrgh	**C**ollins	OPTICKS &c.
Holwel	Dela-Hire	
Hopton	Foster	by
Kircher	Good	
Lawrence	King	**D**Itton
Leybourn	Leybourn	Gravefand
Love	Marius	Gregory
Martindale	Serles	Moxon
Rathborn	Stirrup	Newton
Shaw	Wells	Taylor
Wing	Wilson a 3	FLUXIONS

FLUXIONS or CONIC'S

FLUXIONS or CONIC'S by A Ngelis Apollonius Collins	Dela-Hire Ditton Hayes Hospital Mc. Laurin Milnes Newton	Robinson Schooten Steel Taylor Theodosius Greg. Vincent.

Miscellaneous Tracts, or a Course of the MATHEMATICKS.

BY

B Lundevil Cheyne De-Chales Derham Foster Galtruchius Gravesand Gunter Harris Hawksbee Hawney Herigonius	Johnston Jones Keil La-Motte Leybourn Louthorp Lucar Mandy Maralois Moor Author of Miscellanea Curiosa.	Neve Newton Ozanam Perkins Pickering Rohault The Royal Society Tassius Taylor Ward Wells Wilkins

☞ *Note*, Books Bought and Sold, by the aforesaid *S. Fuller*, at reasonable Rates. Also ready Money for old Libraries.

Book=keeping

THERE was no lack of manuals on book-keeping. Besides the *Young Secretary's Guide, Young Man's Best Companion,* and similar compends, which contained several chapters on book-keeping, there were many books which treated of that subject only. Viewed as an art, book-keeping was first brought to comparative perfection by the merchants of Genoa and other cities in the north of Italy ; and followed up by the merchants of the Netherlands, it has been brought to England and America. John Mellis, who revised Record's Arithmetic as early as 1579, published in 1588 *Bookes of Accompts,* which is reputed to be the oldest English work on double entry book-keeping.

Among the early writers on book-keeping was John Collins, F.R.S., an eminent accountant and mathematician, who was born near Oxford in 1624 and died in 1683. He published a manual entitled, *An Introduction to Merchants Accompts. London, 1652.* He also published, *The Sector or, a Quadrant, 1658 ; Treatise of Geometrical and Arithmetical Navigation, 1659 ; The Mariner's Plain Scale new plained : A Treatise of Navigation, 1659 ;* and other mathematical works.

In 1659 there was published in London, *A most compendious and easie Way of keeping of Merchants Accounts after the Italian manner. By John Carpenter, Merchant.*

A text-book which had passed through the fourteenth edition in 1765, and which was first published in 1719, is entitled *An*

A Perpetual Almanac

By which may be found in two or three Seconds of Time, the Day of the Month in Any Year to come.

Years.   **Sundays.**

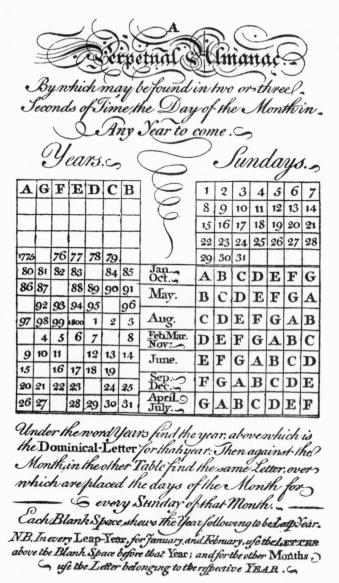

Under the word Years find the year, above which is the Dominical-Letter for that year: Then against the Month, in the other Table find the same Letter, over which are placed the days of the Month for every Sunday of that Month.

Each Blank Space shews the Year following to be a Leap Year.

N.B. In every Leap-Year, for January and February, use the Letter above the Blank Space before that Year; and for the other Months use the Letter belonging to the respective YEAR.

Frontispiece to Cooke's Compting-House Assistant.

THE
COMPTING-HOUSE Affiftant;
OR,
BOOK-KEEPING made eafy:
Being a COMPLETE TREATISE on
MERCHANTS ACCOMPTS,
After the moft approved Method.
WHEREIN
Almoft all the VARIETIES which can happen in that ufeful
ART are introduced, and explained in a concife and eafy
Manner.

THE
Whole being divided into two Sets of Books, principally intended to fupply
the Defects of thofe already publifhed, and for the Perufal of Youth
during their Inftruction at School, and in the Compting-Houfe.

WITH A
SUPPLEMENT,
SHEWING
The Nature of negotiating BILLS of EXCHANGE, PROMISSORY NOTES,
&c. and a COLLECTION of the different BILLS and FORMS of
BUSINESS in Ufe among MERCHANTS.

The SECOND EDITION, corrected, with ALTERATIONS and
AMENDMENTS.

Methodized in the Nature of REAL BUSINESS.

By JOHN COOKE,
*Mafter of the Academy the lower End of Charles-Street,
St. James's Square.*

LONDON:
PRINTED FOR J. NOURSE, AND S. HOOPER, IN THE STRAND.
M.DCC.LXIV.

[Price Two Shillings and Sixpence, bound]

[213]

Essay on Bookkeeping, according to the True Italian Method of Debtor and Creditor, by Double Entry. By William Webster. It is an octavo of eighty-eight pages. The author has added an essay entitled, *An Attempt towards rendering the Education of Youth more Easy and Effectual* in which he advocates teaching children the grounds of grammar in the English tongue before they are perplexed with Latin, and at the same time teaching them to write.

A very compact little manual, which was praised for its "perspicuity and conciseness," and which received the approbation of forty-five schoolmasters who allowed the use of their names, was *A New Introduction to Trade and Business. By Peter Hudson*, the first edition of which was published in 1758. The writer's copy is of the fourth edition and was published in 1775. It is duodecimo in size and contains ninety-five pages. The frontispiece is *A Perpetual Almanac*, and there are also two full-page copper-plate engravings of "Alphabets of the Modern Round, Text, and Running Hands." Peter Hudson was the author of several other school-books, all of which had large sales.

A much more pretentious manual is *The Compting House Assistant ; or Book-keeping made easy : being a complete Treatise on Merchants accompts, By John Cooke, Master of the Academy the lower End of Charles-Street, St. James Square. London, 1764.* It is an octavo of over two hundred pages, and bears the autograph " Arodi Thayer's."

The writer has in his possession a manual which has been used by at least four young students. It is entitled *Book-keeping Methodized ; or A Methodical Treatise of Merchant-Accompts, according to the Italian Form. From the last Edition printed at Edinburgh, and revised by John Mair, A.M. Dublin : Printed and Sold by I. Jackson, at the Globe in Meath-street, 1764.* The sign of the Globe must have been very familiar to the citizens of

A Charles Taylor.

NEW INTRODUCTION

T O

TRADE and BUSINESS;

Very ufeful for the YOUTH of both SEXES.

Wherein is contained great Variety of

RECEIPTS FOR MONEY,	BILLS OF EXCHANGE,
GOODS, &c.	BILLS OF PARCELS, AND
PROMISSORY NOTES,	BILLS ON BOOK-DEBTS.

With ample INSTRUCTIONS how to FORM Them.

A L S O

Several Inftruftive EXERCISES; DISBURSEMENTS;
WEEK's EXPENCES, GOODS bought at SALES, &c.

To which are added,

I. Commercial and Epiftolary Cor-
refpondence, exemplified in various
Forms of Bufinefs, and Familiar
LETTERS.
II. A LIST of the moft common
Abbreviations of WORDS for the
Difpatch of Bufinefs.
III. ARITHMETICAL TABLES
of *Weights* and *Meafures.*

IV. A new Set of QUESTIONS
to exercife the LEARNER in
feveral of the RULES OF
ARITHMETIC, by Way of
AMUSEMENT, as well as
IMPROVEMENT.
V. The EXPLANATION and USE
of the FRONTISPIECE or
Perpetual Almanac.

The FOURTH EDITION, Correfted and Improved,
With the Additio n of COPPER PLATES neatly Engraved.

By PETER HUDSON,

AUTHOR of *The New Englifh Introduftion to the Latin Tongue,*
The French Scholar's Guide, &c.
And other SCHOOLMASTERS.

Defigned for the Ufe of Schools, *and* YOUTH *in General.*

L O N D O N:

Printed for GEORGE KEITH, *Gracechurch-ftreet,*

MDCCLXXV.

[215]

Frontispiece to Webster's Book-keeping.

A N

E S S A Y

O N

BOOK-KEEPING,

According to the

True ITALIAN Method

O F

DEBTOR and CREDITOR,

B Y

DOUBLE ENTRY:

WHEREIN

The THEORY of that EXCELLENT ART
is clearly laid down in a few plain Rules;
And the Practice made evident and easy, by Variety of
intelligible Examples.

The Whole in a Method New and Concise.

By WILLIAM WEBSTER.

The FOURTEENTH EDITION, *Carefully Corrected*
By ELLIS WEBSTER, Writing-Master and Accomptant.

LONDON,
Printed for H. WOODFALL, J. RIVINGTON, L. HAWES,
W. CLARKE, and R. COLLINS, R. HORSFIELD, T
CASLON, T. LONGMAN, J. PRITCHARD, R. and C. WARE,
and W. NICOLL.

MDCCLXV.

[217]

Dublin, for in this same shop Samuel Fuller sold all kinds of mathematical books in 1726. The names of the former owners are recorded in the book as follows : "Samuel Smallcorn His Book 1765 given by his father in the year 1764 ; " " Ebenr Tebbets Property ; " " James Grayson ; " " John H. White, Dover, N. H."

English Grammar

THE manuals by which grammar was first taught in English were not properly English grammars. They were translations of the Latin Accidence, and were designed to aid the pupils in acquiring a knowledge of the Latin language rather than accuracy in their own. Both languages were combined in one book for the purpose of teaching, sometimes both together and sometimes one through the medium of the other.

The oldest manual from which English grammar was taught is supposed to be *Paul's Accidence*. The English *Introduction to the Eight Parts of Latin Speech*, which forms the first part of *Lily's Grammar*, or *The Grammar of King Henry the Eighth*, was written by Dr. John Colet, Dean of St. Paul's, and dedicated to William Lily, the first high master of that school, in 1510, for which reason it has usually gone by the name of *Paul's Accidence*. It was first published in 1513. It was not, however, properly an English grammar, as it was particularly designed for the teaching of Latin.

The honor of producing the first genuine English grammar is claimed for William Bullokar, whose relative, John Bullokar, was the author of the first English dictionary. Being the first English grammar, we feel bound to give the title in full, which reads : —

Bullokar's at large, for the amendment of Orthograthie for English Speech: wherein a most perfect supplie is made for the wantes and double sounds of Letters in the Olde Orthographie, with Examples for the same. With the easie conference and use of both

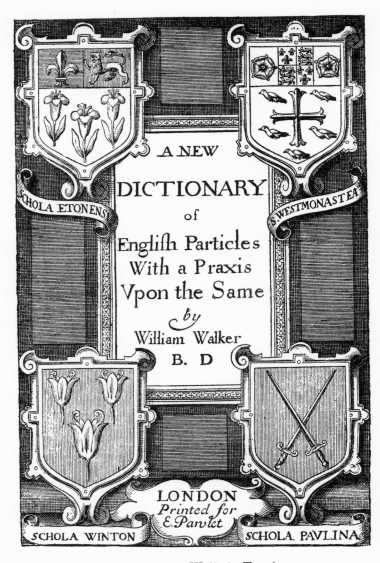

A NEW

DICTIONARY

of

Englifh Particles
With a Praxis
Vpon the Same

by

William Walker
B. D

SCHOLA ETONENSI
S. WESTMONASTEA
SCHOLA WINTON
SCHOLA PAVLINA

LONDON
Printed for
E. Pawlet

Frontispiece to Walker's Treatise.

A
TREATISE
OF
English Particles,

SHEWING

Much of the Variety of their Significations and Uses in English: And how to render them into Latine according to the Propriety and Elegancy of that Language.

With a PRAXIS *upon the same.*

By *WILLIAM WALKER*, B.D.
Formerly Master of *Louth* School, and of the Free-School in *Grantham*.

The Twelfth Edition.

Non sunt contemnenda quasi Parva, sine quibus constare Magna non possunt. D. Hieronym. *Ep.* 89.

LONDON,
Printed by *J. H.* for *E. Pawlett*, at the *Bible* in *Chancery-Lane*, near *Fleetstreet*, 1703.

Orthographies, to save Expence in Bookes for a time, until this amendment grow to a generall use, for the easie, speedie, and perfect reading and writing of English, (the Speech not changed, as some untruly and maliciously, at the least, ignorantly blowe abroad,) by the whiche amendment, the same Author hath also framed a ruled Grammar to be imprinted hereafter for the same Speech, to the no small commoditie of the English nation, not only to come to easie, speedie, and perfect use of our own languages but also to their easie, speedie, and perfect entrance into the secretes of other lan-guages, and easie and speedie pathway to all strangers to use our language, heretofore very hard unto them, to the no small profite and credite to this our nation and stay thereunto in the weightiest causes. [By William Bullokar] London: H. Denham 1580.

The " ruled Grammar " was published in 1586 under the title *Abbreviation of hiz Grammar for English, extracted out of hiz Grammar at large, for the spedi parcing of English spech, and the eazier coming to the knowledge of Grammar for other languages.* [By William Bullokar.] London: Edm. Bullifant. 1586.

In the Preface he says this is " the first Grammar for English that ever waz except my Grammar at large."

The progress of English grammar was greatly assisted by William Walker, a teacher and grammarian of extraordinary learning. He was born in Lincolnshire in 1623, and died in 1684. He was educated at Trinity College, Cambridge. He became master of the South Grammar School, from which he resigned for that of the Free School in Grantham, Lincolnshire, where he had Isaac Newton for his pupil. In 1653 he published *A Treatise of English Particles*, a work of great labor and merit. It was very popular and passed through several editions, the writer's copy being of the twelfth edition published at London in 1703. It bears the autographs of " John Taylor, 1716 " and " Joseph Taylor, 1761," both pupils of the Boston Latin

THE

London Vocabulary,

ENGLISH and LATIN:

Put into a NEW METHOD, proper to
acquaint the Learner with Things
as well as pure *Latin* Words.

Adorned with Twenty-fix PICTURES.

For the Ufe of SCHOOLS.

The TWENTIETH EDITION.

By JAMES GREENWOOD,

Author of the *Englifh Grammar*, and late
Sur-Mafter of St: PAUL's SCHOOL.

LONDON:

Pyinted for J. F. & C. Rivington, T. Longman, B. Law,
R. Baldwin, S. Bladon, and G. & T. Wilkie,

MDCCXCI,

[223]

School. It is a duodecimo of five hundred and twenty pages and shows the marks of hard study.

In 1653 John Wallis, D.D., published in London an English grammar in Latin concerning which Dr. Noah Webster says: " Since the days of Wallis, who published a *Grammar of the English Language in Latin*, in the reign of Charles II. from which Johnson and Lowth borrowed most of their rules, little improvement has been made in English grammar." Dr. John Wallis was born at Ashford in Kent, Nov. 23, 1616, and died Oct. 28, 1703. He was educated at Emmanuel College, Cambridge, and in 1649 was chosen Professor of Geometry at Oxford. He was one of the founders of the Royal Society, and one of the secretaries of the Westminster Assembly of Divines in 1644. Besides the grammar he published several books on mathematics and natural philosophy. The sixth edition of his grammar was published in 1765, and Mr. William B. Fowle, a well-known teacher of Boston, made it the basis of his *Common School Grammar*, published in 1842.

James Greenwood, a " Sur-Master of St. Paul's School," published, in 1711, an *English Grammar*, which was reprinted in 1722. His *London Vocabulary* was a much more popular book, of which the twentieth edition was published in 1791. Although the author claims to have used " a New Method," he has followed exactly the method of Comenius in *Orbis Sensualium Pictus*, but whose name he does not mention. The little book contains thirty-three chapters headed *Minerals*, *Fishes*, *Birds*, *Beasts*, *Buildings*, *Country and Country Affairs*, etc., twenty-six of which have at the beginning a picture illustrating the subject treated of, and the text has two columns of words explanatory of the objects represented in the picture, one column in English and the other in Latin. As the seven remaining chapters treat of Time, Adjectives, Verbs, Pronouns, Adverbs, Conjunctions, and Interjections, there is no attempt to illustrate them. Naturally this book would be very popular with children, who could easily disregard the Latin portion. This book was reprinted in Philadelphia in 1787, as the *Philadelphia Vocabulary*.

In 1753, there was published the first edition of a very popular grammar entitled, *A Practical New Grammar with Exercises of bad English: or, An Easy Guide to Speaking and Writing the English Language Properly and Correctly. By A. Fisher. London, 1753.* The writer's copy, which is of the seventeenth edition, printed at Newcastle in 1773, has the following poetical (?) stanza written on the inside of the cover:

> " James Graham his Book
> God give him Grace on it to Look
> not to Look but to understand
> Learning is better than houses and Land
> when houses and Land is almost Spent
> Learning is most excelent.
>
> Ja.^s Graham
> April 5 1834"

In 1760, there was published the second edition of *A Practical Grammar of the English Tongue. First compiled by James Gough, of Mountmelich. Revised, digested, and enlarged with sundry material Rules by John Gough, of Cole-Alley, Dublin. Dublin: printed by Isaac Jackson, at the Globe in Meath-street, 1760.* It is a duodecimo of two hundred and thirty-two pages, ninety-six of which are devoted to a Dictionary or *Compendious Expositor of English Words derived from the Latin, Greek, and French.* The former owners were " Samuel Walker, 1784," and " Joseph Cabot, 1787."

John Ash, LL.D., published, previous to 1758, *Grammatical Institutes; or an easy Introduction to Dr. Lowth's English Grammar.* He also published, in 1775, *A New and Complete English Dictionary* in two volumes. He was a Baptist minister

A PRACTICAL NEW

GRAMMAR,

WITH

Exercifes of bad Englifh:

OR, AN

EASY GUIDE

To SPEAKING and WRITING the

ENGLISH LANGUAGE

PROPERLY and CORRECTLY.

CONTAINING,

I. ORTHOGRAPHY; or True Spelling, which treats of the Sounds and Ufes of the feveral Letters in all Pofitions; of the Divifion of Words into Syllables, and the Ufe of Points.

II. PROSODY; or the Art of Pronouncing Syllables in Words truly, with Tables of Words properly accented.

III. ETYMOLOGY; or the Kinds of Words, which explains the feveral Parts of Speech; their Derivations and different Endings; Change and Likenefs to one another.

IV. SYNTAX; or Conftruction, which teaches how to connect Words aright in a Sentence, or Sentences together.

To which is added, a Curious and Ufeful

APPENDIX.

The SEVENTEENTH EDITION, ENLARGED and much IMPROVED.

By A. FISHER.

NEWCASTLE:

Printed for THO. SLACK. 1778.

[Entered in Stationers' Hall according to Act of Parliament.]

at Pershore in Worcestershire, and died in 1779, in the fifty-fifth
year of his age. Both the Dictionary and Grammar passed
through several editions and were reprinted in America.

In the *Advertisement* to the fourth edition of the Grammar,
edited by the author, he says the second and third editions were
published under the direction of the Rev. Mr. Ryland, of Northampton, who styled it, " The Easiest Introduction to *Dr. Lowth's
English Grammar*, which Title, in part, it still retains ; though
the Author is apprehensive, it was first printed before the earliest
edition of that valuable Book." In the Preface he speaks of the
importance of an English education and the changes in public
opinion as follows : —

" The importance of an English Education is now pretty well
understood; and it is generally acknowledged, that, not only for
Ladies, but for young Gentlemen designed merely for Trade,
an intimate acquaintance with the Proprieties, and Beauties of
the English Tongue, would be a very desirable and necessary
Attainment; far preferable to a Smattering of the learned
Languages. But then, it has been supposed, even by Men of
Learning, that the English Tongue is too vague, and untract-
able to be reduced to any certain Standard, or Rules of Construction; and that a competent Knowledge of it cannot be
attained without an Acquaintance with the Latin. For my Part,
I hope these Gentlemen are mistaken, because this would be an
invincible Obstacle to the Progress of an English Education.
This vulgar error, for so I beg leave to call it, might perhaps
arise from a too partial Fondness for the Latin, in which about
two Centuries ago, we had the Service of the Church, the Translation of the Bible, and most other Books ; few, of any Value,
being then extant in our Mother Tongue. But now the Case
is happily altered. Nor do I think the Error above-mentioned
would have been so long indulged under the Blessings of the
Reformation had it not been for the many fruitless Attempts

THE
YOUNG LADY's
ACCIDENCE:
OR,

A SHORT AND EASY
INTRODUCTION
TO
English Grammar.
DESIGNED PRINCIPALLY FOR THE USE OF
YOUNG LEARNERS,
More especially those of the FAIR SEX, though
proper for either.

BY CALEB BINGHAM, A. M.

AUTHOR OF THE CHILD'S COMPANION, AMERICAN PRECEP-
TOR, AND COLUMBIAN ORATOR.

" Delightful task ! to rear the tender thought,
" To teach the young idea how to shoot,—"

THE *NINETEENTH* EDITION.

BOSTON :
PRINTED BY LINCOLN & EDMANDS,
FOR THE AUTHOR, NO. 44, CORNHILL.
1813.

which have been made to fix the Grammatical Construction of the English Tongue."

Robert Lowth, LL.D., Bishop of London, born 1710, died 1787, published a manual entitled, *A Short Introduction to English Grammar : with Critical Notes, London, 1758.* It was often reprinted and used in the schools in the United States. The writer's copy was printed at Wilmington, Delaware, in 1800. Dr. Cheever says, " Although Lowth's treatise was written so early as 1758, yet we doubt whether there is at the present day a single work of equal excellence in the same compass."

The first English grammar by an American author was written by Noah Webster and published in 1784. The title reads : *A Grammatical Institute of the English Language ; comprising an Easy, Concise and Systematic Method of Education. Designed for the use of English Schools in America. In Three Parts. Part Second. Containing a plain and Comprehensive Grammar grounded on the true Principles and Idioms of the Language.*

The Grammar was the least successful of the three books composing the Grammatical Institute. Mr. Webster in a letter to Mr. Lemuel Shattuck written in 1829 says : " My Grammar passed through many editions, and continued to be used, till Murray's appeared ; but the number of editions and copies cannot be ascertained." It met with a formidable competitor in Bingham's *Young Lady's Accidence*, which was published about two years after the *Grammar*. The title reads : *The Young Lady's Accidence : or a short and easy Introduction to English Grammar. By Caleb Bingham, A.M.* It was first published by Mr. Bingham for the use of the female pupils in his private school, but when he became master of one of the public schools his book followed him, and was the first English grammar ever used in the Boston schools. It continued to be used until the substitution of *An Abridgment of Murray's Grammar, by a Teacher of*

Youth (Asa Bullard) was substituted. In 1832 the *Accidence* had passed through twenty editions, and one hundred thousand copies had been sold. It was a small duodecimo bound in boards, and contained sixty pages. Martha Stevens used the copy now in the possession of the writer.

Latin Grammars

HAVING acquired a knowledge of reading, writing, and a smattering of arithmetic, the school-days of the greater portion of the children were ended, the boys were apprenticed to a trade, and the girls began to be instructed in the mysteries of housekeeping. A few of the boys, more fortunate than their playmates, proceeded to the grammar school, where they were to be prepared for college, and eventually to enter one of the professions.

Grammar teaching meant the teaching of Latin Grammar. There were practically no English courses in the grammar schools. Macaulay says : " In the time of our Henry VIII. and Edward VI., a person who did not read Greek or Latin could read nothing or next to nothing. The Italian was the only modern language which presented anything that could be called literature. All the valuable books extant in all the vernacular dialects of Europe would hardly have filled a single shelf. England did not yet possess Shakespeare's *Plays* and the *Fairy Queen*, nor France Montaigne's *Essays*, nor Spain *Don Quixote*. In looking round a well-furnished library, how many English or French books can we find which were extant when Lady Jane Grey and Queen Elizabeth received their education. Chaucer, Gower, Froissart, Rabelais, nearly complete the list. It was absolutely necessary to be uneducated, or classically educated. Latin was then the language of courts, as well as of the schools ; of diplomacy, and of theological and political controversy." In 1630 the condition had not materially changed. It is stated that no quotations from Shakespeare appear in the school text-books previous to 1660.

Therefore in order to become an accomplished scholar, a thorough education in Latin was inevitable.

On this point Chambers' Encyclopædia speaks very clearly as follows : " Grammar Schools received their name at a time when the grammar of the English language was not written, and when all knowledge of the principles of language could be obtained only through a study of the grammar of the ancient tongues, particularly Latin. The idea which lay at the basis of these institutions still pervades them, and the ancient languages are the principal subjects of instruction. History, geography, and modern languages have of late years been admitted into the curriculum of these schools, but these subjects still hold a subordinate place and distinction in Latin and Greek gives preeminence, and is the great object of ambition both to masters and pupils. Nor can it be otherwise so long as universities recognize the ancient tongues as the only sound basis of a liberal education."

It was as difficult to change the method of teaching as it was to extend the curriculum. In 1859 Andrews and Stoddard's *Latin Grammar* was one of the text-books used in the Boston Latin School, which, according to the system of education then in vogue, the pupil was required to commit to memory, page by page, and then repeat orally in the class. This was the old, established custom, and although the text-books of John Clarke, the famous Master of the Public Grammar School in Hull, England, were used in the Public Latin School of Boston, New England, for many years, and as early as 1740 Master Clarke had protested against the memorizing method of teaching, yet so difficult is it to change an established custom, the old method was still kept up with no signs of change in the immediate future.

The writer remembers very distinctly his first lesson in that grammar. Quoting from memory, it began : " The Latin language is the language spoken by the ancient Romans. Latin Grammar teaches the principles of the Latin language. These relate, first, to its written characters; second, to its pronunciation; third, to the classification and derivation of its words; fourth, to the construction of its sentences; fifth, to the quantity of its syllables and versification. The first part is called Orthography; the second Orthoëpy; the third, Etymology; the fourth, Syntax; and the fifth, Prosody."

Although these principles were the foundation-stones upon which the Latin structure was erected, the formulæ used in the construction of the grammars of all languages, the steps of the ladder which it was necessary to ascend in order to become an accomplished scholar, and the divisions by which the school was graded into forms or classes, yet the writer committed them to memory and repeated them like a parrot. The master offered no explanation, and it was many years after that their full meaning was grasped and their true significance understood.

In the grammar schools the boys were taught first the grounds or rudiments of the Latin language, and the text-book used was a comparatively simple affair known as an *Accidence.* Then they were taught to write and speak Latin, which required the use of the larger book or Grammar and the Colloquies of Corderius. Later they were taught Greek, Hebrew, rhetoric, elocution, and versification, and the text-books were the Latin and Greek Testaments and the works of the classical authors.

Dionysius Thrax, who had been trained in the Alexandrian school, and who had become a grammaticus, or teacher of Greek, at Rome, published the first systematic Greek grammar for the use of his Roman pupils about 80 B. C. This work became the basis of all subsequent grammars, both Greek and Latin.

About 335 A. D. Ælius Donatus, a well-known grammarian and commentator, taught grammar and rhetoric at Rome. Among his pupils was Saint Jerome, who later produced a new

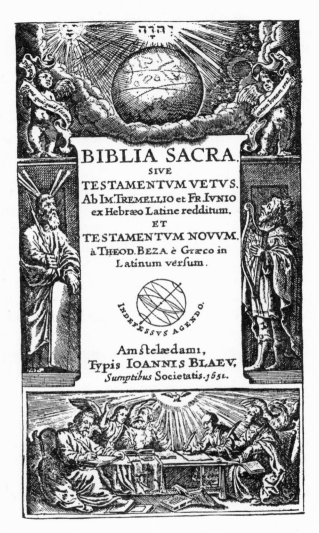

Titlepage to the Bible by Theodore Beza.

version of the Old Testament. Dissatisfied with the Italic Version of the Old Testament, Saint Jerome undertook to revise and amend it, but ultimately made a new Latin translation from the Hebrew text itself, which was adopted by the Romish Church and is known as the Vulgate.

Donatus wrote several treatises which together form a pretty complete course of Latin grammar and in the middle ages was the only text-book used in the schools, so that Donat came to be synonymous with grammar, or with the elements of the science. The Latin grammar of Donatus, *De Octibus Partibus Orationis*, has formed the groundwork of the elementary treatises on that subject to the present day. An abridged Donatus was one of the first books on which the art of printing by means of letters cut on wooden blocks was tried. It made a thin quarto. When printed in the largest letters it occupied thirty-four pages; when printed in small letters, only nine pages were used. Naturally they were very perishable, and if it were not that some of the leaves, being printed on parchment, were used by the binders as stiffness in the covers of books, we should have very few specimens. Fragments of these Donatuses are reckoned among the greatest of bibliographical curiosities. Gotthelf Fischer in his *Essai sur les monuments typographiques* says two leaves of an early typographic edition of a Donatus, twenty-seven lines to the page, printed on vellum from the types of the *Bible of thirty-six lines* have been discovered near Mentz, in the original binding of an old account-book of 1451.

More than fifty editions of this Latin primer were printed from types before 1500, and a revised edition is said to be used in the schools of Italy to-day.

An early Latin grammar, the titlepage of which is given in facsimile, is entitled, *Exercitiũ grammaticale puerorum per dietas distributum* or Grammatical Exercises for boys arranged by days or courses. The colophon reads: " Finit feliciter Anno salutis

Exercitiũ grãmaticale pue/
roxz per dietas diſtributum

Titlepage to Boy's Latin Grammar, 1500.

Die Sabbati

vicinitatē aut sitlitudinē quā habet cū aduerbijs in determina/
tiōibȝ ꝗborȝ. Sed Donatꝰ ponit in fine: ꝗsiderās eoȝ differētiā
Interiectioni ꝗ accidūt. Dico vnuȝ. vt significatio. Quot sunt eꝰ
significatiōes. Dico ꝓm Donatū ꝗtuor. Nā aut leticiā mētis si/
gnificamus. aut doloꝛē. aut ammiratiōeȝ. aut metū. Sed sunt
alie ꝗ ad istas reducunꝛ. vt patet in figura sequēti.

    ⌠Aut significat leticiā mētis. vt euaȝ euge ꝑobeȝa.
    Ad queridentis vt baba bebe reducunꝛ.
    Aut doloꝛē. vt beu beubeu o ab bey ꝓbdoloꝛ
Dis in/ Aut timoꝛē vel metū. vt atatat atat ast
teriectio Aut admiratiōē. vt pape bem bobē.
    Aut indignatiōē. vt ve vah ꝓb nefas infandū
    Aut blādientȝ. vt sodes amabo media breui.
    ⌡Aut ploꝛantis. vt au obiobi. et si qua sunt similia.

Notandū est ꝗ interiectio dr ab inꝰ Ꟊ iacio. qꝛ sermoniȝ nostrȝ est
interiecta: ad affectū mentȝ significādū inuēta. Per interiectio/
nē ponit qñcȝ ꝛbū. vt amabo. interdū ꝑticipiū vt infandū. nō/
nūcȝ integra oꝛatio. De ꝑticipio Virgilius. Nos tua ꝓgenies
nauiȝ infandū amissis ꝓdimur. De oꝛōne Therentiꝰ. Hocci/
ne est officiū patrȝ: ꝓb deū atcȝ hoiem fidē. qd est si nō ꝓtume/
lia est: ꝗ nō ꝓceptū sed affectū animi indicāt. Sic est. Tāta est
infandū dei blaspbemia: beu nos infelicissimos vt ferre debeat
nemo. Luāt ne amabo: penas blaspbemi: luent vticȝ. Nec au/
diēt illud interiectionis leticie. Euge serue bone in modico fide/
lis: sup multa te ꝓstituā intra in gaudiū dñi tui. Ad ꝗ nos eter
naliter ꝑfruēda ꝓducat ꝗ sup oia bñdictꝰ cum gꝇiosissima ma/
tre sua in seculoȝ secula regnat. Amen.

Tractatus secundus exercitij pueroȝ grāmaticalis in ꝗ de regi/
mine Ꟊ ꝓstructione oim dictionū ꝓm oꝛdinē octo ꝑtiȝoꝛōis ꝓ
cessum est ꝑ regulas Ꟊ ꝗstiūculas adeo lucidas faciles atcȝ bꝛe
ues: doctissimoȝ viroȝ exēplis creberrimis roboꝛatas vt ꝗscȝ
sine ꝓceptoꝛe eas discere scire Ꟊ intelligere possit In ꝗ si ꝗ gram/
matica studiosi cuiuscūcȝ status fuerint: pueri: fratres: soꝛoꝛes:
mercatoꝛes: Ꟊ riȝcȝ seculāres aut religiosi legerint studuerint
atcȝ se oblectauerint: fine grāmatice (ausim dicere) breuissime
sine magno laboꝛe ꝓseqnꝛ Impꝛssus de nouo summacȝ cū di/
ligentia coꝛrectus Finit feliciter Anno salutis nostre Milꝇesi/
mo quingentesimo: altera die Marcij

Last page with colophon of Boy's Latin Grammar, 1500.

nostre Millesimo quingentesimo: altera die Marcii." It seems to have been a very popular book, as at least six editions were printed within ten years in various cities, the first in 1491 and the sixth in 1500. The edition of 1493 was printed at Haguenau at the celebrated press of Heinrich Grau.

Another favorite Latin grammar, *Grammatices Institutiones . . . pro pueris*, was written by Lucius Johannes Scoppa and printed at Naples in 1520. It was reprinted in 1537, 1543, and 1558.

Both volumes were octavo in size and printed with Gothic type, the first containing one hundred and thirty-one unnumbered leaves and the second four hundred pages.

The first grammar printed in England was published in 1497 by John Holt, of Magdalen College and usher of Magdalen School, in Oxford. It was entitled *Lac puerorum*, and dedicated to John Morton, Archbishop of Canterbury.

The most popular Latin grammar used in the schools was the one commonly called *Lily's Latin Grammar*. It was edited by William Lily, a celebrated grammarian and successful teacher of the learned languages. He was born at Oldham, in Hampshire, about 1466, studied at Oxford, and died in London Feb. 25, 1523. The title reads: "Brevissima Institutio, seu Ratio Grammatice cognoscendæ, ad omnium puerorum utilitatem præscripta. Londini, 1513." It is in use to-day in St. Paul's School, London. *Lily's Grammar*, or *The Grammar of King Henry the Eighth*, as it was sometimes called, was not put together in its present form until about twenty years after Lily's death.

From an introductory preface in a comparatively modern edition, 1732, written by John Ward, we learn that the English introduction was written by Dr. John Colet, Dean of St. Paul's, for the use of the school he had lately founded there, and was dedicated by him to William Lily, the first master of that school,

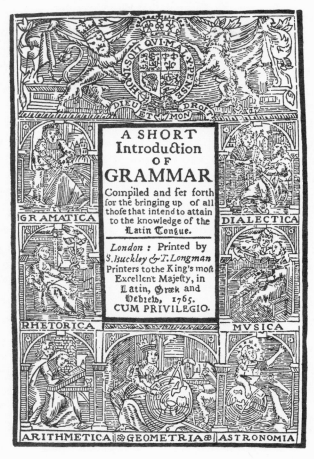

Titlepage of Lily's Latin Grammar.

in 1510, for which reason it has usually gone by the name of *Paul's Accidence*. The preface to the first edition was probably written by Cardinal Wolsey; the Latin Syntax chiefly by Erasmus; and the remainder by Lily. Thus the book may have been the joint production of four of the greatest scholars of the age.

There were in England contemporary with Lily several other persons famous for their skill in grammar, and who likewise wrote upon the art, as John Holt, John Stanbridge, and Robert Whittington. Although the celebrated character which Lily's writings soon gained secured to them the preference over others, yet the many and different compositions written by persons famed for their learning could not but occasion a diversity of teaching, since each of them had his followers. Whereof to prevent this inconvenience and to introduce a right grammatical institution, which is of so great consequence to the public, as being the foundation of all other literature, King Henry VIII. caused "one kind of grammar by sundry learned men to be diligently drawn, and so to be set out, only everywhere to be taught for the use of learners and for the hurt in changing of schoolmasters." The work was completed and published certainly as early as 1542, and possibly in 1541. Since then many alterations and large additions have been made, and great care and attention has been employed to improve the work from time to time. But because some of the first and chief parts of it were both written and published for the use of St. Paul's School and Lily had so considerable a hand in their composition, the whole grammar as it is now modelled has generally gone under his name.

As this grammar was at first enjoined by the king's authority to be the only one taught in schools, so for a long time bishops at their visitations used to inquire of the schoolmasters within their respective dioceses whether they taught any other. One of the articles of inquiry of Bishop Juxon in 1640 is, " Doth he teach them any other grammar than that which was set forth by King Henry VIII. and has since continued." Promulgated by the king's authority and supported by the ecclesiastical sanction of bishops, *Lily's Grammar* had almost a monopoly in England and was used extensively in New England.

There was, however, no lack of grammars by other authors, as in *A Grammar of the Latin Tongue* written by Solomon Lowe and published in 1726, there are enumerated no less than one hundred and eighty-six writers of Latin grammars which either were or had been in use in England. Very few of these grammars were used in New England, and we must confine ourselves to those which were connected with the colonial and provincial schools.

The earliest Latin grammar used in New England by the beginners in Latin is supposed to have been the *Latin Accidence. By John Brinsley*, which was first printed in London in 1611. In the second year *Lily's Grammar* was substituted.

John Brinsley, a Non-conformist divine, was born in Leicestershire in 1600, and died in 1665. He was a noted grammarian, sometime schoolmaster and minister in Great Yarmouth in Norfolk. Besides the *Accidence* he published in 1612 *Sententiæ Pueriles*, translated grammatically; in 1614, Corderius *Colloquies*, translated grammatically; and in 1622, an English grammar entitled *A Consolation for Our Grammar Schooles*. All of these publications were used undoubtedly in the New England schools, but it would be exceedingly difficult to find copies to-day. He also published, in 1612, *Ludus Literarius; or the Grammar School*, which is exceedingly valuable for the minute details it gives of the manner of conducting a grammar school at the beginning of the seventeenth century.

Contemporary with Brinsley as a teacher, but somewhat later as a publisher, was Charles Hoole, whose name was famous in scholastic circles in New England.

Maturinus Corderius's

SCHOOL-COLLOQUIES,

ENGLISH and *LATIN*,

Divided into feveral Claufes:

Wherein the Propriety of both Languages is kept.

That Children, by the Help of their Mother-Tongue, may the better learn to fpeak *Latin* in ordinary Difcourfe.

By *CHARLES HOOLE*, Mafter of Arts of *Lincoln-College*, *Oxford* : And late School-mafter in *London*.

This fame fpeaking Latin *is a Thing indeed to be highly commended, but not fo much of it felf, as becaufe very many neglect it : For it is not fuch a gallant Thing to underftand* Latin, *as it is a bafe to be ignorant of it.* Cic. de clar. Orator.

L O N D O N,
Printed by *J. Read,* for the Company of *Stationers,*
1719.

Charles Hoole, a well-known and successful teacher in London for more than twenty years in the seventeenth century, wrote several text-books which were so highly prized that they were printed for the use of the college at Eton, and some of them were used in the Boston Latin School.

A short biography of Hoole reads as follows: " Charles Hoole, a native of Wakefield, Yorkshire, was educated at Lincoln College, Oxford. He was elected master of Rotheram school but during the Civil wars came to London and acquired some celebrity as a public teacher. His services to literature and education were acknowledged by the gratitude of Bishop Saunderson who gave him the rectory of Stock in Essex and a prebend in Lincoln cathedral. He died in 1666."

In 1652, while master of a school in Goldsmiths-Alley, he published, *Maturinus Corderius's School Colloquies, English and Latin, divided into several Clauses: wherein the Propriety of both Languages is kept. That Children, by the help of their Mother-Tongue, may the better learn to speak Latin in ordinary Discourse.*

For more than one hundred years Hoole's edition of Corderius's Colloquies was used in the schools. The writer possesses two copies each bearing the imprint, " London, printed by F. Read, for the Company of Stationers, 1719." On the fly-leaf of one is written, "John Cleves Symms and Timothy Symms their book 1753." On the titlepage of the other is written, " Johannis Taylor hunc Librum jure tenet. Anno 1748." The Colloquies of Corderius was a standard text-book which was in use until very recent times. The writer possesses a copy edited by John Clarke, " A New Edition carefully Corrected and Compared with the Twenty-Sixth London Edition," which was " Printed at Exeter by H. Ranlet for I. Thomas & E. T. Andrews. Sold at their Bookstore, Faust's Statue, No. 45, Newbury Street, Boston. 1800."

Joseph Taylor

The COMMON

ACCIDENCE

Examined *and* Explained

B Y

Short Questions and Answers,

According to the very

WORDS of the BOOK.

Conducing very much to the Eafe of
the Teacher, and the Benefit of the
Learner.

Being helpful to the better Underftanding
of the *Rudiments* and *Grounds* of *Grammar,*
delivered in that and the like Introdu-
&ion to the Latin Tongue.

Written heretofore, and made ufe of in
Rotheram School, and now publifhed for the Profit
of young Beginners in that and other Schools.

By CHARLES HOOLE, Mafter of Arts:
lately Teacher of a private *Grammar-School* near
the *Token-houfe* Garden in *Lothbury, London.*

LONDON:
Printed by *M. C.* for *John Clark,* and are to
be fold at *Mercers-Chappel* in *Cheapfide.* 1695.

[244]

In 1659 Charles Hoole published *The Rudiments of the Latin Grammar usually taught in all Schools. Delivered in a very plain method for young beginners. London: printed by T. Mabb for John Clarke, jun., and are to be sold at his Shop at the entring in of Mercers Chappel.*

In 1695 there was published *The Common Accidence Examined and Explained by Short Questions and Answers, according to the very Words of the Book. By Charles Hoole, Master of Arts: lately Teacher of a private Grammar-School near the Token-house Garden in Lothbury, London. London: printed by M. C. for John Clark, and are to be sold at Mercers-Chappel in Cheapside. 1695.* It is a duodecimo of about three hundred and fifty pages. The plan is very similar to Lily's, as it consists of three parts separately paged. The first contains " The Introduction of the Eight Parts of Speech;" the second, " Hoole's Accidence and Terminations;" the third, " Propria Quæ Maribus," " Quæ Genus," and " As in Præsenti."

The writer's copy was used by John Taylor in 1715 and in 1761 by his relative Joseph Taylor. On the recto of the flyleaf is written " John Taylor. Ejus Liber. bought November ye 16 1715." On the verso

" Hujus Si Cupias Dominum Cognoscere Libri
Inferius Legito Nomen habebis ibi
Johannes Taylor Hunc Librum jure tenet
Millesimo Septingentesimo Decimo Sexto."

Another book by Hoole which is seldom seen is the first American edition of *Sententiæ Pueriles,* or *Sentences for Children,* which Hoole translated into English from the Latin of Leonard Culman. It is a small octavo, contains seventy-four pages, and is bound in calf. It is one of the earliest school-books printed in New England. If we omit catechisms and primers and *The Spelling-Book,* printed by Day, the earliest school-book printed in New England known to the writer is an *Epitome of English Orthography*, printed in Boston in 1697. It was an octavo of thirty-nine pages. No copy is known, but the title is given by Rev. Thomas Prince in his manuscript list.

In the centre of the facsimile title of the *Sententiæ* appears some faint handwriting. It reads : " Joshua Lamb, his book." Joshua Lamb, the son of Samuel Lamb, a captain in the Revolutionary Army, was born Dec. 12, 1781. He became a millwright by trade, a captain in the militia, and at his death, Oct. 14, 1868, left a large property. This little book of Latin and English sentences was used by him when he was studying with the Rev. Zenas Lockwood Leonard in Sturbridge, Mass.

Charles Hoole also made his name famous in all English-speaking countries by his translating into English a book which had an enormous sale in Europe, and was published in many languages. For more than a century after its first publication the most popular text-book for young Latinists in Europe was Comenius's *Orbis Sensualium Pictus*, by which children were taught Latin by means of pictures the descriptions of which were given in German and Latin. The English portion of the title of the eleventh London edition reads : *Joh. Amos. Comenius's Visible World: or A Nomenclature, and Pictures of all the Chief Things that are in the World, and of Mens Employments therein; in above 150 Copper Cuts written by the Author in Latin and High Dutch, being one of his last Essays ; and the most suitable to Children's Capacity of any he hath hitherto made. Translated into English by Charles Hoole, M.A., for the Use of Young Latin Scholars. London, 1728.*

Each chapter began with a picture. Over each picture was its title in English and Latin. Underneath was a description of every part of the picture in English, and in a parallel column its equivalent in Latin.

Sententiæ Pueriles

Anglo Latinæ.

Quas e diverſis Authoribus olim collegerat,

Leonardus Culman ;

Et in Vernaculum Sermonem nuperrime tranſtulit,

Carolus. Hoole :

Pro primis Latinæ Linguæ Tyronibus.

P. Anteſignanus in Epiſt ad Saræos Fratres.
Doctrinæ opinionem aff.ctont alii ; ego pro mea virili parte, me puerorum & formandis & promovendis ſtudiis omnem meam operam addixiſſe, aperte & ingenue fateor.

~~ojorum sum hiſco~~

Sentences -for Children,

Engliſh and Latin.

Collected out of ſundry Authors long ſince,

By Leonard Culman ;
And now Tranſlated into Engliſh :
By Charles Hoole :
For the firſt Entrers into Latin.

P. Anteſignanus in his Epiſt to the Setæi Brethren.
Let others affect the Opinion of Learning : I do plainly and ingenuouſly confeſs I have ſeriouſly addicted my ſelf both to faſhion and promote Childrens Studies all that ever I can.

BOSTON in N E. Printed by B Green, & J Allen, for *Samuel Phillips* at the Brick Shop. 1702

The ninety-eighth picture represents a school, showing the master at his desk and the scholars busy with their books. Over the picture is printed, " A School. Schola." Underneath are parallel columns, which read as follows, the numbers referring to similar numbers in the picture : —

A *School,* 1.
is a Shop in which
Young Wits are fashioned
to vertue, and it is
distinguished into *Forms.*
    The *Master,* 2.
sitteth in a *Chair,* 3.
the *Scholars,* 4.
in *Forms,* 5.
he teacheth, they learn.
    Some things
are writ down before them
with *Chalk* on a *Table,* 6.
    Some sit
at a Table, and write, 7
he mendeth their Faults, 8.
    Some stand and rehearse
things committed to
memory, 9.
    Some talk together, 10
and behave themselves
wantonly and carelessly ;
these are chastised
with a *Ferrula,* 11.
and a Rod, 12.

Schola, 1.
est Officina, in quâ
Novelli Anim formantur
ad virtutem, &
distinguitur in *Classes.*
    Præceptor, 2.
sedet in *Cathedra,* 3.
Discipuli, 4.
in *Subselliis,* 5.
ille docet, hi discunt.
    Quædam
præscribuntur illis
Cretâ in *Tabella,* 6.
    Quidam sedent
ad Mensam, & scribunt, 7.
ipse corrigit Mendas, 8.
    Quidam stant, & reci-
tant mandata
memoriæ, 9.
    Quidam confabulantur,
10. ac gerunt se
petulantes, & negligentes ;
hi castigantur
Ferulâ (baculo), 11.
& *Virgâ,* (12).

It was a duodecimo and contained two hundred pages. The first edition was published at Nuremberg in 1657 ; soon after a translation was made into English by Charles Hoole. The last English edition appeared in 1777, and this was reprinted in America in 1810. It was the first illustrated school-book, and has served as a model for the innumerable illustrated books

JOH. AMOS COMENII
ORBIS SENSUALIUM PICTUS:
HOC EST

OMNIUM PRINCIPALIUM IN MUNDO RERUM, ET IN
VITA ACTIONUM,

PICTURA & NOMENCLATURA.

JOH. AMOS COMENIUS'S
VISIBLE WORLD

OR

A NOMENCLATURE, AND PICTURES

OF

ALL THE CHIEF THINGS THAT ARE IN THE WORLD,

AND OF

MEN'S EMPLOYMENTS THEREIN;

In above 150 Cuts.

Written by the Author in Latin and High Dutch, being one of his last
Essays, and the most suitable to Children's Capacities of
any he hath hitherto made.

Translated into English
BY CHARLES HOOLE, M. A.
For the Use of Young Latin Scholars.

THE FIRST AMERICAN, FROM THE TWELFTH LONDON
EDITION, CORRECTED AND ENLARGED.
And the English made to answer Word for Word to the Latin.

Nihil est in intellectu, quod non prius fuit in sensu.
Arist.

New-York:
Printed and sold by T. & J. Swords, No. 160 Pearl-Street.

1810.

By permission of Rev. Samuel E. Herrick, D.D.

[249]

which have been made for the schools. It was universally popular and had an enormous circulation. Notwithstanding many editions were published, copies are difficult to find, as it was a book children were fond of and wore out in turning the leaves over and over to see the pictures.

The author, John Amos Comenius, a distinguished educational reformer, was born in Germany March 28, 1592. He was educated at Herborn and Heidelberg, after which he travelled through Holland and England and at last settled at Lissa, in Poland, where he was chosen bishop of the Moravian Brethren. In 1631 he published his *Janua Linguarum Reserata*, which was translated into many European and some Oriental languages. He instituted reforms in the system of public instruction in England, Sweden, and Hungary. Cotton Mather in his *Magnalia* says: " That brave old man Johannes Amos Commenius was indeed agreed withal, by one Mr. Winthrop in his travels through the Low Countries, to come over to New England, and illuminate their Colledge and Country, in the quality of a President, which was now become vacant. But the solicitations of the Swedish Ambassador diverting him another way, that incomparable Moravian became not an American." In Hungary he composed the celebrated *Orbis Sensualium Pictus*, which has often been reprinted and imitated. Finally he settled at Amsterdam, where he published several other works. He died at Naarden, Oct. 15, 1671.

Brinsley's Latin Accidence and *Hoole's Rudiments* were superseded by *Cheever's Latin Accidence*. The Rev. Samuel Bentley, D. D., of Salem, who died in 1819, in his *Notes for an Address on Education*, speaks of Mr. Cheever's book as follows: —

" His Accidence was the wonder of the age, and though, as his biographer and pupil Dr. Cotton Mather observed, it had not excluded the original grammar, it passed through eighteen editions before the Revolution, and had been used as generally as any elementary work ever known. The familiar epistles of this master to his son, minister of Marblehead, are all worthy of the age of Erasmus, and of the days of Ascham.

" Before Mr. Cheever's Accidence obtained, Mr. John Brinsley's method had obtained, and this was published in 1611, three years before Cheever was born. It is in question and answer and was undoubtedly known to Cheever, who has availed himself of the expression, but has most ingeniously reduced it to the form of his Accidence, — 134 small 4to pages to 79 small 12mo., with the addition of an excellent Table of Irregular Verbs from the great work of the days of Roger Ascham."

Mr. Bentley's statement as to the number of pages does not apply to the earlier editions of the *Accidence*. In making his comparison he must have used the eighteenth edition, published in Boston in 1785, which is the only edition known to the writer which contains seventy-nine pages. The writer's copy of this edition bears the autograph " Abiel Abbot, 1786."

Although it has been stated that the *Accidence* was composed by Mr. Cheever during his residence in New Haven, 1638 to 1650, the writer has found no evidence to corroborate this statement, nor the other statement that it had been used in the schools since 1650. It is possible that Mr. Cheever in the early years of his teaching may have composed a scheme for teaching beginners in Latin, which he was constantly revising and correcting during his seventy years of teaching, but this scheme remained in manuscript and was not printed in his lifetime.

The titlepage of the earliest edition known to the writer and which very probably is the first edition reads: *A Short Introduction to the Latin Tongue: For the Use of the Lower Forms in the Latin School, Being the Accidence Abbridg'd and Compiled in that most easy and accurate Method, wherein the Famous Mr.*

Ezekiel Cheever taught; and which he found the most advantageous by Seventy years experience. To which are added a Catalogue of Irregular Nouns and of Verbs disposed Alphabetically. Boston in N. E. Printed by B. Green, for Benj. Eliot. 1709.

Collation; Titlepage, verso blank, pp. (2). A Short Introduction to the Latin Tongue, pp. 1–46; A Catalogue of Verbs in common use, pp. 1–15; Mistakes, 1 page.

We are greatly indebted to the Rev. Samuel Edward Herrick, D. D., of Boston, who has kindly loaned a superb copy of the third edition printed in 1724 and has generously permitted a facsimile of the titlepage to be made. It differs from the edition of 1709 in that previous to "A Short Introduction" have been inserted "Of the Latin Letters, Points, &c.," pp. i–iv; the number of pages in "A Short Introduction" and "Catalogue of Verbs" has been increased from 61 to 66, while the pagination, instead of being broken, is continuous from 1 to 66; the leaf of "Mistakes" is omitted; and the following words have been inserted in the titlepage; namely, "The Third Edition Revised and Corrected by the Author." These would seem to be positive proofs that Ezekiel Cheever who died in 1708 was not the author. It will be noticed that the wording of the titlepage of the edition of 1709 is non-committal as to authorship. Mr. Cheever's name is mentioned only as having used this method, "which he found the most advantageous by seventy years experience." It was written "for the use of the Lower Forms in the Latin School," which meant the Latin School in Boston. "The Short Introduction" occupied forty-six pages, which may have been edited from a manuscript left by Mr. Cheever or composed by some one intimately acquainted with his method. To the "Introduction" were added fifteen pages of "Nouns and Verbs" evidently not by Mr. Cheever, and one page of "Mistakes." On the titlepage of the third edition it is plainly stated that it was "revised and corrected by

A Short
I N TRODUCTION
TO THE
Latin Tongue.
For the Use of the Lower Forms in the *Latin School.*

Being the Accidence Abbridg'd and Compiled in that moft eafy and accurate Method, wherein the Famous Mr. *Ezekiel Cheever* taught; and which he found the moft advantageous by *Seventy* years experience.

The Third Edition Revifed & Corrected by the Author.
To which are added a Catalogue of Irregular Nouns and of Verbs difpos'd Alphabetically.

BOSTON in *N. E*
Printed by *B. Green,* for *Benj. Eliot,* at his Shop in King Street. 1 7 2 4.

By permission of Rev. Samuel E. Herrick, D.D.

the author," and a comparison of the two editions shows the revisions and additions, and that the " mistakes " have been corrected.

Who then was the author of this little manual whicn for so many years haş been known as *Cheever's Latin Accidence?* Evidently it must have been composed by some one who had been associated with Mr. Cheever, and being published so soon after his death was probably projected during his life and composed with his approbation and supervision. Could it have been his son, the Rev. Samuel Cheever, of Marblehead, who died May 29, 1724, who, says Rev. John Barnard, was a man of great classical learning ? Was it Mr. Nathaniel Williams, who was appointed assistant to Mr. Cheever in 1703, who " made a handsome Latin Oration in his Honour " at his funeral, and who was chosen his successor as master of the Latin School ? Do not the indications point very strongly towards his grandson Ezekiel Lewis, who at a meeting of the selectmen of Boston August 28, 1699, " pursuant to a Vote of the Town, May 8th, was agreed with, and admitted an assistant to his grandfather Mr. Ezekiel Cheever in the Latine free school, his salary at present to be forty pounds per year " ?

Here was a person competent to compile the *Accidence*, teaching " the lower forms of the Latin school," and in close companionship with Mr. Cheever, as will appear from the following order of the selectmen ; namely, —

" Sept. 6, 1708. Ordered that Mr. Nathaniel Williams be invited to remove into the House where Mr. Cheever dwelt and that Mr. Minot and Mr. Powning do Speak with him about it, and to Mr. Lewise about Cleering the Said House."

The last edition was published in Boston in 1838, under the title of *Cheever's Latin Accidence.* It was preceded by a prospectus containing commendations from Hon. Josiah Quincy, Hon. John Pickering, Rev. Nathaniel Thayer, and others. President Quincy says: " A work which was used for more than a century in the schools of New England, as the first elementary book for learning of the Latin language; which held its place, in some of the most eminent of those schools, nearly, if not quite, to the end of the last century; which has passed through at least twenty editions in this country; which was the subject of the successive labor and improvement of a man who spent seventy years in the business of instruction and whose fame is second to that of no school-master New England has ever produced, requires no additional testimony to its worth or its merits."

Samuel Walker, who revised and corrected this edition, says: " His (Cheever's) Latin Accidence, which was the favorite little book of our youthful days, has probably done more to inspire young minds with the study of the Latin language than any other work of the kind, since the first settlement of this country. I have found it to be the best book, for beginners in the study of Latin, that has ever come within my knowledge; and no work of the kind have I ever known, that contains so much useful matter in so small a compass."

Ezekiel Cheever was born in London, Jan. 25, 1614. He was educated at Christ's Church hospital and in consequence was " a blue coat boy." He came to Boston in New England in June, 1637, but soon removed to New Haven, Conn., where he married and taught school for twelve years. In 1650 he removed from New Haven to Ipswich, Mass., where he taught in the grammar school for eleven years, and married in 1652 his second wife Ellen Lathrop, sister of Capt. Thomas Lathrop of Beverly. He again removed in 1661 to Charlestown, Mass., where he was master of the grammar school for nine years. Having been chosen master of the Latin School in Boston, he removed to that town in 1670 and taught for thirty-eight years. Cotton Mather records his death as follows: " He died on

Ingenio manus est et cervix cæsa

TULLYS OFFICES
in 3 Books.

Turn'd out of Latin
into English
By
ROGER L'ESTRANGE

LONDON Printed
for Henry Broome.

Frontispiece to Tully's Offices.

TULLYS
OFFICES
IN
Three Books,
Turned out of
LATIN
INTO
ENGLISH.

By Ro. L Estrange.

𝕿𝖍𝖊 𝕾𝖊𝖈𝖔𝖓𝖉 𝕰𝖉𝖎𝖙𝖎𝖔𝖓 𝕮𝖔𝖗𝖗𝖊𝖈𝖙𝖊𝖉.

LONDON,
Printed for *Henry Brome,* at the Gun in
St. *Paul's* Church Yard, 1681.

Saturday morning, August 21, 1708, in the ninety-fourth year
of his age; after he had been a skilful, painful schoolmaster
for seventy years; and had the singular favour of Heaven, that
though he had usefully spent his life among children, yet he
had not become twice a child; but held his abilities, with his
usefulness, in an unusual degree to the very last."

The following lines are taken from a poetical tribute to the
memory of Ezekiel Cheever, by his pupil Cotton Mather not
only because they are laudatory, but also because they contain
the titles of many of the school-books used by Mather in the
Latin School: —

> " 'T is Corlet's pains, & Cheever's we must own,
> That thou, *New England*, art not *Scythia* grown.
> The *Isles* of *Silly* had o're-run this Day
> The *Continent* of our *America*.
> *Grammar* he taught, which 't was his work to do :
> But he would *Hagar* have her place to know.
> The *Bible* is the Sacred *Grammar*, where
> The *Rules of speaking well*, contained are.
> He taught us *Lilly*, and he *Gospel* taught;
> And us poor Children to our *Saviour* brought.
> *Master of Sentences*, he gave us more
> Than we in our *Sententiae* had before.
> We Learn't Good Things in *Tullies Offices*;
> But we from *him* Learn't Better things than these.
> With *Cato's* he to us the *Higher* gave
> Lessons of Jesus, that our Souls do save.
> We Constru'd *Ovid's Metamorphosis*
> But on ourselves charg'd, not a *Change* to miss.
> Young *Austin* wept, when he saw *Dido* dead,
> Tho' not a Tear for a *Lost Soul* he had :
> Our Master would not let us be so vain,
> But us from *Virgil* did to *David* train,
> *Textors Epistles* would not *Cloathe* our Souls;
> *Pauls* too we heard; we *went to School at Pauls.*"

For the more advanced pupils *Lily's Grammar* was not the only one. William Walker, who published in 1652 *A Treatise of English Particles*, published a Latin grammar entitled, *Some Improvements to the Art of Teaching, especially in the First Grounding of a Young Scholar in Grammar Learning. Shewing a Short, Sure, and Easie way to bring a Scholar to Variety and Elegancy in Writing Latin.* The imprint of the seventh edition reads, *London Printed for George Sawbridge*, at the *Three Golden Flower-de-Luces in Little Britain, 1706.* On the inside of the cover is written, " E Libris Johannis Taylor, 1716."

John Clarke, " master of the Publick Grammar School in Hull," published in London in 1733, " An Introduction to the Making of Latin," an edition of which was used in the Boston Latin School in 1800. The writer's copy is the twenty-second edition, printed in London in 1775, and bears the autograph " Charles Taylor, 28th Dec. 1778."

A very handsomely printed grammar, with a rubricated titlepage, the first edition of which was printed in 1729, and was used to some extent in New England, is entitled, *A Practical Grammar of the Latin Tongue : wherein all the Rules are expressed in English, in the Method of Text and Notes ; and thrown into the most agreeable View, for the Benefit of Learners.* It is a large octavo of four hundred and eight pages. The writer's copy is the second edition, printed in London in 1742, and has the book-plate of Charles Taylor.

A manual which was very extensively used was, *English Exercises for School-Boys to translate into Latin. Comprising all the Rules of Grammar and Other Necessary Observations ; ascending gradually from the Meanest to Higher Capacities. By J. Garretson, Schoolmaster. The Twenty-First Edition Corrected. London, 1755.* It is a duodecimo of two hundred and fourteen pages, and bears the autograph " John Fletcher, 1750."

Nathan Bailey, who published the popular dictionary, also

SOME
IMPROVEMENTS
TO THE
Art of Teaching,
Especially in the
FIRST GROUNDING
OF A
YOUNG SCHOLAR
In Grammar Learning.

Shewing a Short, Sure, and Easie way
to bring a SCHOLAR to *Variety*
and *Elegancy* in Writing *LATIN*.

Written for the Help and Ease of all *Ushers* of
SCHOOLS, and *Country School-Masters*, and
for the Use and Profit of all *Young-Scholars*.

The Seventh Edition.

By *WILLIAM WALKER*, B. D. Author
of the Treatise of *Idioms* and *English Examples*.

Fundamenta tota domus nititur, Cic.

LONDON,
Printed for *George Sawbridge*, at the Three *Golden
Flower-de-luces* in *Little-Britain*, 1706.

ENGLISH *and* LATIN
EXERCISES,
FOR
SCHOOL-BOYS:

Comprifing all the

RULES of SYNTAXIS.

WITH

Explanations, and other neceffary Obfervations on each RULE.

And fhewing

The *Genitive Cafe,* and *Gender* of *Nouns*
and *Prɔnouns* ; as alfo the *Preterperfeƈt
Tenfe, Supine,* and *Conjugation* of *Verbs.*

ANSWERING

Perfeƈtly to the Defign of Mr. *Garretfon,*
and *Hermes Romanus,* in bringing on Learners moft
gradually and expeditioufly to the Tranflating of
Englifh into *Latin.*

By N. BAILEY, *School-Mafter.*

The NINTH EDITION, Correƈted.

LONDON:
Printed for R. WARE, at the *Bible* and *Sun* in *Amen-
Corner.* MDCCXXXIV.

T H E

R U D I M E N T S

O F

LATIN PROSODY:

W I T H

A *Diſſertation* on L E T T E R S,

A N D

The Principles of H A R M O N Y,

I N

Poetic and *Proſaic* Composition.

Collected from ſome of the Best Writers.

Dii probos mores docili juventae,
Dii ſenectuti placidae quietem,
Romulae genti date remque, prolemque,
Et decus omne.

Hor. Carm. Secul.

B O S T O N, *N. E.*

Printed and Sold by Benj. Mecom, at the *New*
Printing-Office, near the Town-Houſe.

M,DCC,LX.

Titlepage of " The Rudiments " by James Otis.

[262]

published *English and Latin Exercises for School Boys : comprising all the Rules of Syntaxis.* The imprint of the ninth edition reads, *London ; printed for R. Ware, at the Bible and Sun in Amen-Corner. MDCCXXXIV.* On the inside of the cover of the writer's copy is written, " Samuel Turell Ejus Liber, 1739."

Rev. Thomas Dyche, Schoolmaster at Stratford-le-Bow, who published in 1723 his *Dictionary of Words commonly used in the English Tongue,* also published *Vocabularium Latiale : or, A Latin Vocabulary,* the twelfth edition of which was published in London in 1780. " Thomas Gardner, Jun'r His Book " is inscribed in the writer's copy.

In 1760 James Otis, who later became the great defender of the rights of the colonies, published *The Rudiments of Latin Prosody.* The name of the author does not appear on the titlepage. It is in two parts, separately paged, the second part being, *A Dissertation on Letters and the Principles of Harmony, in Poetic and Prosaic Composition.* It is a small octavo, the *Prosody* occupying sixty pages and the *Dissertation* seventy-two. " Only a few months after its publication, Otis, ' with a tongue of flame and the inspiration of a seer,' was arguing the question of the Writs of Assistance in the council-chamber in Boston, and leading the van of American Patriots."

In 1786 was published the first American edition of *Rudiments of the Latin Tongue ; or a Plain and Easy Introduction to Latin Grammar. By Thomas Ruddiman, M.A., Philadelphia, MDCCLXXXVI.* It is a small octavo, containing one hundred and thirty pages.

Thomas Ruddiman was born in Aberdeenshire in 1684, and educated at Aberdeen. He was made overseer of the king's privy purse, Edinburgh, and for fifty years continued keeper of the Advocates library there. He distinguished himself for the many valuable books which he edited, particularly for his Latin

Henry S. Nightingale.

RUDIMENTS

OF THE

LATIN TONGUE;

OR, A

PLAIN AND EASY INTRODUCTION

TO

LATIN GRAMMAR:

WHEREIN

The PRINCIPLES of the LANGUAGE are methodically
digested, both in ENGLISH and LATIN.

WITH

USEFUL NOTES and OBSERVATIONS, explaining the TERMS of
GRAMMAR, and farther improving its RULES.

BY THOMAS RUDDIMAN, *M. A.*

To this new *American* Edition is annexed,

P R O S O D Y;

Particularly adapted to this *Introduction* to *Latin Grammar.*

P H I L A D E L P H I A:
Printed and Sold by YOUNG, STEWART, and M'CULLOCH, the
Corner of *Second* and *Chefnut-ftreets.*
M.DCC.LXXX.VI.

Grammar, which is much admired. He died at Edinburgh in 1757.

In 1772 was published the first edition of *The Rudiments of Latin and English Grammar. By Alexander Adam, LL.D.* It was a popular manual and passed through several editions. In 1799 the University in Cambridge, New England, was meeting with the same difficulty which troubled King Henry the Eighth more than two hundred and fifty years before. The difficulty was overcome in much the same way as the king overcame his, as will be seen by the following Advertisement of the Cambridge University: "Whereas the University in Cambridge for several years past has suffered much inconvenience, and the interest of Letters no small detriment from the variety of Latin and Greek Grammars used by the Students, in consequence of that diversity, to which, under present instructors, they have been accustomed in their preparatory course; to promote, so far as may be, the cause of Literature, by preventing those evils in future, the Government of the University, on due consideration of the subject, has thought it expedient to request all instructors of Youth, who may resort to Cambridge for education, to adopt *Adam's Latin Grammar* and the *Gloucester Greek Grammar*, with reference to such pupils, as Books singularly calculated for the improvement of students in these languages. The University has no wish to recommend, much less to dictate, to any other institution, but only facilitate the acquisition of Literature by promoting uniformity within itself. These being the Grammars which will be used at this College by all classes, admitted after the present year, it seems necessary, to prevent future difficulty, by giving this public and timely notice; for though a knowledge of the Grammar is not at present made indispensably necessary to admission into the University, yet every Scholar, who may be accepted after the present Commencement without such knowledge, will be required immediately to form a radical and intimate acquaintance with them, as no student will be permitted at the classical exercises to use any other Grammar.

" Cambridge, July 7, 1799."

Accordingly an edition of Adam's *Latin Grammar* was printed, on the titlepage of which was printed *First American from the Fifth English Edition, with Improvements. Recommended by the University at Cambridge, (Mass.), to be used by those who are intended for that Seminary. Boston : Printed by Manning & Loring, December, 1799.*

Alexander Adam was born at Rufford in the shire of Moray, in 1741, and died in 1809. He obtained the degree of LL.D., and was for many years Head Master of the High School at Edinburgh. He compiled Roman Antiquities, Latin Lexicon, Latin Grammar, and other school-books.

Caleb Alexander not only compiled the first English Dictionary by an American author, but also was the first American author to compile a Latin Grammar. Its title reads : *A New Introduction to the Latin Language : being an attempt to Exemplify the Latin Syntax and render familiar to the Mind the Grammatical Construction of this Useful Language. By Caleb Alexander, A.M., Worcester, (Massachusetts). Printed by Isaiah Thomas, Jun., for Isaiah Thomas, 1795.*

In his Preface the author says : " Two reasons were influential to begin and finish the following *Introduction.* 1. Some apparent deficiencies in Mr. Clarke's *Introduction to the Making of Latin.* 2. To prevent the necessity of sending to Europe for books, that are wanted and used in American schools." Concerning the second reason he offers the following remarks : " To the Republican Sons of America this reason will appear not only plausible, but conclusive. As an independence is now fully established, as the arts and sciences are now flourishing among us, as men of literature and genius are constantly rising up and appearing on the glorious and extensive theatre of knowledge, so we ought not to be dependent on European pens, for the composition of books, that may be composed by our own sons. If, by a blinded partiality for British productions, we neglect our own, the *stimulus* to genius and exertion will be blunted, and our servility will too clearly appear."

He further remarks: " Although the following collection has no originality, yet it is *the first* of the kind, that has been written and published in the United States."

That Caleb Alexander's warning has been heeded from that day to this is shown by the long list of American writers of text-books, by the bulky catalogues of American school-books, by the great publishing houses dealing in American manuals of education, and by the erection of immense printing-offices engaged almost exclusively in manufacturing the products of American brains, of which the great establishments on the banks of Charles River are remarkable examples.

For many years the master mind of one of these establishments was our late honorary member, John Wilson, whose excellent taste and superior skill in printing made the name of the University Press famous among the readers of English and American literature.

Caleb Alexander, D. D., was born in Northfield, Mass., and graduated at Yale College in 1777. He was first settled as a Congregational minister at New Marlborough, and afterwards at Mendon, Mass. His continuance in each of these situations was less than two years. The remainder of his life was spent in teaching and kindred pursuits. He published several grammatical books, a dictionary, and other small works. He died in April, 1828.

Greek Grammars

WHAT Lily's *Grammar* was to Latin, Camden's was to Greek. It was based upon the *Græcæ Linguæ Spicilegium* of Edward Grant, his predecessor in the Head Mastership of Westminster School. The *Spicilegium* was a small quarto written in the form of a dialogue between master and pupil, and was first published in 1575. Camden's *Grammar* was first published in 1597, and was long popular, remaining in use over two hundred years. It was not until 1800 that the University at Cambridge, New England, substituted for it the *Gloucester Greek Grammar*. The title of the writer's copy, which bears the autograph " Luther Laurence's Book, 1795," reads, *Institutio Græcæ Grammatices Compendaria, in usum regiæ scholæ Westmonasteriensis. Londini: 1793*. With the exception of the date this title does not differ from that of the first edition.

William Camden, the celebrated antiquary, was born at London, May 2, 1551. In 1575 he received the appointment as second master of Westminster School. In 1586 he published his valuable work on Britannia which secured for him the degree of M. A. In 1593 he succeeded Dr. Grant in the headship of Westminster School. In 1597 he was appointed Clerencieux king of arms, an employment more congenial to his tastes, and which afforded ample opportunity to continue his literary pursuits. He died at Chiselhurst in Kent, Nov. 9, 1623, and his remains were deposited in Westminster Abbey.

In 1663 was published the celebrated Westminster *Græcæ Grammaticæ Rudimenta*. Its author was Richard Busby, the

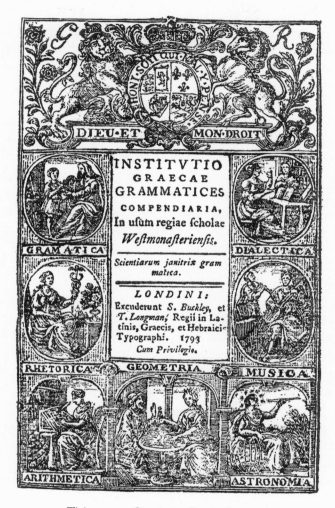

Titlepage to Camden's Greek Grammar.

most famous of English schoolmasters, who was born at Lutton, Northamptonshire, Sept. 22, 1606. Educated at Westminster School and Oxford, in 1640 he was appointed Head Master of Westminster School, which office he retained until his death in 1695. He was a most successful teacher, and has the reputation of having " bred up the greatest number of learned scholars that ever adorned any age or nation."

In 1684 a very elaborate Greek grammar was published by Joannes Verwey, a learned Dutchman who presided with great reputation over the school at Gaude, and afterwards that of the Hague, where he died about 1690. It is entitled, *Nova Via Docendi Græca*. The writer's copy is a beautifully printed octavo volume, with a rubricated titlepage, and contains five hundred and eighty-eight pages. It was printed at Amsterdam in 1710. Verwey was the author not only of *Nova Via*, but also of *Medulla Aristarchi Vossiani*, two grammars of singular merit and general utility.

In 1688 John Leusden published *Compendium Græcum Novi Testamenti*, the seventh edition of which was published in 1726. The writer's copy of this edition has a page of one of the flyleaves covered with a description of the book in the handwriting of Dr. Jonathan Homer of Newton, Mass. He says in part: " This oft published work of Professor Leusden is divided into thirty-six lessons, to be learnt in thirty-six days or six weeks. It contains all the words of the Greek New Testament. . . . A scholar who can thoroughly understand this work is, or may be, master of the whole Greek New Testament."

A little manual for learning to write and speak Greek is entitled *Familiarum Colloquiorum Libellus ; Græce et Latine, auctus & recognitus. Auctore Johanne Posselio. Londini, 1710.* On the fly-leaf of the writer's copy is written " Wm. Rand His Book. Began June Y^e 30, 1737." It is a small octavo containing fifty-six unnumbered leaves.

'Ο Ι Κ Ε Ι' Ω Ν *Taylor*

Δ Ι Α Λ Ο Γ Ω Ν

ΒΙΒΛΙΟΝ ΕΛΛΗΝΙΣΤΙ

ΚΑΙ ΡΩΜΑΙΣΤΙ.

FAMILIARIUM COLLO-
QUIORUM LIBELLUS;
GRÆCE ET LATINE,
Auctus & recognitus.

Accessit & utilis Dialogus de ratione
studiorum recte instituenda.

I T E M
Oratio de ratione discendæ, ac docendæ Linguæ
LATINÆ & GRÆCÆ.

Autore *Johanne Posselio.*

L O N D I N I,
Excudebat *Gulielmus Redmayne* pro
Societate Stationariorum, 1710.

Titlepage of Posselio's Colloquies.

John Holmes, Master of the Public Grammar School in Holt, published a little manual for beginners in Greek entitled, *Græcæ Sententiæ E variis Græcorum Libris hinc inde excerptæ quibus insuper adduntur Aurea Carmina Pythagoræ; cum Epitaphio Adonidis*, the seventh edition of which was published in London in 1775, and which Charles Taylor used in 1779.

In 1794 there was published in London the third edition of *A Grammar of the Greek Language; originally composed for the College-School at Gloucester*. This grammar had largely superseded Camden's Grammar in England, and in 1799 the University at Cambridge, New England, gave notice that in 1800 no other Greek grammar than *Gloucester Greek Grammar* would be permitted to be used at the classical exercises of that institution. In April, 1800, Isaiah Thomas and E. T. Andrews printed at Boston an edition of the *Gloucester Greek Grammar*, being, as stated on the titlepage, the "First American from the Third London Edition," which superseded Camden, Wettenhall, and Milner's grammars.

Hebrew Grammars

THE principal writers of Hebrew text-books used in the New England schools were William Schickard, John Buxtorf, John Leusden, and Judah Monis.

William Schickard's Grammar was first published in 1625. The writer's copy, of which a facsimile titlepage is given, was published in London in 1639. On a fly-leaf is written, "Pretiũ 3ˢ 6ᵈ. Deodatus Lawsonus Anno Domini 1677." Also in Lawson's handwriting, "Mo. 1; 2 Die; 79. I agreed with Chᵉ Bennett to keep my horse to give him ½ peck oats a day from hence & is due to him this day 5ˢ 5ᵈ

I say agreed at 1ˢ p'diem."

Rev. Deodat Lawson was pastor of the First Church in Salem Village, now Danvers, in 1684, but in 1688 became pastor of the church in Scituate. He was a firm believer in the witchcraft delusion of 1692. In 1696 he went to England, and probably gave the book to Rev. Mr. Wadsworth, as on another fly-leaf is written, "Bn. Wadsworths Book 1701."

William Schickard was a professor of Hebrew at Tubingen and died of the plague in 1635, aged forty-three.

Besides a grammar John Buxtorf wrote *Synagoga Judaica de Judæorum Fide, Vita, Ritibus et ceremoniis,* the first edition of which was published in 1604. The writer's copy was printed at Basle in 1641, and was edited by his son, Professor of Hebrew at Basle Academy. It bears the autographs of Jere Davis and John White.

John Buxtorf was an eminent Hebrew grammarian and lexicographer. He was born at Camen in Westphalia, and became

WILHELMI SCHICKARDI

HOROLOGIVM
HEBRÆVM,

SIVE

Confilium, quomodo fancta lin-
gua fpacio xxiv. horarum, a totidem col-
legis, feu eorundem femiffe fufficienter ap-
prehendi queat,

Septies comprobatum, & impreffum
iam quantâ fieri potuit diligentiâ.

Quum priùs
Ab innumeris mathematicis mendis emendatum,
Ab aliquâ breviloquij obfcuritate annotatiunculis elucidatum,
Et lexici compendium ad juftum pene dictionarium exauctum-
fuiffet

A N. H. S.T.D.

Næ vide   Ne ride

LONDINI,
Typis THOMÆ PAINE!
Venit apud Philemonem Stephanum, & Chriftopho-
rum Meredith, *fub leone aureo, in* D. Paulj
Cæmteriô; quorum impenfis, excufum
fuit. 1 6 3 9.

Titlepage to Schickard's Hebrew Grammar.

Johannis Buxtorfi

SYNAGOGA
JUDAICA,

Auſpiciis Authoris jam olim
Latinitate donata,

*Nunc primum in vulgus
emiſſa.*

BASILEÆ,

Impenſis Ludovici König.
M. DC. XLI. *14·4*

CLAVIS GRÆCA
Novi Testamenti,
opera ac cura
IOHANNIS LEUSDEN
in lucem edita.

Ultrajecti
ex Officina
Georgii à Poolsum

Anno
1672.

FONS

CLAVIS

SAPIENTIÆ

POTENTIÆ

דִּקְדּוּק

לְשׁוֹן עִבְרִית

DICKDOOK LESHON GNEBREET.

A

G R A M M A R

OF THE

𝕳𝖊𝖇𝖗𝖊𝖜 𝕿𝖔𝖓𝖌𝖚𝖊,

BEING

An E S S A Y

To bring the 𝕳𝖊𝖇𝖗𝖊𝖜 𝕲𝖗𝖆𝖒𝖒𝖆𝖗 into 𝕰𝖓𝖌𝖑𝖎𝖘𝖍,

to Facilitate the

I N S T R U C T I O N

Of all thofe who are defirous of acquiring a clear Idea of this

Primitive Tongue

by their own Studies ;

In order to their more diftinct Acquaintance with the SACRED ORACLES of the Old Teftament, according to the Original. And

Publifhed more efpecially for the Ufe of the STUDENTS of *HARVARD-COLLEGE* at *Cambridge*, in NEW-ENGLAND.

נֶחְבַּר וְהוּגַת בְּעִיוּן נִמְרָץ עַל יְדֵי

יְהוּדָה מוֹנִישׁ

Compofed and accurately Corrected,

By J U D A H M O N I S, M A.

B O S T O N, N. E.

Printed by JONAS GREEN, and are to be Sold by the AUTHOR at his Houfe in *Cambridge*. MDCCXXXV.

By permission of Mr. Frederick L. Gay.

professor of Hebrew at Basle, where he died of the plague in 1629, aged sixty-five.

In 1672 John Leusden published at Utrecht *Novi Testamenti Clavis Græca in qua et Themata Novi Test. referantur, & ejusdem Dialecti, Hebraismi, ac multæ constructiones explicantur.* The writer's copy carries the autograph of J. P. Westewelt.

John Leusden, eminent as a grammarian and a biblical scholar, was born at Utrecht, where he became Professor of Hebrew and died in 1699, aged seventy-five.

In 1735 was published the first Hebrew grammar written in America. It was entitled, *A Grammar of the Hebrew Tongue, being an Essay to bring the Hebrew Grammar into English, to facilitate the instruction of all those who are desirous of acquiring a clear idea of this primitive tongue by their own studies. Published more especially for the use of the students at Harvard College at Cambridge in New England. By Judah Monis, Boston, N. E. printed by Jonas Green 1735.* It was a small quarto of one hundred pages.

Judah Monis was the first Hebrew instructor in Harvard College. He was a native of Italy, and after his arrival in this country began his instructions about the year 1720. Though a Jew, he embraced the Christian religion and was publicly baptized at Cambridge in 1722. After the death of his wife in 1761 he resigned his office and retired to Northborough, Massachusetts, where he passed the remainder of his life in the family of the Rev. James Martyn, who married a sister of his wife. He died April 25, 1764, aged eighty-one.

French Grammars

IN the early days in England great attention was paid to teaching the French language, and many text-books were written for that purpose. On this side of the Atlantic, in New England, there was little use for that language, and very few of the children in Colonial or Provincial days were taught it. The writer, however, possesses a few text-books which were used by New England boys in the eighteenth century. The earliest one is entitled, *The Complete French Master for Ladies and Gentlemen. For the Use of His late Highness the Duke of Glocester. By Mr. A. Boyer. The Eighteenth Edition. London, 1756.* It is a small octavo, containing four hundred and sixteen pages. Although the date of its use, "Anno Domini 1781," is written on the fly-leaf, the owner's name has been cut off. Abel Boyer, the author, was born at Castre in France in 1664. By the edict of Nantes he was banished and went to Geneva. Some years later he went to England, where he spent the greater part of his life, and died at Chelsea, November, 1729. He is chiefly known by his useful *French and English Dictionary*, first published in 1702, and his *French Master*, first published in 1694, both of which have passed through many editions. The Author's Preface to the eighth edition, dated Nov. 26, 1720, reads in part: —

"I published, about twenty-six years ago *The First Rudiments of the French Tongue*, calculated for the tenderest capacities, and chiefly designed for the late Duke of Glocester, to whom they were inscribed. That Essay was so favourably entertained, that I was soon after encouraged by that great Patroness of Arts and

ANNA
D.G. Angliæ Scotiæ Franciæ
et Hiberniæ Regina Fidei defens &c.

Frontispiece to Queen Anne's Prayerbook.

B Barnes

LITURGIA,
SEU LIBER
PRECUM COMMUNIUM,
Et Adminiſtrationis
SACRAMENTORUM
Aliorúmque
Rituum atque Ceremoniarum ECCLESIÆ,
JUXTA USUM
ECCLESIÆ ANGLICANÆ:
UNA CUM
PSALTERIO
SEU
PSALMIS *DAVIDIS,*
Ea Punctatione diſtinctis, qùa Cantari aut
Recitari debent in ECCLESIIS.
Itémque
Forma & Modus Faciendi. Ordinándi & Conſecrandi
Epiſcopos, Presbyteros, Diaconos.

Huic Editioni Precum Formula' acceſſit quæ durante Comitiorum Eccleſiaſticorum Conſeſſu, utriq; Domui Convocationis uſui eſſe ſolet;
Triginta Novem Ecclefiæ *Anglicanæ* Articulis inſuper adjectis.

LONDINI,
Excudebat *E. Jones,* Impenſis *D. Brown, T. Benskin, J. Walthoe,* & *F. Coggan,* MDCCIII.

Titlepage of Queen Anne's Prayerbook.

Sciences, the late Queen Anne (then Princess of Denmark) to compose not only a *Methodical French Grammar*, but likewise a *Dictionary*, for the use of her Royal Son. His untimely and justly lamented death deprived me of the honour and credit I had some reason to expect from my contributing to some part of the education of that promising young prince. But yet I had the satisfaction to see those two compositions so well received, that, in a few years, they bore several impressions and almost entirely drowned all other works of the same kind." The facsimile portrait of Queen Anne is taken from the frontispiece of *Liturgia, seu Liber Precum Communium, et Administrationis Sacramentorum Aliorumque Rituum atque Ceremoniarum Ecclesiæ, juxta usum Ecclesiæ Anglicanæ. London, MDCCIII.* It is a small octavo, bound in full morocco, and is a fine specimen of early eighteenth-century binding. On the titlepage is the autograph " B. Barnes."

Previous to 1774 John Perrin had written ten text-books relating to the French language, two of which were used in the New England schools and are in the possession of the writer. In 1769 he published *A Grammar of the French grounded upon the Decisions of the French Academy London, printed for B. Law, No. 13, in Ave-Mary-Lane, Ludgate-Street. MDCCLXIX.* It is a duodecimo of three hundred and sixty pages, and on the titlepage is the autograph "Samuel Rogers, 1772." To accompany the *Grammar*, John Perrin published *The Elements of French Conversation, with new, familiar, and easy Dialogues, each preceded by a suitable Vocabulary in French and English. London : printed for the Author, and sold by B. Law, Ave-Maria-Lane, MDCCLXXIV."* It is a thin duodecimo of one hundred and sixty-one pages. It will be noticed that the author was his own publisher. In the Preface of the *Elements* he claims that the French Tongue is confessedly an essential part of a liberal education.

NEW

FRENCH

AND

ENGLISH

GRAMMAR

Wherein the Principles are Methodically digefted, with ufeful Notes and Obfervations, explaining the terms of Grammar, and further improving its Rules.

By J O H N   M A R Y,

French Inftructor of the Univerfity of Cambridge

B O S T O N:
Printed for and Sold by the Author, and by J Norman, at his fhop in Marfhall's Lane, near the Bofton Stone.

M,DCC,LXXXIV

[283]

Previous to 1766 the instructors in French at Harvard College were not regularly appointed, but were permitted by the Corporation to teach such students as so desired. In 1766 the students were forbidden to attend the instruction of unauthorized teachers, and the position of the licensed teacher became more defined. Their charges were included in the quarter-bills, and they shared with the tutors the privileges of the Library, Commons, etc. In 1780 the instructor was appointed. The study, however, was at first an extra, and afterwards the only substitute for Hebrew, and in all cases involved an extra charge for tuition.

In 1783 John Mary was appointed French instructor and immediately proceeded to carry out a long-cherished plan of publishing a grammar. In the Introduction to his grammar he says, " From the moment I had the honour of being appointed French Instructor of the University of Cambridge, it has been my ambition to give to the publick a new Grammar, collected from the newest and best authors." The titlepage reads, *A New French and English Grammar. By John Mary, French Instructor of the University of Cambridge. Boston: Printed for and Sold by the Author, and by J. Norman, at his shop in Marshall's Lane, near the Boston Stone, MDCCLXXXIV.* It is a large octavo divided into two parts. The first part, containing the *Grammar, and Familiar Dialogues,* has one hundred and sixty-two pages. The second part, composed of *Instructive and Entertaining Exercises with the Rules of French Syntax,* has eighty-eight pages. Both at the beginning and end of the volume are several blank leaves evidently to be used in taking notes. On the first blank leaf is written, " Jacob Corey, Jr. Ejus Liber." " I began to study this Grammar March 26th 1804 at Rev. Mr. Leonards. J. Corey, Jr."

Letter=Writing, Themes, Rhet=oric, and Oratory

THE books whose titles are given in this chapter were used in the highest forms of the grammar schools or in the college. They are noticed because they furnish some information concerning the text-books used in the highest institutions of learning in early days.

What was apparently a very desirable and handy little dictionary was entitled, *Tirocinium Linguæ Græcæ Primiginias Voces, sives Radices complexum. Autore P. Philippo Labbe Biturico è Societate Jesu. Cadomi. MDCCXIII.* It is a very small octavo, contains three hundred and seventy-one pages, and is bound in vellum. It does not give definitions. It contains a list of about twenty-five hundred Greek words alphabetically arranged with the Latin equivalent in a parallel column.

It was the custom with such masters as Roger Ascham and Charles Hoole to cause their pupils to make most extensive use of manuscript common-place books in which were to be collected all sorts of phrases, adages, emblems, witty sentences, etc., from the classical authors, which caused compilations to be printed which were very helpful to the pupils and relieved them of much drudgery.

One of these compilations is entitled, *Epitheta Joannis Ravisii Textoris, Nivernensis. Genevæ, MDCXXXII.* It is a thick octavo of eleven hundred and fifty pages, one hundred and thirty-four of which relate to Prosody, and the remainder contain quotations from classical authors. The writer's copy bears

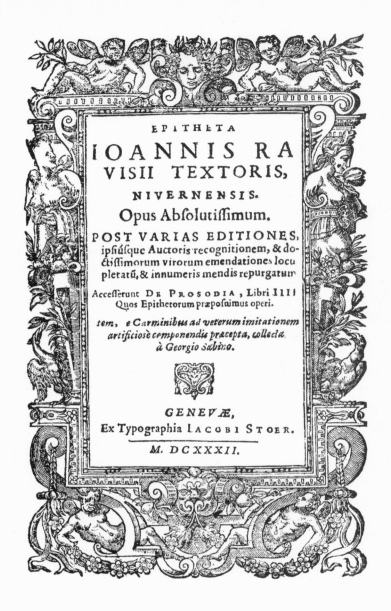

EPITHETA

IOANNIS RA VISII TEXTORIS,

NIVERNENSIS.

Opus Abſolutiſſimum.

POST VARIAS EDITIONES,
ipſiúſque Auctoris recognitionem, & do-
ctiſſimorum virorum emendationes locu
pletatū, & innumeris mendis repurgatum

Acceſſerunt DE PROSODIA , Libri IIII
Quos Epithetorum præpoſuimus operi.

*tem, e Carminibus ad veterum imitationem
artificioſe componendis præcepta, collecta.
à Georgio Sabino.*

GENEVÆ,
Ex Typographia IACOBI STOER.

M. DCXXXII.

the autographs, " J. Recompense Wadsworth, ejus Liber " and
" Benjamin Wadsworth me jure tenet a dono fratris sui."

Another compilation which was of use in writing themes
was, *Idiomatologia Anglo-Latina, or, A Dictionary of English and
Latine Idiomes, wherein phrases of the English and Latine tongue
answering in parallels each to the other are ranked under severall
heads. By William Walker, London, 1670.* On the fly-leaves
of the writer's copy are the autographs of Nathaniel Rogers,
Barratt Dyre, Daniel Oliver, and " John Taylor His Book
Anno Domini 1721."

In 1664 was published the tenth edition of *Symbola Heroica
in Tribus Classibus. Quarum Primâ continentur Illa Impp. ac
Cæsarum Romanorum-Italicorum, à Caio Julio Cæsare, usque ad
Flavium Constantinum Magnum. Secundâ verò, Impp. & Cæsarum
Romanorum-Græcorum, ab eodem Constantino usque ad Carolum
Magnum I, Cæsarem Germanicum. Tertià autem Classe, Impp.
Cæsarumque Romanorum-Germanicorum, à Carolo illo Magno, us-
que ad Ferdinandum II. Cæsarem Austriacum. Auctore Nicolao
Reusnero Leorino, J. C. Palat. Cæs. Londini, MDCLXIV.*
It is a small octavo of six hundred and thirty pages. It is
styled *Opus Aureum & verè Politicum, ac Regium,* and *Opus Jucun-
dissimæ & utilissimæ lectionis.* The former owners have written
as follows, " George Day His Booke Anno Domini 1676 ; "
" John Winslow ; " " John Wallys ; " and " John Taylor," who
" bought at an auction of Mr. Fletcher's books 1720."

Another book which was highly recommended was John
Clarke's edition of *Colloquiorum Desiderii Erasmi Roterodami Familiarum Opus Aureum,* the first edition of which was published in
1631. The writer's copy was published in London in 1717. It
is an octavo of four hundred and eighty-three pages. On the fly-
leaf are found the following autographs, " W^m. Royall, 1723 ; "
" Benjamin Dolbeare, Junr, 1757 ; " " Francis Gardner, Jr. ; "
" Ch. K. Dillaway, Dec. 20, 1872."

COLLOQUIORUM
Desiderii Erasmi Roterodami
FAMILIARIUM
OPUS AUREUM.

Cum Scholiis quibusdam perquam eruditis, quæ difficiliora passim loca diligenter explicant.

Editio triplici nomine commendatissima.

1. *Collatis optimis usquequaque Exemplaribus.*
2. *Additis seorsim in fronte Argumentis unicuique Colloquio.*
3. *Adjecto Indice novo rerum & verborum memorabiliorum locupletissimo.*

Denuo Recensita & Emendata.

LONDINI,

Impensis R. Bonwicke, Tim. Goodwin, J. Walthoe, M. Wotton, S. Manship, R. Wilkin, B. Tooke, R. Smith, T. Ward. 1717.

Titlepage of " Colloquies of Erasmus."

L. ANNÆI
SENECÆ FIL.
PHILOSOPHI:
Nec non
M. ANNÆI SENECÆ PAT.
RHETORIS
opera omnia.

Accedunt etiam
L. SENECÆ, ac P. SYRI MIMI,
Sententiæ aureæ.

Nunc primum centum aliquot versibus
auctiores correctioresq̨;
Studio
IANI GRVTERI.

In Bibliopolio Commeliniano.
cIɔ Iɔ cIV. 115

Titlepage of Seneca's Works.

Seneca's Works was also used, the titlepage of the writer's copy reading, *L. Annæi Senecæ Fil. Philosophi: nec non M. Annæi Senecæ Pat. Rhetoris opera omnia. Accedunt etiam L. Senecæ as P. Syri Mimi Sententiæ aureæ. Studio Iani Gruteri. In Bibliopolio Commeliniano.* CIƆIƆCIV. It is an octavo of six hundred and seventy-six pages. On the titlepage is written, "George McNish," and on the inside of the cover is the book-plate of Charles Taylor.

John Sturm, who was Rector of the famous School of Strasburg from 1538 to 1583, published a treatise on oratory and rhetoric entitled, *Hermogenis Tarsensis Rhetoris Acutissimi de ratione inveniendi oratoria libri IIII. Latinitate donati & Scholis explicati atque illustrati a Joanne Sturmio. (Argentorati) MDLXX.* Bound with it is *Joanni Sturmii Scholæ in Partitiones Rhetoricas Hermogenis.* It is an octavo bound in vellum and contains seventeen hundred and fourteen pages.

The titlepage of a treatise on rhetoric, first published in 1657, which in 1706 had reached its ninth edition, reads: *The Mystery of Rhetorick Unveil'd. Wherein above 130 of the Tropes and Figures are severally derived from the Greek into English. . . . Eminently delightful and profitable for young Scholars, and others of all sorts enabling them to discern and imitate the Elegancy in any Author they read, &c. The Ninth Edition. By John Smith, Gent. London, 1706.* It is a small octavo of two hundred and fifty-four pages, and bears the autograph, "John Taylor's Book, 1718."

Great pains were taken in the early schools in teaching the boys to write and speak Latin, and the ability to compose and deliver a Latin oration would insure high rank. In 1633 Thomas Farnaby, the great classical scholar and schoolmaster, to show the method of oratorical composition, published his *Index Rhetoricus*, which passed through many editions. The title reads, *Index Rhetoricus, scholis et institutioni tenerioris ætatis accom-*

The Myſtery
OF
RHETORICK
UNVEIL'D.

Wherein above 130 of
The *Tropes*, and *Figures* are ſeve-
rally derived from the *Greek* into
Engliſh; together with lively Definitions, and Variety

Of $\begin{cases} \textit{Latin,} \\ \textit{Engliſh,} \\ \textit{Scriptural,} \end{cases}$ Examples;

Pertinent to each of them apart.

Eminently delightful and profitable for
young Scholars, and others of all ſorts,
enabling them to diſcern and imitate the
Elegancy in any Author they read, *&c.*

The Ninth Edition.

By *JOHN SMITH*, Gent.

Ut hominis decus eſt ingenium :
Sic ingenii lumen eſt Eloquentia, Cic.

London, Printed for *Robert Clavel* at the *Pea-*
cock in St. *Paul's* Church-yard, 1706.

modatus. Cui adjiciuntur formulæ oratoriæ. The writer's copy, published in London in 1689, contains also an *Index Poeticus.* It is a small octavo, the *Index Rhetoricus* containing one hundred and twenty pages, and the *Index Poeticus* fifty-four pages.

No book gives the idea of the oration as a school exercise so clearly as *Formulæ Oratoriæ*, published by John Clarke in 1627. The titlepage of the writer's copy reads, *Formulæ Oratoriæ in Usum Scholarum concinnatæ. Cum Praxi & Usu earunden in Epistolis, Thematibus, Declamationibus contexencis. Accessit Dux Poeticus. Editio Octavo. Londini. 1659.* It is written in Latin and intended for the use of schools. In his address to the reader, Clarke quotes Alsted " that teachers should not teach what is to be done merely, but that they teach what is to be done, by doing it. The illustrious Erasmus descended into the minutest details when, for the sake of youth, he compiled his *Copia Verborum.*" Clarke follows him by presenting a treatise of Formulæ and Transitions of Oratorical Compositions, which, being for the use of schools, should not be meagre in hints and suggestions. Clarke used the oration for a public display before the chief people of the city and parents of the pupils in what was known in the Lincoln School as " Declamation Day." The Boston Latin School had similar exercises on " Public Saturday."

The writer's copy bears the autographs, " Nathaniel Gookins," " John Higginson," and " Jonathan Mitchell Sewall." Duyckinck says that Jonathan Mitchell Sewall " is a name that should be better known and cherished, for it was borne by one whose lyrics warmed the patriotism and cheered the hearts of the soldiers of the Revolution in the peril of battle and the privations of the camp. His *War and Washington* was composed at the beginning of the American Revolution and sung by the army in all parts of the country." He was the author of the famous couplet, —

" No pent-up Utica contracts your powers,
But the whole boundless continent is yours,"

which is found in the epilogue to the tragedy of *Cato* written
in 1778.

Another book used in the study of oratory is entitled, *Enchi-
ridion Duplex: Oratorium: Nempe & Poeticum. Hoc ab Alex-
andro Rossæo: illud à Theodorico Morello concinnatum: sed ab
eodem Rossæ recognitum & auctum. Londini, 1650.* It is a
small octavo of five hundred and ninety-eight pages. The following autographs appear in the book ; namely : " James Russell
Ejus Liber Anno 1682," and " J. Norton 1803."

Geography and History

G
EOGRAPHY and History had an insignificant place
in the curriculum of the common schools, and the
little that was learned was found in the reading lessons of the spellers, grammars, and readers. The
grammar schools and colleges had courses of study in these
branches, but they were confined almost wholly to ancient
geography and history and mythology.

A book which received the special mark of an Order in
Council for the public reading and teaching in all the grammar
and free schools in England and Wales was *Ockland's English
Battles*. Although John Winthrop and his associates may have
read it in their school-days, it is not probable that it was read in
a New England grammar school. It was written by Christopher Ockland, Head Master of the Southwark School, and
published in 1580. It is a Latin poem, martial in tone, cele-
brating the English victories, from Edward III. to Philip and
Mary, especially Crecy and Agincourt. It was reprinted in
1582, with the addition of the author's second poem, *De
pacatissimo Angliæ statu imperante Elizabetha, compendiosa Narratio*. At least three editions were published in this year. As
showing the reason for the Order in Council, we quote the
" Tenour of the Letters directed by the Lords of his highnesse
privie Counsell to his Majesties high commissioners in causes
Ecclesiastical, for the publike receyving and teaching of
Ch. Ocklande's Booke in all Grammer and freeschooles within
this Realme.

ANGLORVM PRÆLIA
ab anno Domini.1327.anno
nimirùm primo inclytifsimi Princi-
pis Eduardi eius nominis tertij,vſque ad annũ
Domini.1558.Carmine ſummatim perſtriĉta.

ITEM.
De pacatiſſimo Angliæ ſtatu, imperante Eliza-
betha,compendioſa Narratio.

Authore CHRISTOPHORO OCLANDO, primò
Scholæ Southwarkienſis propè Londinum,dein
Cheltennamenſis,quæ ſunt à ſereniſsima ſua
Maieſtate fundatæ,Moderatore.

Hæc duo Poemata, tàm ob argumenti grauitatem,
quàm Carminis facilitatem, Nobiliſſimi Regiæ Maieſtatis
Conſiliarij in omnibus huius regni Scholis præ-
legenda pueris præſcripſerunt.

Hijs Alexandri Neuilli K E T T V M : tùm propter argumenti ſimilitudinem,tùm propter orationis
elegantiam adiunximus.

LONDINI:
Apud Radulphum Nubery, ex aſsignatione
Henrici Bynneman Typographi.ANNO.1582.
Cum priuilegio Regiæ Maieſtatis.

Titlepage of Ockland's English Battles.

" After our right hartie commendations. Whereas there hath beene of late, a Booke written in Latine by one Christopher Ocklande, entituled *Anglorum prælia*, aboute halfe a yeare sithence imprinted and published, and nowe againe lately reprinted with the addition of a short treatise or appendix concerning the peaceable government of the Queenes Majestie : Forasmuche as his travaile therein, with the qualitie of the verse, hath received good commendation, and that the subject or matter of the saide Booke, is such, as is worthie to be read of all men, and especially, in common schooles, where divers heathen Poets are ordinarily read and taught, from the which the youthe of the realme doth rather receive infection in manners than advancement in vertue : in place of some of which Poets we think this Booke fit to be read and taught in the Grammar schooles : We have therefore thought good as well for the encouraging of the saide Ockland and others, that are learned, to bestowe their traveil and studies to so good purposes, as also for the benefit of the youth, and the removing of such lascivious Poets as are commonly read and taught in the saide Grammar schooles (the matter of thys Booke being heroical and of good instruction) to praye and require you upon the sight hereof, as by our special order, to write your Letters unto all the Bishops throughout this realme, requiring them to give commaundement, that in all the Grammer and free schooles within their several Diocesses, the saide Bookes, *de Anglorum Præliis*, and peaceable governement of his Majestie, may be in place of some of the heathen Poets, receyved and publiquely read and taught by the Scholemaisters unto their Scholers in some one of the fourmes in their schoole, fittest for that matter. Whereof praying you there may be no defaulte, so as this our direction may take place accordingly, we bidde you hartily farewell : from the Court of Greenwich the 21. of Aprill, 1582."

For a full appreciation of Homer, Ovid, and Virgil it was

necessary to know something about the personages concerning whom these poets wrote, and many books were written to explain the mythology and fables of the ancients. Compends, or abridgments, were compiled for the use of schools, and it was by reading these compends that the boys acquired much of their knowledge of history and geography. One of the best of these compends was *l'Explication Historique des Fables*, published by Anthony Banier at Paris in 1711. He was an ecclesiastic of the diocese of Clermont in Auvergne, who acquired by his industry and the patronage of his friends those means of education which the poverty of his parents could not supply. He was intrusted with the care of the children of Monsieur de Metz, president of the chamber of accounts at Paris, and it was for their education and improvement that he applied himself to mythological studies and soon produced his "Historical Explanation of Fables." This work on its appearance was universally admired, and procured the author admission to the academy of inscriptions. The fruits of his literary labors were numerous and valuable, the last ten years of his life being devoted to his favorite study of mythology. In 1740 he published *The Mythology and Fables of the Ancients*, in three volumes, quarto, a work abounding in erudition and much admired, an English translation in four volumes being published in London in 1741. Banier was born in 1673 and died November 19, 1741.

William King, a humorous English writer, born in London, 1663, and educated at Westminster School and Christ Church, Oxford, published *Historical Account of Heathen Gods and Heroes* for the use of Westminster School, and which was long used in the Boston Latin School. Dr. King's literary attainments secured for him in 1694 the appointment of secretary to the Princess Anne of Denmark, and in 1702 as judge of the high court of the admiralty in Ireland and vicar-general to the

A Compendious

DICTIONARY

OF THE

Fabulous History

O F

HEATHEN GODS

and HEROES:

Defign'd for the more ready Underftanding of

Poets, Paintings and Statues.

To which are Annex'd,

References to the feveral AUTHORS, from
which their Characters are deduc'd.

Peculiarly Adapted to the Ufe of

LATIN and FRENCH Schools,

And to Perfons who Read, or Attend

THEATRICAL ENTERTAINMENTS.

LONDON:

Printed for J. CLARK in *Duck-lane*, L. GIL-
LIVER at *Homer's Head*, and F. COGAN at
the *Middle Temple Gate* in *Fleet-ftreet*. 1731.

primate. He died December 25, 1712, and was interred in the north cloisters of Westminster Abbey.

Francis Pomey, a Jesuit of Lyons, born 1618, died 1673, besides a French and Latin Dictionary wrote *Pantheum Mysticum*, which was first published in 1669. Andrew Tooke translated it into English and published it as his own performance under the title *Pantheon, or History of the Heathen Gods*, which was in use in the Boston Latin School as late as 1825. Tooke was born in London in 1673, and was educated at the Charterhouse and Clare Hall, Cambridge, where he took his degrees in arts. In 1695 he was made usher of the Charter-house, in 1704 Professor of Geometry at Gresham College, and in 1728 Master of Charter-house. He died Jan. 20, 1731, and was buried in the Charter-house chapel.

The titlepage of the writer's manual reads *A Compendious Dictionary of the Fabulous History of Heathen Gods and Heroes. London : 1731.* It will be noticed by reference to the facsimile titlepage that it was " Peculiarly adapted to the use of persons who attend Theatrical Entertainments." It is a small octavo of two hundred and thirty-six pages.

John Clarke in his *Essay upon Education* says, " after Cornelius Nepos let them proceed to the *Roman* History, beginning with Eutropius, which must be followed by Florus. These three authors they must read entirely through ; which, with translations as literal as can conveniently be made, they will do in less time than is usually spent upon poor miserable scraps of them to little or no purpose ; as all things they will meet with in the Histories of *Greece* and *Rome* are not equally remarkable." Mr. Clarke was a firm believer in the use of translations. John Clarke's educational books were published in the early part of the eighteenth century. They were very popular and remained in use for many years. They were republished in New England and were used in the first half

EUTROPII

HISTORIÆ ROMANÆ Breviarium;

CUM

VERSIONE ANGLICA,

IN QUA VERBUM DE VERBO EXPRIMITUR:

NOTIS quoque & INDICE:

OR,

EUTROPIUS's

COMPENDIOUS

HISTORY of ROME;

TOGETHER WITH

AN ENGLISH TRANSLATION,

AS LITERAL AS POSSIBLE,

NOTES AND AN INDEX.

BY JOHN CLARKE,
AUTHOR OF THE ESSAYS UPON EDUCATION AND STUDY.

THE FIRST AMERICAN EDITION.

PRINTED AT BOSTON, BY PETER EDES,
FOR THOMAS & ANDREWS, JAMES WHITE, DAVID WEST,
AND EBENEZER LARKIN, JUN.
MDCCXCIII.

[300]

of the nineteenth century. The first American edition of Eutropius was printed in Boston in 1793 by Peter Edes. It is a duodecimo of one hundred and twenty-eight pages and is printed in double columns, the first column in Latin, the second in English. On the last fly-leaf is written, "Price 75 cents. — 4/6 Bought of Nath'l Peabody, Preceptor of Franklin academy Andover 1803." On page thirteen is written, "William I. Page began this book Jan. 11th. A. D. 1804."

The English portion of the titlepage of Florus reads, *A Compendious History of Rome. By L. Florus. With an English Translation, as Literal as possible. By John Clarke. The Third Edition London: MDCCXXXIX.* It is an octavo of two hundred and one pages in excellent condition, as are nearly all the books from the Taylor library. On the titlepage is the autograph "Joseph Taylor's," and on the inside of the cover is the book-plate of Charles Taylor.

G. Meriton published in London in 1679 a *Geography*, and in 1699 Laurence Echard published *A Compend of Geography*, both of which were used in New England schools. Laurence Echard, born 1671 (?), died 1730, was a native of Suffolk and educated at Christ Church, Oxford. In 1702 he published *Roman History* in five volumes, and in 1715 *Classical Geographical Dictionary*. He also published several other historical works, all of which were favorably received.

Another geography used in the New England schools was published in 1713 by Edmund Bohun. The titlepage of the fourth edition reads: *A Geographical Dictionary; representing the present and ancient Names and States of all the Countries, Kingdoms, Provinces, remarkable Cities, Universities, Ports, Towns, Mountains, Seas, Streights, Fountains, and Rivers of the whole World; their Distances, Longitudes, and Latitudes. Begun by Edmund Bohun, Esq. London, 1717.* The published price was 12*s.*

Isaac Watts, the well-known theologian and writer of hymns, born 1679, died 1748, published in 1725 a manual of astronomy and geography. The titlepage of the writer's copy reads : *The Knowledge of the Heavens and the Earth made easy; or the First Principles of Astronomy and Geography explained by the Use of Globes and Maps. By I. Watts. The Second Edition Corrected. London MDCCXXVIII.* It is an octavo of two hundred and forty-four pages. On the titlepage is written, "John Barnard's 1761 given him by his father," and " Thos. Barnard's 1731."

Daniel Fenning, a well-known author of school-books, published in 1754, *A New and Easy Guide to the Use of the Globes; and the Rudiments of Geography.* The third edition was published in 1770 with six maps of the World, two of which relate to America. It is a small duodecimo of one hundred and eighty pages.

The Solar System had another popular text-book entitled, *The Description and Use of Globes and the Orrery. To which is prefixed by Way of Introduction a Brief Account of the Solar System. By Joseph Harris, Teacher of Mathematics. The Sixth Edition. London, 1745.* It is an octavo of one hundred and ninety pages and contains five folding plates illustrating the motions of the Planets and two plates of the Globes and Orrery. On the fly-leaf is written, " Guillame Saxton's Livre 1766," and on one of the folding plates, " Jane Lambert."

In 1740 John Holmes, Schoolmaster in Holt, published *The History of England; Being a Compendium adapted to the Capacities and Memories of Youth at School. And likewise useful for all Others who have weak Memories and would willingly retain what they read of English History.* This manual was very popular, and used as a text-book for fifty years or more.

In 1754 was published, *A New History of England by Question and Answer. Extracted from the most celebrated English Historians, particularly M. Rapin de Thoyras. The Eighth Edition*

(*By John Lockman.*) *Adorned with Thirty-two Copper-Plates representing the most remarkable Incidents in the English History, for the Entertainment of Youth. London 1754.* On the fly-leaf is written, " Ex Libris Josephi Taylor." Uniform with the History of England Mr. Lockman published *A New Roman History by Question and Answer.*

The titlepage of the writer's copy of a Geography which passed through many editions reads, *Geography Anatomized or the Geographical Grammar. Being a short and exact Analysis of the Whole Body of Modern Geography. By Pat. Gordon. The Twentieth edition. With a new Set of Maps engraved by Emanuel Bowen, Geographer to his Majesty. London 1754.* It is an octavo of four hundred and twenty-six pages.

Another favorite geography, which passed through more than ten editions, was, *A New Geographical and Historical Grammar. By Mr. Salmon.* The third edition was published in Dublin in 1752, and a tenth in London in 1766. It is an octavo of over five hundred pages. Thomas Salmon, the author, was a writer of reputation, having published, besides the *Grammar, A Chronological History of England, Present State of all Nations, Examination of Burnet's History of his own Times*, and rendered valuable assistance in the *Universal History.* He died April, 1743, and was buried in St. Dunstan's Church.

The first edition of *Guthrie's Grammar*, which was an enlargement of *Salmon's Grammar*, was published in London in 1770. The titlepage of the writer's copy reads, *A New Geographical, Historical and Commercial Grammar and Present State of the several Kingdoms of the World. By William Guthrie. Illustrated by a correct set of Maps, engraved by Mr. Kitchen, Geographer. The Twelfth Edition, London, 1790.*

William Guthrie was born in 1708 at Brechin, educated at King's College, Aberdeen, settled in London as an author, was pensioned by the government, and died in 1770. He published

GEOGRAPHY MADE EASY:

BEING

An ABRIDGMENT

OF THE

American Univerſal Geography.

CONTAINING

ASTRONOMICAL GEOGRAPHY;

DISCOVERY and GENERAL DESCRIPTION of

AMERICA;

GENERAL VIEW of the UNITED STATES ;

PARTICULAR ACCOUNTS of the UNITED STATES of AMER-
ICA, and of all the KINGDOMS, STATES, and REPUBLICS
in the known WORLD.

In regard to their *Boundaries, Extent, Rivers, Lakes, Mountains,
Productions, Population, Character, Government, Trade, Manufactures, Curioſities, Hiſtory, &c.*

TO WHICH IS ADDED,

An improved CHRONOLOGICAL TABLE of REMARKA-
BLE EVENTS, from the Creation to the preſent Time.

Illuſtrated with a MAP *of the* WORLD, *and a* MAP *of*
NORTH AMERICA.

Calculated particularly for the

USE and IMPROVEMENT of SCHOOLS and ACAD-
EMIES in the UNITED STATES of AMERICA.

By JEDIDIAH MORSE, D. D.

*Miniſter of the Congregation in Charleſtown, Maſſachuſetts—Author of the American
Univerſal Geography, and the American Gazetteer.*

SEVENTH EDITION, corrected by the *AUTHOR.*

Publiſhed according to Act of Congreſs.

There is not a Son or Daughter of Adam but has ſome concern both in GEOG
RAPHY and ASTRONOMY.   *Dr. Watts.*
Among thoſe Studies which are uſually recommended to young people, there
are few that might be improved to better uſe than GEOGRAPHY.,
                                                          Eſſays on various Subjects.

PRINTED AT *BOSTON*,

By I. THOMAS and E. T. ANDREWS,

FAUST & STATUE, No. 45, NEWBURY STREET.

Sold by ſaid *Thomas & Andrews*, and other Bookſellers, in Boſton ; r. *Thomas*,
Worceſter ; *Thomas, Andrews & Penniman*, Albany ; and *Thomas,
Andrews & Butler*, Baltimore.————*October*, 1800.

History of England, History of Scotland, and *A Universal History.*
The Geographical Grammar which bears his name is believed to
have been compiled by Knox, the bookseller.

The first geography by an American author was *Geography
made Easy. By Jedidiah Morse, New Haven (1784).*

Jedidiah Morse, LL.D., clergyman and geographer, was
born at Woodstock, Conn., August 23, 1761; graduated at Yale
College, 1783; died at New Haven, June 9, 1820. He was
installed minister of the First Congregational Church in Charlestown, Mass., April 30, 1789, which position he resigned in
1820. Dr. Morse is the father of American Geography, having
prepared at New Haven in 1784, while a tutor in Yale College,
for the use of schools, the first work of the kind in America.

Mr. W. B. Fowle, a prominent author and educator, says:
" No geography was prepared for the schools until Mr. Bingham left them. Morse's abridgment began to be a reading-
book about the year 1800. When geography began to be read
in our public schools, and class-books were read long before any
lessons were recited or any maps used, Mr. Bingham prepared
the small *Astronomical and Geographical Catechism* based upon Dr.
Morse's School Geography, which was read occasionally by the
highest class in the Boston reading schools. Many copies of
the Catechism were sold (over one hundred thousand), and
meagre though it was, it was the only book used, and was recited literally, without any explanation or illustration by teacher
or pupil."

English Dictionaries

ICTIONARIES are a comparatively modern invention, and have become such necessities that it is difficult to imagine ourselves without them. The ancients had little if any notion concerning them. Neither the word Lexicon or Dictionarium belongs to the classical languages of Greece or Rome. The Greeks and Romans had no idea of a book embracing all the words of their own or any other foreign tongue. Glossaries, however, or collections of glosses, or explanations of words or passages of a work or author, were early current. The work known as the Homerica Lexicon, or in English *Homeric words*, of Apollonius, an Alexandrine grammarian of the time of Augustus, was a glossary of Homer. This glossary is the oldest work extant of the kind, and Apollonius is considered the oldest Greek lexicographer.

The earliest dictionaries we possess were compiled to teach the English a foreign tongue, and were bilingual or trilingual. Purely English dictionaries followed after a long interval, but for many years were merely lists of hard words; and it was not until Edward Phillips published in 1658 *The New World of Words* that we began to have a dictionary which was approximately a complete collection of all the words in the English language.

" The earliest *printed* vocabulary with which we are acquainted, in which the words of any modern language answering to the Latin are inserted, is the *Promptorius Puerorum*, printed by

Pynson in 1499, in which English words are followed by their supposed Latin equivalents."[1] It was also printed by Julian Notary in 1508, and from 1510 to 1528 Wynkyn de Worde printed six editions.

The authorship has been attributed to Richard Francis, a Preaching, or Black Friar, of Norfolk, but there is better evidence in favor of the claims of Galfridus Grammaticus, also a Black Friar, of Norfolk.

The first edition has no title, but the Prologue is printed on the reverse of the first leaf; and then on signature aii " Incipit liber qui dicitur Promptorium parvulorum sive clericorum." The colophon reads : " Ad laudem et ad honorem omnipotentis dei, et intemerate genitricis eiuo. Finit, excellentissimum opus exiguis manisq; scholasticis vtillisimum, quod nuncupator Medulla Grammatice. Impressum per egregium Richardum pynson in expensis virtuosorum virorum Frederice egmont et Petri post pascha anno domini m.cccc nonagesimo nono decima v^e die mensis Maii."

It is a folio of forty leaves. The printing is in double columns with the English before the Latin.

Few books have gone through so many editions or have been so frequently edited as Withals' Dictionary. It was first printed by Wynkyn de Worde, "Imprynted in the late house of William Caxton," but the year is unknown. The title of a later edition reads, *A shorte dictionarie for yonge beginners. Gathered out of good authours, specially Columel, Grapald, and Plini. Anno MDLXVIII.* The colophon reads : " Thus endeth this Dictionarie very necessary for children. Compiled by J. Withals. Imprinted at London in Fletestrete by Henry Wykes." The title of one of the latest editions reads in part : *A Dictionarie in English and Latine devised for the capacity of children, and young Beginners. At first set foorth by M. Withals, with Phrases*

---

[1] *Quarterly Review*, September, 1855.

both Rhythmical and Proverbial. Printed at London by Thomas Purfoot, 1616.

In 1573 John Baret compiled one of the most pleasing of the early dictionaries, to which he gave the curious name, *An Alvearie*, because it was really compiled by his scholars. In the *Address to the Reader* he says : " About eyghteene yeares agone having pupils at Cambridge studious of the Latin tongue I used them often to write epistles and themes togither and daily to translate some peece of English into Latin, for the more speedy and easie attaining of the same. And after we had a little begunne, perceyving what great trouble it was to come running to mee for every word they missed (knowing then of no other Dictionarie to help us, but Sir Thomas Eliots Librarie, which was come out a little before) I appoynted them certaine leaves of the same booke every day to write English before ye Latin, and likewise to gather a number of fine phrases out of Cicero, Terence, Caesar, Livie, &c., and to set them under several tytles, for the more ready finding them againe at their neede. Thus within a yeare or two they had gathered togethir a great volume, which (for the apt similitude betweene the good scholers and diligent Bees in gathering their wax and hony into their hive I called then their Alvearie, both for a memoriall by whom it was made, and also by this name to incourage other to the like diligence, for that they should not see their worthy prayse for the same, unworthily drowned in oblivion."

The title reads : —

An Alvearie or Triple Dictionarie, in Englishe, Latin, and French: very profitable for all such as be desirous of any of these three Languages. Also by the two tables in the ende of this booke, they may contrariwise finde the most necessary Latin or French wordes, placed after the order of an alphabet, whatsoever are to be founde in any other Dictionarie: and so to turne them back-

wardes againe into Englishe when they reade any Latin or French aucthors, & doubt of any hard word therein. Imprinted at London by Henry Denham, dwelling in Paternoster rowe, at the signe of the Starre, [n. d. 1573].

John Baret was Fellow of Trinity College, Cambridge, B. A. 1555, M.A. 1558, M.D. 1577.

A second edition was published in 1580 which contains Greek in addition to the Latin and French. The author was dead when this edition was published, as is seen by the lines, " To the Reader" signed " Tho. M.," which begin as follows :

> " When Barret liude, yᵗ first this worke did frame,
> In sort you seé, with long and tedious toile,
> A Beehive heé did deéme it best to name,
> Because like Beé he manie a yeére did moile,
> In large wide fields, that far dissundred beé,
> Adornde with floures most beautifull in gleé."

In a recent London catalogue a copy is priced at £9 9s., and the bookseller adds the following note : " This very rare volume is of great service in enabling us to trace the meaning of Elizabethan words and phrases that are now obsolete, since it is the earliest English dictionary, and is especially valuable on that account to the Shakespearian student."

The first purely English dictionary was compiled by John Bullokar and published in 1616. The title reads: *An English Expositor; teaching the interpretation of the hardest words used in our Language, with sundry explications, descriptions, and discourses. By I[ohn] B[ullokar] Doctor of Physic. London, 1616.* It passed through several editions, the thirteenth being published in Dublin in 1726.

In 1658 Edward Phillips published his *New World of Words*, a dictionary which Sir John Hawkins speaks of as the basis of English lexicography. Its title reads: *The New World of*

Words: or a Universal English Dictionary: containing the proper significations and derivations of all words from other Languages . . . as now made use of in our English tongue; together with the definitions of all those terms that conduce to the understanding of any of the Arts or Sciences, etc., etc. Collected and Published by E[dward] P[hillips]. London, *1658.* The sixth edition, revised by John Kersey, was enlarged by the addition of near twenty thousand words. Edward Phillips was the son of Edward Phillips and Anne, sister of John Milton, under whose care he received his earlier education. He was born in 1630 and died about 1698.

A dictionary which was popular both in England and America was Elisha Coles' Dictionary, which was first published in 1676 and republished as late as 1732. Its title reads: *An English Dictionary, explaining the difficult terms that are used in Divinity, Husbandry, Physick, Phylosophy, Law, Navigation, Mathematicks and other Arts and Sciences. Containing many thousands of hard Words (and proper names of Places) more than are in any other English Dictionary or Expositor; together with the etymological derivation of them from their proper fountains, whether Hebrew, Greek, Latin, French, or any other Language. In a method more comprehensive than any that is extant. By E. Coles, School-master and Teacher of the English Tongue to Forreigners, London, 1676.*

We can obtain some idea of the size of these dictionaries by reference to his Preface in which he says: " The addition that is made to the number of words in former authors of this kind is almost incredible (considering the bulk) being raised from seven in the Expositor to almost thirty thousand here, which are some thousands more than there are in Mr. Phillips World of Words."

The author was born about 1640 and educated at Magdalen College. He taught Latin and English in Russell Street, Covent Garden, and later was an usher in Merchant Tailors' School. He died in 1680.

Another dictionary which was very popular in America was Nathan Bailey's, the first edition of which was published in London in 1721. It was styled, *An Universal Etymological English Dictionary*, and was for many years the standard until displaced by Johnson's. This was the first English dictionary illustrated with woodcuts. The author, who was a schoolmaster at Stepney, died in 1742. Dr. Johnson's immortal work was first published in 1755. The title reads, *A Dictionary of the English Language: in which the words are deduced from their originals, and illustrated in their different significations by examples from the best writers. To which are prefixed, a History of the Language and an English Grammar. By Samuel Johnson, A.M., London, 1755.* It was in two folio volumes. The fourth and the last edition corrected by the author was published in 1773. An octavo edition without the quotations was published in 1756, the seventh and last author's edition being published in 1783.

Regarding this work, H. B. Wheatley in Philological Society's Transactions, 1865, says: " It is not necessary to dwell upon the merits of this great work, which is now pretty well estimated at its true value; and there are few in the present day who put that implicit faith in it which the majority formerly did. It has, however, three grand characteristics, of which no time or successor can ever deprive it.

"1. It was the first English Dictionary that could in any way be considered as a standard, all its predecessors being mere lists of words in comparison.

" 2. Johnson was the first to illustrate his meanings by quotations from standard authors.

" 3. His definitions are above all praise in their happy illustration of the meanings of words. It is possible to quibble at them now, but this department is one of the most difficult in Lexicography, and he had no assistance from his precursors, whose explanations are usually miserable in the extreme."

An Univerſal Etymological

ENGLISH
DICTIONARY;

COMPREHENDING

The Derivations of the Generality of Words in the *Engliſh* Tongue, either Ancient or Modern, from the Ancient *Britiſh*, *Saxon*, *Daniſh*, *Norman*, and Modern *French*, *Teutonic*, *Dutch*, *Spaniſh*, *Italian*; as alſo from the *Latin*, *Greek*, and *Hebrew* Languages, each in their proper Characters.

AND ALSO

A brief and clear Explication of all difficult Words, derived from any of the aforeſaid Languages, and Terms of Art, relating to ANATOMY, BOTANY, PHYSICK PHARMACY, SURGERY, CHYMISTRY, PHILOSOPHY, DIVINITY, MATHEMATICKS, GRAMMAR, LOGICK, RHETORICK, MUSICK, HERALDRY, MARITIME AFFAIRS, MILITARY DISCIPLINE, HORSEMANSHIP, HUNTING, HAWKING, FOWLING, FISHING, GARDENING, HUSBANDRY, HANDICRAFTS, CONFECTIONARY, CARVING, COOKERY, &c.

TOGETHER WITH

A large Collection and Explication of Words and Phraſes uſed in our Ancient STATUTES, CHARTERS, WRITS, OLD RECORDS, and PROCESSES in Law; and the Etymology, and Interpretation of the Proper Names of MEN, WOMEN, and remarkable *Places* in *Great-Britain*: Alſo the DIALECTS of our different Countries.

Containing many Thouſand Words more than either *Harris*, *Philips*, *Kerſey*, or any *Engliſh* Dictionary before extant.

To which is added,

A Collection of our moſt common PROVERBS, with their Explication and Illuſtration.

The whole WORK compil'd and methodically digeſted, as well for the Entertainment of the Curious, as the Information of the Ignorant; and for the Benefit of young Students, Artificers, Tradeſmen, and Foreigners, who are deſirous thoroughly to underſtand what they Speak, Read. or Write.

The Sixteenth Edition, with conſiderable Improvements.

By N. BAILEY, Φιλόλογος.

LONDON:

Printed for R. WARE, W. INNYS and J. RICHARDSON, J. and P. KNAPTON, T. and T. LONGMAN, S. BIRT, C. HITCH and L. HAWES, J. HODGES, B. DOD, J. and J. RIVINGTON, J. HINTON, W. and D. BAKER, J. WARD, W. JOHNSTON, C. CORBETT, and M. COOPER.
M.DCC.LV.

[Price SIX SHILLINGS.]

Samuel Johnson was born at Lichfield Sept. 18, 1709. In 1728 he went to Pembroke College, Oxford, but was prevented by poverty from taking his degree. He died Dec. 13, 1784, and was buried in Westminster Abbey close by the grave of his celebrated pupil David Garrick.

In 1772 was published a dictionary which had a large sale in America. It was entitled: *The Complete English Dictionary: or General Repository of the English Language; containing a copious explanation of all the words in the English Language, together with their different significations . . . to which will be prefixed, a complete English Grammar. By the Rev. Frederick Barlow, M.A., Vicar of Burton, assisted by several other gentlemen. London, printed for the Author.*

It is in two octavo volumes and includes a Gazetteer and a Biographical Dictionary. It was originally published in numbers, and contains many plates, one of which, the frontispiece, represents the author kneeling before the king and offering him his book.

Other compilers of English dictionaries which were extensively used in America were Thomas Dyche, 1723; Daniel Fenning, 1761; Rev. James Barclay, 1774; Rev. John Ash, 1775; Thomas Sheridan, 1780; and John Walker, 1791.

The first dictionary published in the British Colonies was: *The Royal Standard English Dictionary. By William Perry, Lecturer in the Academy at Edinburgh,* the first edition of which was printed in Edinburgh in 1775. It was reprinted in 1788 in Worcester, Mass., by Isaiah Thomas. On the recto of the second leaf appears the following: —

"Dedication to the FIRST American Edition. To the American Academy of Arts and Sciences, this Edition of Perry's Royal Standard English Dictionary, (being the FIRST Work of the Kind printed in America) intended to fix a Standard for the Pronunciation of the English Language, conformably to

The Editor presenting to his Majesty the Complete English Dictionary.

Frontispiece to Barlow's Dictionary.

THE
Complete English Dictionary:

OR,

GENERAL REPOSITORY

OF THE

ENGLISH LANGUAGE,

CONTAINING

A COPIOUS EXPLANATION

OF ALL THE

WORDS in the ENGLISH LANGUAGE;

TOGETHER WITH

Their different SIGNIFICATIONS, VIZ.

I. The WORDS, and the various Senses in which they are used.

II. The TRUE PRONUNCIATION pointed out by being properly accented.

III. INITIAL LETTERS placed to denote the Part of Speech to which each Word belongs.

IV. A geographical DESCRIPTION of the four Quarters of the World.

V. A more particular DESCRIPTION of the Counties, Cities, and principal Towns in England and Wales, than has ever appeared in any Book of this Kind.

VI. As the LIVES of the ENGLISH POETS, and others, celebrated for their Learning and Genius, can no where be introduced with more Propriety than in a DICTIONARY of the ENGLISH LANGUAGE, we have enriched our Performance with the most entertaining and authentic Memoirs of those illustrious Men who have flourished in these Kingdoms.

To which will be prefixed,

A COMPLETE ENGLISH GRAMMAR.

By the Rev. FREDERICK BARLOW, M. A.
Vicar of BURTON.
Assisted by several other GENTLEMEN.

LONDON

Printed for the AUTHOR,

And Sold by T. EVANS, at No. 54, in Pater-noster Row; F. BLYTH, at the Royal Exchange; Mr. JACKSON at Oxford; Mess. FLETCHER and HODSON, at Cambridge; Mr. WILSON, at Dublin; Mr. ETHERINGTON, at York; and all other Booksellers, &c. in Great Britain and Ireland.

[315]

THE ROYAL STANDARD
ENGLISH DICTIONARY.
IN WHICH THE
WORDS are not only rationally DIVIDED into Syllables, accurately ACCENTED,
their PART of SPEECH properly diftinguifhed, and their various SIGNIFICATIONS
arranged in one Line ; but, likewife, by
A *KEY* to this WORK,
Comprifing the VARIOUS SOUNDS of the VOWELS and CONSONANTS,
Denoted by *TYPOGRAPHICAL* CHARACTERS, and
Illuftrated by EXAMPLES, which render it intelligible to the weakeft Capacity,
IT EXHIBITS THEIR
TRUE PRONUNCIATION,
According to the PRESENT PRACTICE of
MEN of LETTERS, EMINENT ORATORS, and POLITE SPEAKERS, in LONDON.
Upon a PLAN perfectly PLAIN, and entirely NEW.
To which is PREFIXED, a COMPREHENSIVE
GRAMMAR of the *ENGLISH* LANGUAGE.
TO THE WHOLE IS ADDED,
The SCRIPTURE proper NAMES in the *Old* and *New Teftaments* ;
NAMES of the principal CITIES, RIVERS, MOUNTAINS, *&c.* in the known world :
Alfo, the Ancient and Modern POETS, PHILOSOPHERS, and STATESMEN, *&c*
With their PROPER *PRONUNCIATION* pointed out.

The THIRD *WORCESTER* EDITION,
Carefully Revifed and Corrected.

By WILLIAM PERRY, Lecturer in the Academy at *Edinburgh,*
Author of The *Only Sure Guide to the Englifh Tongue,* The *Man of Bufinefs,* The *Orator,* &c. &c.

PRINTED at *WORCESTER,* MASSACHUSETTS, by LEONARD WORCESTER,
For ISAIAH THOMAS. Sold at his BOOKSTORE,
By faid THOMAS, & WALDO, in *Brookfield,* and faid THOMAS, & CARLISLE, in *Walpole.*
Sold alfo, in BOSTON, by faid THOMAS, and ANDREWS, S. HALL, B. LARKIN, J. WHITE,
D. WEST, E. LARKIN, jun. J. WEST. and at the BOSTON BOOKSTORE.

MDCCXGIV.

THE
COLUMBIAN DICTIONARY
OF THE
ENGLISH LANGUAGE:

IN WHICH

Many NEW WORDS, peculiar to the *United States*, and many WORDS of GENERAL USE, not found in any other *English Dictionary*, are inserted.

THE WORDS ARE

Divided as they are pronounced, and each Word is accented according to the most approved* *Authors* and *Speakers;* with ABBREVIATIONS used to denote each Part of Speech all the IRREGULAR VERBS are properly arranged, and made plain to the reader.

THE WHOLE IS CALCULATED TO

Assist FOREIGNERS in acquiring a just Pronunciation of the *English Language:* and to be used as a *School Book,* by any who wish to study the Language grammatically.

TO WHICH IS PREFIXED,

A PROSODIAL GRAMMAR,

Containing, a short DISSERTATION on VOWELS and CONSONANTS.

TO THE WHOLE IS ADDED

HEATHEN MYTHOLOGY
OR, A CLASSICAL PRONOUNCING DICTIONARY.

BY CALEB ALEXANDER, A. M.

Author of " Virgil's Works translated into literal English Prose," &c. &c. and Teacher of the English Language

Published according to Act of Congress.

PRINTED AT BOSTON,

BY ISAIAH THOMAS AND EBENEZER T. ANDREWS.

Sold by them and the other Booksellers in Boston: by L.THOMAS, in *Worcester;* by THOMAS, ANDREWS & PENNIMAN, in *Albany;* and by THOMAS, ANDREWS & BUTLER, in *Baltimore.*————AUG. 1800.

the Present Practice of Polite Speakers in Great Britain and the United States; is humbly inscribed by their most obedient and very humble servant,

ISAIAH THOMAS.

WORCESTER, January 1, 1788.'

It is a square duodecimo, printed with double columns, and contains five hundred and ninety-six pages.

The first English Dictionary by an American author was: *The Columbian Dictionary of the English Language. By Caleb Alexander. Printed at Boston by Isaiah Thomas and Ebenezer T. Andrews, Aug. 1800.*

The author offers the following Advertisement: " This Dictionary is not offered to the *public*, with an expectation of *fixing* an *uniform* and permanent standard of pronunciation. If a Roman Emperor, at the head of his legions, could not introduce *one* letter into the alphabet, much less can an obscure individual persuade, or compel men to pronounce alike. Could any means be used, or any plan devised, to alter and unite Americans, in giving similar sounds to all the vowels and consonants, and their various combinations, the event would be happy. In doing this, a man would have to encounter *prejudice*, *ignorance*, *malice*, and *pedantry*, four powerful enemies. In spite of the most learned dissertation, and the best rules, some would pronounce *tūne*, others *tshône*; some tūesday, others tshôsday; some vô'lum, vôl'yum; pĭc'ture, others pĭc'tshur; some vĕn'due, and others wĕn'due; and each word would have his admirers and followers. Not despairing however, of doing a little to fix an *uniform* and permanent standard of pronunciation, no pains have been spared in dividing and accenting the words according to the practice of the most *approved* and *polite* speakers."

It is a square duodecimo, printed in double columns, and contains five hundred and fifty-six pages.

Latin Dictionaries

THE earliest Latin-English Dictionary was the *Medulla Grammaticæ*, which is supposed to have been compiled by the author of the *Promptorium Parvulorum*. The first Latin-English Dictionary printed in England was founded upon the *Medulla* and printed in London by Wynkyn de Worde in 1500. The title reads:

Ortus Vocabulorum : alphabetico ordine fere omnia quæ in Catholico breviloquio. Cornucopia. Gemma Vocabulorum atque Medulla Grammatice ponuntur cum perpulchris Additoribus Ascens. Et vernaculæ Linguæ Anglicanæ expositionem continens.

Colophon reads, —

Impressus per virum laudabilem civem providum magistrum Wynandum de Worde prope celeberrimum monasterium quod Westmynstre appellatur M D.

It is a small quarto containing about two hundred leaves. The author was John Stanbridge, who was born in the County of Northampton, and was educated at the College founded by William of Wykeham, near Winchester. In 1481, he was admitted a Fellow of New College, Oxford, receiving his degree of B. A. in 1486. In 1488 he was first Usher of the Free School adjoining Magdalen College, Oxford, of which he became chief Master.

In 1531 there was printed in Paris the first edition of *Dictionarium seu Latinæ Thesaurus. Roberto Stephano, auctore.* This work was adopted by the University of Paris, and, superseding the existing Latin dictionaries, remained for many years the standard authority on its subject. The author was of the second generation of the famous family of the Estiennes, whose members were not only among the great publishers of their time, but were also distinguished scholars.   He was born in 1503, became proprietor of his father's press in 1524, and died in 1559, having rendered honorable service during thirty-five years in the production in Paris of scholarly Latin and Greek texts.   Mr. G. H. Putnam, in *Books and their Makers during the Middle Ages*, gives a glimpse of his home life: "Shortly after his majority, Robert married Petronilla, a daughter of the famous publisher Jodocus Badius, and the co-operation of his wife proved of no little service in the management of the editorial portion of his business, as she was herself a thorough scholar, and could read, write, and speak Latin fluently.   The publisher's household included for many years, in addition to the members of his family circle, a number of his editors and press-correctors. These assistants represented a number of nationalities, and they had, as a convenience, adopted Latin as their common tongue. Through the example of these permanent guests, aided by the facility of the mistress of the house, Latin became the language first of the table and finally of the whole domestic establishment, even the servants and children having gained a sufficient mastery of the idioms."

In 1548 there was published in London the first edition of the Latin and English Dictionary of Thomas Cooper.   It is a work of considerable merit and deservedly held in high esteem as one of the earliest and best attempts in the promotion of lexicographical literature.

The foundation of Cooper's Dictionary was taken from Sir Thomas Elyot's Dictionary, first published in London in 1538, and the materials for the most part from Robert Stephens's Thesaurus and John Frisius' Latin and German Dictionary.   In 1622, when in the seventeenth year of his age, John Winthrop, Jr., the eldest son of John Winthrop, and later the Governor of

Connecticut, was sent as a student to Trinity College, Dublin. May 26, 1623, he wrote to his father a letter in Latin requesting him to send some books, among them Cooper's Dictionary. It was received some time in July. In a letter written June 26, 1623, John Winthrop says, "For Cooper's Dictionary I will send it to you as soon as I can: but it is so difficult and hazardable (especially, now, since Mr. Goad died) as I cannot tell how to convey that or anything else." In a letter dated August 12, he says the book had been sent. The titlepage reads, *Bibliotheca Eliotæ. Eliotes Dictionarie by Thomas Cooper, the third tyme corrected and with a great number of phrases enriched, as to him that conferreth the other editions, it may easely appeare. Londini in ædibus nuper Tho. Bertheleti. Anno Domini, 1559. Cum privilegio.* It is a small folio, printed in black letter. A copy sold in New York recently for $40. John Winthrop, Jr.'s copy, which bears the autographs of John and Adam Winthrop, is now in the library of the Massachusetts Historical Society.

In 1565 Thomas Cooper published *Thesaurus Linguæ Romanæ Et Britannicæ*, which is said by Dr. White Kennett to be a verbatim transcript of *Dictionarium Latino-Gallicum*, published in Paris in 1552, by Charles Stephens, the brother of Robert.

Thomas Cooper was born about 1517, and died in 1549. He was educated at Magdalen College, Oxford; became Dean of Gloucester, 1569; Bishop of London, 1570; and of Winchester, 1584. He was much admired by Queen Elizabeth, and was by her advanced to the bishopric.

The dictionaries of Stephens and Cooper passed through many editions and were frequently edited, revised, and enlarged, but were finally superseded by Ainsworth's *Latin and English Dictionary*.

Robert Ainsworth was born at Woodyale, near Manchester, September, 1660, and educated at the grammar school in Bolton, of which he became master. A few years later he went to London, where he opened a school at Bethnal Green, at Hackney, and other places. Having secured a competency, he retired from teaching and engaged in literary pursuits, devoting several years to the compilation of his dictionary, which was founded upon the *Ortus Vocabulorum* of John Stanbridge. He also published a grammar and some other classical compositions. He died at London, April 4, 1743.

The first edition of his dictionary was published in London in 1736. It was reprinted many times, and was very popular both in England and America, until superseded by Andrews' *Latin Lexicon*.

Greek Dictionaries

ETYMOLOGICUM MAGNUM is the name of a Greek lexicon, the oldest of the kind, professing to give the roots of words, and appears to have been compiled in the tenth century. An edition was printed in the last part of the fifteenth century, the titlepage reading, *Etymologicon Magnum Græcum, cum Græca Præfatione M. Musuri.* The imprint reads: *Venet. sumptibus Nic. Blasti, opera Zachariæ Calliergi, 1499*, both the title and imprint being in Greek. It is a folio containing two hundred and twenty-three leaves. Brunet says it is a "très belle édition, rare et recherchée." It was reprinted in 1549, 1594, 1710, and at Leipsic in 1816.

The Lexicon of Suidas is the name given to a lexicon compiled some time during the Byzantine Empire. Who Suidas was, or where he lived, no one can say, but it is customary to place him about the tenth or eleventh century. The lexicon is valuable in the eyes of scholars on account of its numerous extracts from ancient Greek writers, grammarians, scholiasts, and lexicographers, whose writings have perished. It is a folio of five hundred and sixteen pages. The first edition appeared at Milan in 1499. It has been several times reprinted, an edition having been printed at Oxford in 1834.

In 1572 there was published in Paris a work which has been described by Greswell as an "admirable and unrivalled monument of ardent zeal for the advancement of learning, and as an example of unwearied diligence and of colossal erudition." The title reads:

Thesaurus Græcæ Linguæ, ab Henrico Stephano constructus, in quo præter alia plurima quæ primus præstit (paternæ diligentia æmulus) vocabula in classes distribuit, multiplici derivatorum serie ad primigenia, tanquam ad radices unde pullulant, revocata. Thesaurus Lectori.

> *Nunc alii intrepide vestigia nostra sequantur;*
> *Me duce, plana via est quæ salebrosa fuit.*

Anno MDLXXII excudebat Henr. Stephanus, cum privilegio Cæs. Majestatis et Christianiss. Galliarum Regis.

Four volumes folio, with two supplementary volumes containing an appendix and an index. In 1573 a seventh volume was issued containing two glossaries and a treatise on the dialects of Attica.

Henry Estienne was the son of Robert, and after the death of his father carried on the press which his father had established in Geneva, but after a few years removed to Paris and established a second Estienne Press, in which he produced books which in beauty of typography and excellence of text surpassed his father's publications. He was the most finished scholar of this remarkable family, and his father had taken great pains with his education, causing him to travel as a young man in Italy, England, and the Low Countries. He edited many of his publications, and in 1572 published the great *Thesaurus*. He gives to his father the credit of having conceived and planned this gigantic undertaking, who had collected before his death a large amount of material for the great etymological and lexicographical enterprise. Concerning this publication Mr. George H. Putnam speaks as follows: " This Thesaurus Græcus was completed by Henry at about the same age as that at which his father Robert had published his Latin Thesaurus. The two works would have been for any generation of publishers creditable examples of scholarly and public spirited enterprise, but when we remember that the publishers were the compilers, and were also the authors of the notes, commentaries, and separate treatises which make up a large portion of the bulk of the volumes, and that their work as editors and authors was done amidst the engrossing cares of the management in stormy times of a complex and absorbing business, the Thesauri remain magnificent monuments to the scholarship, the capacity, and the persistent energy of the two Estiennes." The publication of this work involved Henry in serious pecuniary difficulties. The sale was injured by unscrupulous lexicographers who made epitomes or abridgments and sold them as their own. Stephens vented his indignation in the *Latinity of Lepsius*, but found no redress. He died at Lyons in 1598, aged seventy.

In 1579 there was published at Basle a *Lexicon Græco-Latinum*, by Joannes Scapula. It is claimed that this was no more nor less than an abridgment of Stephens's *Thesaurus Græcæ*. Scapula had been employed by Henry Stephens as a corrector, and has been charged with taking advantage of his position to compile this abridgment. In his Preface Scapula claims to have begun his book and to have made considerable progress before Stephens's book was printed, yet whole pages of his *Lexicon* are almost identical with the *Thèsaurus*. Mattaire says that Dr. Busby forbade his pupils, on the ground of indignation at literary larceny, to use what he called "the surreptitious lexicon" of Scapula.

Notwithstanding the charges against Scapula, his Lexicon, being in a smaller and less costly form, was found to be more convenient to students, and large sales were made which brought to the compiler a considerable sum, but dishonorably ruined in some degree the laborious *Thesaurus* of Stephens, which found few purchasers.

Scapula's dictionary was reprinted several times, the writer possessing a copy the title of which reads: *Joannis Scapulæ Lexicon Græco-Latinum; ex probatis autoribus locupletatum, cum indicibus, et Græco et Latino, auctis et correctis. Glasguæ; 1816.* It makes two large quarto volumes, containing over two thousand pages.

A lexicon which met with considerable success was *Constantini Lexicon Græco-Latinum. Londoni, 1592.* Robert Constantine was a professor of physic and belles-lettres at Caen University, born at Caen, 1502, died 1605. His knowledge of Greek was very extensive, as was evinced by this lexicon. As a useful and correct dictionary, this work of Constantine greatly surpassed all that had preceded it, and is still deservedly in request amongst students for the valuable interpretations which it furnishes of many passages in the Greek prose writers, especially Thucydides. Besides the lexicon Constantine wrote three books on Greek and Roman antiquities.

A very popular dictionary, which was used both in England and America well into the nineteenth century, was the Greek Lexicon compiled by Cornelius Schrevelius, the first edition of which was printed in 1654. Schrevelius was born at Harlem, Holland, in 1615, and died in 1667.

Favorini Thesaurus Universæ Linguæ Græcæ, per Ant. Bartoli castigatus et copia dictionum auctus. Venet. 1712, is the title of a dictionary concerning which Roscoe says: "This great work will always secure to Favorinus an honorable rank among the promoters of Grecian literature, and yet retains its rank among those useful and laborious compilations of which it set the first laudable example."

Benjamin Hedericus, born at Grosen-hayn in Misnia in 1675, died in 1748, was the author of a well-known Greek lexicon which was first published at Leipsic in 1722. It was republished in England and had a large sale in America.

Thomas Morell, born 1701, died 1784, an able divine who edited the dictionaries of Ainsworth and Hedericus, published a Greek poetical dictionary the title of which reads,

Thesaurus Græcæ Poeseos sive Lexicon Græco-Prosodiacum Versus et Synonyma (tam ad explicationem vocabulorum, quam ad compositionem Poeticam pertinentia,) Epitheta, Phrases, Descriptiones, etc., ad Parnassum complectens. . . . Cui præfigitur de Poesi, seu Prosodia, Græcorum Tractatus. Auctore T. Morell, S. T. P. S. S. A. Etonæ MDCCLXII.

This lexicon was based upon *Thesaurus Græcæ Poeseos ex omnibus Græcis collectis. Moguntiæ, MDCXIV,* compiled by Nicholas Caussin, a learned Jesuit, born at Troyes in 1580, who became counsellor to Louis XIII., but opposed by Richelieu, was banished from Paris. After the cardinal's death he returned to Paris, where he died at the Jesuit convent, July, 1651. His book *De sacrâ et profanâ eloquentiâ* is well known in England, and his *Courte Sainte* has been translated into almost every language in Europe.

An edition of Morell's *Thesaurus* was published in London in 1824, edited by Edward Maltby. It is a large quarto, containing more than a thousand pages.

The Greek dictionaries most commonly used in England and America in the nineteenth century were Donnegan's, which was based upon Schneider's Greek-German Lexicon, and Liddell and Scott's, which was based upon the German work of Francis Passow.

Here we close our story of the early New England school and the books used by the scholars, not because we have exhausted the subject, or have no more books to describe. As for the subject, we have only scratched the surface, and a rich reward awaits any one who wishes to know more of the story, if he will but plough a little deeper. As for the books, we still possess many others which once belonged to the Taylor family of Boston and which were used by several generations of that family in their younger days. We are well aware, however, that bibliographical details soon become tiresome. Viewed independently, they are dry and uninteresting. But if we consider them as signboards on the long road to learning, they soon change their appearance and afford us a vast amount of information as to how our ancestors passed their school-days and what were the tools they used in trying to secure an education. The writer is very strongly of the opinion that the facilities for instruction in the colonial and provincial periods were greater than is generally supposed.

Index

Index